About Development Dimensions International

DEVELOPMENT DIMENSIONS INTERNATIONAL (DDI) IS A LEADING provider of human resource programs and services designed to create high-involvement organizations.

Founded in 1970, we now provide services to more than 9,000 clients around the world, spanning a diverse range of industries and including more than 400 of the Fortune 500 corporations.

Our products/services fall into three general areas:

- Assessment and selection, ensuring organizations select and promote team members and leaders most capable of working in high-involvement organizations.

- Organizational change, involving a wide range of consulting services and expertise in implementing teams.

- Training and development, including proven and comprehensive skill-building systems for teams and their leaders.

DDI's corporate headquarters and distribution facilities are located in Pittsburgh, Pennsylvania. We maintain offices around the world, including regional training centers in Atlanta, Chicago, Dallas, Denver, Hong Kong, London, Los Angeles, Montreal, New York, Singapore, Sydney, Tokyo, and Toronto. International in the truest sense, DDI is represented in 19 countries, and our programs have been translated into 21 languages.

DEVELOPMENT DIMENSIONS INTERNATIONAL, INC.
World Headquarters—Pittsburgh
1225 Washington Pike
Bridgeville, PA 15017-2838
800/933-4624

Other Books by the Authors About Empowerment and Teams

BENCHMARKING TEAM IMPLEMENTATIONS WITH OTHER ORGANIZATIONS provides only part of the information one needs to implement teams successfully. In addition to the various resources that are available, we recommend the following books:

• *Zapp! The Lightning of Empowerment* (**William C. Byham, Ph.D., with Jeff Cox. Fawcett, 1992**)

This easy-to-read book, written in the form of a fable, provides a definition of what empowerment is, why it is important, and what it takes to achieve empowerment—including the development of teams—within an organization.

• *Empowered Teams: Creating Self-Directed Work Groups That Improve Quality, Productivity, and Participation* (**Richard S. Wellins, William C. Byham, and Jeanne M. Wilson. Jossey-Bass, 1991**)

This is a how-to book on starting teams. It focuses on getting teams off to the right start and explores why empowered teams work, how they operate, and what's needed to make them survive and prosper.

• *Leadership Trapeze: Strategies for Leadership in Team-Based Organizations* (**Jeanne M. Wilson, Jill George, and Richard S. Wellins, with William C. Byham. Jossey-Bass, 1994**)

This book defines the leadership behaviors required of an empowering leader and the changes those requirements go through as individuals in teams take on more organizational responsibility.

• *HeroZ—Empower Yourself, Your Co-workers, and Your Company* (**William C. Byham, Ph.D., and Jeff Cox. Harmony Books, 1994**)

This sequel to *Zapp! The Lightning of Empowerment* deals with empowering yourself and continuous improvement. It focuses on overcoming barriers to implementing change from the bottom up and working effectively in teams with representatives of all functional areas to accomplish specific projects. Written as a fable, it is easy and fun to read for individuals at all levels in the organization.

• *Succeeding with Teams: 101 Tips That Really Work* (Richard S. Wellins, Dick Schaff, and Kathy Harper Shomo. Lakewood Publications, 1994)

This is a handbook, designed primarily for team members and leaders, that contains simple, practical tips for implementing successful teams.

INSIDE TEAMS

Richard S. Wellins

William C. Byham

George R. Dixon

INSIDE TEAMS

How 20 World-Class
Organizations Are Winning
Through Teamwork

Jossey-Bass Publishers • San Francisco

Substantial discounts on bulk quantities of Jossey-Bass books
are available to corporations, professional associations, and other
organizations. For details and discount information, contact the
special sales department at Jossey-Bass Inc., Publishers.
(415) 433-1740; Fax (415) 433-0499.

For sales outside the United States, please contact your local
Paramount Publishing International office.

Manufactured in the United States of America on Lyons Falls
Pathfinder Tradebook. This paper is acid-free and 100 percent
totally chlorine-free.

Library of Congress Cataloging-in-Publication Data

Wellins, Richard S.
    Inside teams : how 20 world-class organizations are winning
through teamwork / Richard S. Wellins, William C. Byham, George R.
Dixon.
        p.   cm.—(Jossey-Bass management series)
    Includes index.
    ISBN 1-55542-574-7
    1. Work groups   2. Benchmarking (Management).   I. Byham, William
C.   II. Dixon, George R.   III. Title.   IV. Series.
HD66.W46   1994
658.4′036—dc20   94-26312
                                                                              CIP

FIRST EDITION
HB Printing   10 9 8 7 6 5 4 3 2 1   *Code 94110*

The Jossey-Bass Management Series

Dedication

To our wives, Ellen Lief-Wellins and Carolyn Byham, whose support and understanding have allowed us the time to write this book, and for their thoughtful contributions to its contents.
Rich Wellins
Bill Byham

To my coauthors and to team members everywhere—all working hard to make a bold new concept of workplace relationships become business as usual.
George Dixon

Contents

Preface xv

The Authors xxi

Introduction: A Guide to Benchmarking World-Class   *1*
Work Teams

PART ONE
Start-Up and Early Stages

1

Focusing on the Patient to Meet the Challenges of   *19*
Health Care Reform
   Cape Coral Hospital
   Cape Coral, Florida

2

The Evolving Role of Leadership in Creating Flexible,   *34*
Productive Teams
   Development Dimensions International
   Canonsburg, Pennsylvania

3

Keeping in Step with a Rapidly Changing Market   *53*
   K Shoes, Ltd.
   Cumbria, United Kingdom

4

Building Teams from the Ground Up by Developing   *66*
New Team Skills
   Miller Brewing Company
   Trenton, Ohio

5

Streamlining Business Processes to Stay Competitive   *79*
   Mine Safety Appliances Company
   Murrysville, Pennsylvania

6

Making a Commitment to Involve Everyone in the Change   *90*
Pfizer, Inc.
Terre Haute, Indiana

7

Using Teamwork to Redesign Core Processes   *106*
Sterling Winthrop, Ltd.
Sydney, Australia

8

Driving Reengineering Through Empowered Teams   *121*
UCAR Carbon
Clarksville, Tennessee

PART TWO
Experienced and Maturing Stages

9

Teams in Fast-Forward: Building Commitment Quickly   *137*
Ampex Systems
Colorado Springs, Colorado

10

Gaining Business Focus Through Mini-Enterprise Units   *151*
Bord na Mona—Peat Energy Division
Leaberg, County Offaly, Ireland

11

The Plant Start-Up That Became the Model for   *164*
High-Performance Teams
Colgate-Palmolive Company
Cambridge, Ohio

12

Making Teams Work in Union and Nonunion Facilities   *179*
Hannaford Brothers Company
Schodack Landing, New York

13

Project-Based Teams: Creating Flexibility and Focus in a   *192*
Matrix Environment
  Harris Corporation
  Melbourne, Florida

14

Achieving Customer Satisfaction by Managing the   *207*
Whole Business with Teams
  Kodak Customer Assistance Center
  Rochester, New York

15

Using Total Quality Management as the Foundation   *221*
for Teams
  Milwaukee Mutual Insurance Company
  Milwaukee, Wisconsin

16

How Empowered Teams Helped Win the   *234*
Malcolm Baldrige Award
  Eastman Chemical Company—Tennesee Eastman Division
  Kingsport, Tennessee

17

The Baldrige and Beyond: Sustaining Systemwide   *248*
Reengineering and Empowerment
  Texas Instruments—Defense Systems and Electronics Group
  Dallas, Texas

18

The Language of Teams Can Be Spoken Anywhere   *262*
  Texas Instruments Malaysia
  Kuala Lumpur, Malaysia

19

Aligning Systems to Keep Teams on the High-Performance   *272*
Track
  Westinghouse Electronic Assembly Plant
  College Station, Texas

20

Leading Teams: Transforming Managers into Coaches   *286*
  Wilson Sporting Goods Company
  Humboldt, Tennessee

PART THREE
Lessons Learned

21

Taking a Deeper Look Inside Teams: A Summary of   *299*
Best Practices

22

The Future of Teams: Predictions About the Journey   *338*
Toward Empowerment

Index   347

Preface

There are good reasons why you should seek the experience of other organizations before adopting teams as a means of employee empowerment. The thought of empowering teams of frontline workers to make major job decisions and, to a large extent, manage themselves both intrigues and frightens most managers. The popular business press reports stories of impressive gains in quality, productivity, and customer service stemming from the use of empowered teams. Yet you realize that a transition to teams will be far from easy. Perhaps you have scars from failed organizational change efforts or you're concerned that teams are just another management fad.

Inside Teams was written to allay your concerns about implementing teams. By learning from the mistakes and successes of other organizations, you can gain the confidence to bring about significant change in your own company.

Swivel Chair Benchmarking was a subtitle we considered for this book—because that is exactly what *Inside Teams* provides. We profile twenty organizations from around the world that have used teams of empowered employees. We describe why teams were chosen as an organizational direction, how they were started, the problems they encountered, the successes achieved, the lessons learned—exactly what one would seek from a benchmarking trip.

Who Should Read This Book?

Inside Teams offers information and advice from some of the best team applications in the world. The following people will benefit from getting to know the organizations we have profiled:

- Senior managers who must make decisions about the transition to teams
- Managers who are attempting to forge a vision of teams in their organization
- Design committee members who are making the transition to teams in their organization
- Supervisors and middle managers who will play a critical role in encouraging teams toward their organization's vision and who must change their job responsibilities and skills along the way
- Team members who are experiencing one of the most rewarding—yet confusing and stressful—times of their lives

Background

Inside Teams is an extension of our book *Empowered Teams: Creating Self-Directed Work Groups That Improve Quality, Productivity, and Participation* (1991), which outlines the ways teams operate and the benefits they provide. *Empowered Teams* is a how-to book for the organization that wants to implement work teams. In fact, several of the teams profiled here used *Empowered Teams* to guide their team implementation. Since we wrote *Empowered Teams,* we have continued to work with a large variety of teams worldwide— as well as within our own organization, Development Dimensions International (DDI). In the past three years more than a thousand organizations have used our training and consulting services as part of their transition to teams.

Our views have changed, however, as we have seen teams

develop and have observed the vast variety of team implementations that are possible. For example, we now think that the terms "self-directed" or "self-managed" work teams are no longer appropriate. These terms do not describe types of teams; they describe how teams function. We also realize that *Empowered Teams* concentrated on teams just getting started. In our more recent book on teams, *The Leadership Trapeze: Strategies for Leadership in Team-Based Organizations* (1994), we felt it important to concentrate on the three stages of team development: preteams, new teams, and mature teams. In that book we give practical advice to those who must meet the challenge of leading in a team-based organization. In *Inside Teams* we deal with teams in two of the three stages—new teams and mature teams—because each provides a unique set of challenges. (We do not include preteam cases because their "history" with teams would not provide you with meaningful benchmarking data.)

What to Expect

Inside Teams has a simple organization. In the Introduction, we tell you who you will visit, why they were selected, and what to look for in each organization. We also explain the rather confusing and overlapping nomenclature used by the various organizations you will visit.

In Parts One and Two, the case studies, we profile the twenty companies. For each case we include similar types of information but do not necessarily adhere to a rigid format. Each case begins with a brief summary of the main facts, so you can make a quick tour if you want, followed by an in-depth visit. When we interviewed representatives of these organizations, we tried to ask the kinds of questions you would ask:

- Why were teams chosen?
- How were teams started?
- Who led the way?
- How was work reorganized?
- What training was provided at each level?
- What compensation changes were made?
- What checks and balances were established?
- How were management's fears of relinquishing power and employees' fears of assuming power handled?
- How long did it take to get teams working?
- How was union involvement handled?
- How long have teams been in operation?
- What are the bottom-line results in terms of quality, productivity, and customer service?
- What are the other results (such as reduced employee turnover, improved morale, and increased cooperation among departments)?
- What problems were encountered?
- What lessons were learned?

In Part Three we summarize common trends and key differences among the twenty cases. We also make some predictions about the future of teams. We think you will enjoy getting to know these twenty companies as much as we did.

Acknowledgments

We want to start by thanking the organizations who were willing to discuss their team implementations with us. Without them, there would be no book. Their honesty in detailing their successes and difficulties will help us all establish more effective teams.

Several DDI associates made important contributions to this book—ranging from ideas for content to the development of the figures and tables. Those who deserve special recognition include Tammy Bercosky, Shawn Garry, Sandra Hilker, Anne Maers, Marcia Medvid, Billie Nestor, Carol Schuetz, Cheryl Soukup, and Mary Szpak. Special appreciation goes to Helene Lautman and Ellen Lief-Wellins, our ever-diligent editors, and Nancy Boyle, who coordinated information gathering from our case organizations. We also wish to thank Kathy Harper Shomo, who pitched in to develop the story on our own team implementation at DDI.

Bridgeville, Pennsylvania　　　　　　　　Richard S. Wellins
July 1994　　　　　　　　　　　　　　　William C. Byham
　　　　　　　　　　　　　　　　　　　George R. Dixon

The Authors

Richard S. Wellins is senior vice president of programs and marketing for Development Dimensions International (DDI). Since joining DDI in 1982, Wellins has focused the majority of his time on new program development, research, and consulting. He formed DDI's start-up group, a special unit responsible for designing team-based work systems for more than fifty new facilities around the world. He was involved in the development and launch of DDI's new teams training system currently being used by over two thousand organizations. He has also consulted with numerous organizations, including International Paper, Laurentian Technology, NYNEX, and Toyota, on culture change, work-system design, performance management, and selection systems. Wellins, who earned a Ph.D. in social-industrial psychology from American University, has published or presented numerous articles or papers on high-involvement work teams. He is lead author of a nationwide study on work teams, *Self-Directed Teams: A Study of Current Practice* (1990), and senior author of *Empowered Teams* (1991), a book on the same subject.

William C. Byham is president and chief executive officer of Development Dimensions International (DDI). He earned a Ph.D. in industrial/organizational psychology from Purdue University and is widely regarded a thought leader in selection, training, and human resource development. He has written more than 150 books, monographs, and articles and has spoken to business and professional groups throughout the world. In recognition of his achievements, he has received more than a dozen professional awards, including the highest professional awards given by the Society of Industrial and Organizational Psychology and the American Society for Training and Development. For more than twenty years, Byham has researched and written about how to create an empowering culture—particularly by developing the behavioral skills of employees, supervisors, and managers. His book *Zapp! The Lightning of Empowerment* (1988) has sold more than 1.5 million copies and is available in nine languages. Byham consults on empowerment as well as management selection and development issues with leading organizations throughout the world.

George R. Dixon is a professional business writer, marketing communications consultant, and researcher who has written about human resource development, information systems, and quality management. He is coauthor of *From This Land* and editor of two business handbooks, *What Works at Work* and *The Total Quality Handbook*.

INSIDE TEAMS

Introduction:
A Guide to Benchmarking
World-Class Work Teams

- At Bord Na Mona, a unique peat harvesting operation in Ireland, output per employee has risen by nearly 100 percent.
- At K Shoes, Ltd., in the United Kingdom, rejects have dropped from 5,000 parts per million to 250.
- At Milwaukee Mutual Insurance Company, employee turnover—once as high as 36 percent—has dropped significantly.
- Texas Instrument's Defense System and Electronics Group (1992 Malcolm Baldrige Award recipient) realized a 50 precent increase in revenues per employee over a four-year period.
- Cycle times for many products have been reduced from twelve weeks to less than two weeks at Westinghouse's Electronic Assembly Plant in Texas.
- At Kodak's team-based customer assistance center, both employee productivity (measured by calls handled per hour) and first-time accuracy levels in helping customers with problems have doubled.

These results are just a sample of what the twenty organizations surveyed here (and others like them) have accomplished thanks to empowered teams. You will see why these organizations implemented teams, how they accomplished such impressive results, and some of the ups and downs they experienced along the way.

1

Before embarking on your benchmarking journey, it will help you to know what to look for. In each case study we present the following information:

- Why and how the organization shifted to teams
- Types of teams used
- Responsibilities offered to teams
- Multiple skilling
- Training
- Titles used to describe team positions (facilitator, coach, team leader)
- Team size
- Leadership roles
- Relationships with unions
- Performance management and reward systems
- Results

Table I.1 lists the twenty organizations profiled here along with some basic facts on team implementation. The table divides the teams into two categories: new team implementation and mature team implementation. While we recommend that you read all the cases to get a broad feel for the variety of implementations in *Inside Teams,* the table will help you focus on those organizations you'd like to visit first.

Types of Teams

As you survey the twenty team cases, you will notice two types of empowered teams: *permanent work teams*—teams organized around a product or service; and *cross-functional teams*—teams charged with problem solving, coordination, and decision making relative to larger organizational issues.

In most of the case studies, employees are involved in both types of teams.

Permanent Work Teams

Permanent work teams can be either natural teams or redesigned teams. *Natural work teams* are the most common type. They are formed of employees who, at the start of the transformation, work on a common product or service—for example, eight people who assemble a product and report to a common group leader. Empowered natural teams make decisions about the quality and quantity of their output (job responsibilities) and how the team operates (governance). In other words, they are largely self-directed. Ideally the team is responsible for an entire operation or a measurable part of the process—for example, dashboard installation on an automobile assembly line. Team members can measure their quality, their productivity, and many other key variables. The main characteristic of natural work teams is that the organization does not have to undertake extensive reorganization or major process redesign.

But sometimes an organization and its processes are not conducive to forming empowered teams. This usually occurs when organizations are structured around functional "silos," have dozens of individual job classifications, or require a multitude of handoffs among departments in order to complete a product or deliver a service. In such organizations, it becomes almost impossible to provide the authority, responsibility, and sense of ownership necessary for empowered teams. No one feels responsible for anything; when something goes wrong, it's someone else's fault. In this case it might be necessary to reconfigure work processes so that teams can take real responsibility and accurately measure their results. These teams, which we call *redesigned work teams,* are formed around a common output (product or

Table I.1. The Twenty Organizations.

New Team Implementations	Business	Location	Union Status	% in Teams	Average Team Size	Total Employees	New Start-Up
Cape Coral Hospital	Health care	Florida	No	10	15	1,300	No
Development Dimensions International	Printing/distribution	Pennsylvania	No	100	2-15	70	No
K Shoes	Footwear manufacturing/retailing	Throughout U.K.	Yes	40	5-8	1,100	No
Miller Brewing	Beer brewing	Ohio	Yes	100	6-19	410	Yes
Mine Safety Appliances	Safety equipment	Pennsylvania	No	21	3-18	530	No
Pfizer Inc.	Specialty food ingredients	Indiana	No	100	4-6	130	No
Sterling Winthrop	Pharmaceuticals	Australia	Yes	30	10-12	500	No
UCAR	Graphite products	Throughout U.S., especially Southeast	Varied	85-90	4-20	1,600 (U.S.)	No

Mature Team Implementations	Business	Location	Union Status	% in Teams	Average Team Size	Total Employees	New Start-Up
Ampex	Electronics	Colorado	No	95	10-12	225	No
Bord na Mona	Peat extraction	Ireland	Yes	85	5-17	1,100	No
Colgate-Palmolive	Detergents	Ohio	No	100	3-10	200	Yes
Hannaford Brothers	Retail food distribution	Maine/New York	Varied	100	5-25	150	Yes
Harris Corporation	Electronics	Florida	No	65	6-10	8,000	No
Kodak Customer Assistance Center	Customer service	New York	No	50	3-20	300	No
Milwaukee Mutual	Insurance	Wisconsin	No	100	8-10	750	No
Tennessee Eastman	Chemicals, fibers, plastics	Tennessee	No	100	10	8,370	No
Texas Instruments	Defense electronics	Texas	No	100	10	13,000	No
Texas Instruments Malaysia	Electronics	Kuala Lumpur	No	100	6-18	3,000	No
Westinghouse	Defense and commercial electronics	Texas	No	100	8-14	185	Yes
Wilson Sporting Goods	Sporting goods (golf balls)	Tennessee	No	75	15	650	No

service) or a group of customers. Like natural work teams, members of redesigned teams are largely self-directed. They are responsible for the quantity and quality of their output and assume many leadership or governance responsibilities.

Figure I.1 shows a traditional, functionally organized manufacturing organization. Figure I.2 shows the same organization after its boundaries were redefined around products. As members of the product teams were given control of all major aspects of manufacturing, they were able to reduce inventory requirements, reduce work in process, increase throughput, and reduce rework and rejects. When team members succeed, they take pride in their accomplishments. When they do not meet specifications, they make improvements because it is *their* product and they want to make it a success.

Figure I.3 shows a parallel example of how functional departments were organized in a large insurance company, while Figure I.4 shows how teams were set up to focus on specific groups of agents (their "customers"). Under the traditional design, field agents often needed to call several departments to gather client information. Information delays

Figure I.1. Synthetic Fiber Manufacturing Facility Before Redesign

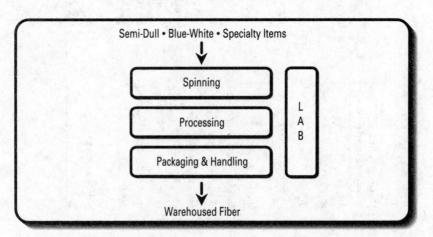

**Figure I.2. The Same Manufacturing Facility
After a Team-Based Redesign**

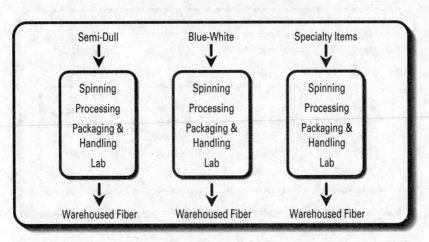

Figure I.3. A Functionally Designed Insurance Company Before Redesign

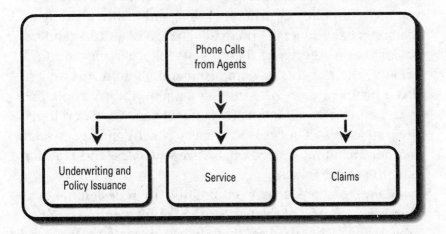

frequently occurred because customer files were in between departments (and thus unavailable), there was little coordination, and the people providing the information had little motivation because they were dealing with faceless agents over the phone. And, importantly, there was no way to measure success except through annual evaluations with supervisors.

Figure I.4. The Same Insurance Company with Regional Teams

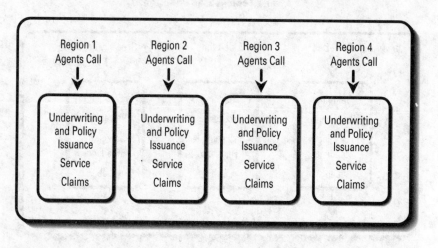

When the company organized teams assigned to specific agents and then cross-trained in all three functions (underwriting and policy issuance, service, and claims), the team members experienced a dramatic change of attitude and behavior. Teams displayed their agents' photographs and took pride in their agents' accomplishments. If an agent's client had a problem or registered a complaint, the team pitched in to help—after all, it was their client too. They developed their measures of success in terms of client and agent satisfaction, including service quality, repeat sales, and reaction time to resolve issues.

Many companies have committed to redesigning their workplaces as one of the first steps in implementing empowered teams. They realize that their current structure and processes present insurmountable barriers to achieving substantial performance gains. Others have decided to use a natural work team approach. The creation of natural teams is easier than reorganizing. With reorganizing, more turf battles occur, heavy equipment might need to be relocated, facility structures might have to change, and employee resistance to the new way of doing things can be very strong

indeed. Besides, as you'll see in many of the twenty implementations, often the work and processes are already organized in a logical fashion.

There is no right or wrong course of action. But one
word of caution: trying to impose natural work teams on
cumbersome bureaucratic processes and structures may increase your risk of a failed implementation.

Cross-Functional Teams

Cross-functional teams consist of members representing
various departments or functions. Most of the organizations
described in this book have some form of *permanent cross-
functional teams*—for example, Figure I.5 illustrates the
multiple governance responsibilities assigned to natural
work teams at the Hannaford Brothers distribution center.
Responsibilities commonly are called "star" assignments because of the shape of the diagram. Everyone on the redesigned work team, either individually or with one or two

**Figure I.5. "Star" Responsibilities—A Graphic Way of Illustrating
Responsibility Areas Allotted to Team Members.**

others, is responsible for a star point area. About once a month, members of a standing cross-functional team meet with their counterparts from the other work teams to coordinate, develop plans, and make decisions affecting the entire organization. For example, about once a month the plant-wide cross-functional safety team meets to discuss safety issues. This cross-functional team is composed of safety star point team members from the various work teams.

Temporary cross-functional teams are set up for special projects: planning a new performance management system, working on a product changeover, solving a key customer problem. These teams might also be assigned to improve a major organizational process or develop a new product. The use of cross-functional teams usually follows the installation of permanent work teams and builds on the skills and confidence developed in those teams. The permanent work team members continue to improve the processes and quality in their own work areas and begin to serve on cross-functional teams that take on bigger challenges and larger projects that cross team boundaries. Many of these cross-functional teams are highly self-directed. They may function without a formal leader, set their own agendas, and take responsibility for action.

The organizations profiled in this book, for the most part, use natural or redesigned work teams *and* cross-functional teams. These teams, when used in combination, maximize both the feelings of empowerment and the achievement of performance gains.

Key Points to Watch

As you read the team cases it will be helpful to pay special attention to the following points. They will make your benchmarking journey much more meaningful.

Enhanced Job Responsibilities. The jobs performed by a team provide opportunities for empowerment and participation in decision making with management. In moving to teams, most organizations significantly broaden their employees' empowerment. Note the wide range of job-related responsibilities handed off to teams on a day-to-day basis—decisions related to quality, productivity, monitoring budgets, vendor selection, and more.

Governance Responsibilities. Empowering people includes giving them more control over areas not directly related to their outputs or services—such as vacation and overtime scheduling, disciplinary authority, and training others. These issues are critical to a person's job satisfaction. If people are treated as adults in terms of job decisions but treated as children in terms of the work environment, it will be difficult to achieve high levels of empowerment. Employees cannot, of course, expect complete responsibility for governance. Anarchy would prevail if everyone governed themselves—scheduling their own work and coming and going as they please. Clearly, coordination must be maintained for work to be accomplished.

Yet allowing teams to make decisions that affect their governance can be highly beneficial. Teams often can make decisions that otherwise would be no-win decisions for leaders—such as deciding who should work overtime or who should be assigned to which tasks. When team members make such decisions, they are more committed to the outcome, feel trusted, and understand all the factors leading to the decision. These responsibilities, however, can be tougher for a team to handle than those associated with work output. Teams can be objective about a quality problem, for example, but might find objectivity difficult when decisions affect their co-workers. Note how our case teams get involved in both enhanced job responsibilities and governance responsibilities, helping team members feel a sense of job ownership and organizational identification.

Multiple Skilling. Many of the case teams have implemented multiple skilling (or cross-training), which requires team members to learn many or all of the skills needed for the team to accomplish its goals. Multiple skilling has several advantages:

- Relieving the tedium of repeating the same task throughout the day.
- Providing increased staffing flexibility and having members who can help each other when problems occur or heavy volume demands arise.
- Giving team members a better understanding of how different jobs fit with each other and how each member contributes to overall output.
- Encouraging team members to help in the development and training of others. (Everyone benefits if everyone is cross-trained.)
- Providing a source of pride and achievement for team members when they are certified in a new task. Posting cross-training accomplishments provides an opportunity for management and peer reinforcement as well as self-reinforcement.

As you read the cases, note the degree of cross-training (both in terms of task depth and breadth), the reduction in voluminous and dysfunctional job classifications, and the connections between cross-training and compensation.

Training. Team members and leaders must make significant changes in behavior to work successfully in an empowered team environment. Some will make the transition easily with little help, but most will need significant assistance. Formal training programs, on-the-job coaching, and reinforcement are key components used by the organizations profiled in this book. Note the commitment to formal (off-the-job) training and informal coaching. Pay particular attention not only to the amount of training but to the range of skills team members and leaders must master in their new environments.

Titles. To reflect changes in responsibility, organizations often change the titles of people when teams are formed. Title changes don't guarantee changes in performance, of course, but they do send a powerful message. The following list will help you equate levels and responsibilities among the organizations profiled:

Titles used in traditional organizations	*Titles used in team-based organizations*
Executive/senior manager	Executive/senior manager
Manager	Manager, coach
Supervisor	Group leader, team leader, facilitator, coach, supporter, counselor, partner, internal consultant
Leader (nonmanagement employee assumes limited responsibility)	Team leader, coordinator, coach (nonmanagement leader of team)
Employee	Team member, associate, technician, team representative, processor

Team Size. There is no magic number relative to team size. The appropriate size depends on the team's function (although there must be a limit to how many people can be on one team).

The Leader's Role. There are several models of leadership within empowered teams. Some organizations opt for a model of shared leadership; others keep a formal (but hopefully empowering) team leader permanently in place; still others rotate leadership responsibilities. Also note how organizations handle the role of leadership outside the team itself: What happens to current supervisors and managers? Where do they go? How are they "redeployed"? What types of special training do they need? Above all, note how organizations involve them as partners in the change process—which, as you will see, is a key ingredient of a successful team implementation.

Use of Resources in Redesign. While most of these organizations have used internal or external consulting help to redesign and implement teams, some have elected to do it themselves through a combination of benchmarking trips, reading, and trial and error. As you will see, the successful implementation is a combination of science and art.

Relationship with Unions. Five of the twenty organizations are unionized. Note how unions are involved in both the team planning phase and the ongoing team process. In some cases unions were stumbling blocks; in others they were active partners in the journey toward empowered teams. Pay attention to management's attitude toward union involvement as well.

Aligning Systems. Many organizations find that successful team implementation demands a change in companywide systems. Two systems we've highlighted are compensation and performance management. Note how organizations have redesigned these systems to better reflect empowerment and the team concept. Team involvement in the appraisal process

and "pay for application of multiple skills" are two trends you
will see in many of the cases.

Team Maturity. The twenty case teams are divided into two
maturity levels: new teams and mature teams. Note the differences among the teams at these levels. Maturity is not
defined in terms of years but in terms of sophistication, confidence, skills, and areas of responsibility handled by teams.

- At the new team level, team members, leaders, and the
  organization still are struggling as teams take on more
  responsibility and the culture shifts toward empowerment. As everyone is learning, there may be confusion
  and even some pain, but there is also a conviction that
  there is indeed a light at the end of the tunnel.
- At the mature team level, the team and its members are
  taking a larger view of responsibility—often involving
  suppliers and customers. Members also are involved
  with cross-functional process improvement or reengineering teams. Watch how mature teams grapple with
  keeping up the momentum and challenge.

Organizations Profiled. You probably will be most interested in learning about organizations similar to your own in
terms of industry, location, or size. Therefore, as shown in
Table I.1, you will see a variety of organizational types:

- Manufacturing/service (across a wide range of
  industries)
- Union/nonunion
- Start-up/existing operations
- United States/international

Sources of Benchmarking Information. All the teams profiled were known to us through site visits, consulting relationships, and meetings. Information for the profiles was obtained through questionnaires and then in-depth interviews of those in the organization responsible for implementing teams. At times, these interviews were supplemented with additional site visits and interviews with team members and leaders. All the organizations have seen draft copies of their profile so they could check its accuracy.

PART ONE

Start-Up and Early Stages

1

Focusing on the Patient to Meet the Challenges of Health Care Reform

Cape Coral Hospital
Cape Coral, Florida

Industry	Health care
Union	None
Type of team implementation	Redesigning teams around patient care and business units
First teams started	1992
Employees	1,300
Percentage in teams	10 percent
Team size	15
Team responsibilities	Once the system is fully implemented, teams will cross-train so that primary caregivers can learn to administer patient services normally handed off to a multitude of specialists—for example, registered nurses eventually will be drawing blood and performing intravenous, respiratory, and physical therapies. Teams will also be expected to work on continuous improvement projects, monitor budgets, and determine schedules.

Organization-wide team responsibilities	Implementation teams are focusing on patient care and business units. Currently teams do not have organizationwide duties other than team implementation. Future responsibilities have not yet been determined.
Team leadership and governance	Implementation teams rotate leadership monthly. Leaders are primarily responsible for keeping meeting agendas and reporting to the steering team. Once the implementation is complete, extended patient care teams will be fully self-directed and will rotate their own leaders. Leaders' responsibilities will include record keeping, communicating with other teams, and facilitating team meetings.
Leadership outside teams	A steering team composed of the vice president and other executives worked with the implementation teams to establish team boundaries and had ultimate authority over redesigned systems and processes.
Team compensation	No change to the compensation system; team members are not compensated for participation.
First-year team member training	All team members are trained in team meeting skills, quality and problem-solving techniques, team interaction skills, decision-making skills, and facilitation and coaching skills. All team members and most employees have received twenty-five hours of culture change training to become familiar with empowered work environments.

Subsequent team member training	Not applicable at this time.
First-year leadership training	Same as first-year team member training.
Subsequent leadership training	Not applicable at this time.
How team members are selected	Design team members were selected by managers from volunteers. Once the team implementation is complete, team members will interview and select new members.
How team performance is evaluated	Extended patient care teams will be evaluated on their ability to meet patient care standards and continuous improvement goals. Specific systems have not yet been worked out.
Team impact on organization	Too soon to tell. Anticipated results include lower operating costs and more time spent with patients rather than administrative chores.
Key lessons	• Culture change training is an indispensable step in preparing for major reorganization. • Team charters must be realistic and clear. Team members must review their charters periodically to ensure they are headed in the right direction. • Clear boundaries should be established between steering and imple-

mentation teams in a restructuring effort. Unclear boundaries caused resentment when the steering team vetoed the implementation teams' efforts to redesign processes that were "off limits." At times both teams had different notions about their boundaries—undermining the trust and cooperation both teams needed to be effective.

Background

Located just inland from the southwest "Shell Coast" of Florida, Cape Coral is a pleasant, somewhat insular community that attracts many retirees. Cape Coral Hospital, a nonprofit community hospital with 1,300 employees, is the community's sole health care provider; few residents want to travel outside the community for health care. But Cape Coral Hospital's strength in its home market does little to shield it from the forces that are transforming the health care business. In 1993, a third of the nation's 900,000 hospital beds were empty each night. Hospitals have been closing, merging, or laying off large numbers of employees. Group purchasing alliances, insurance companies, and federal and state governments are squeezing hospitals from all sides. Meanwhile, costs continue to rise.

With more than 70 percent of its patients currently covered by Medicare and most of the rest covered by insurance companies (which limit what they will pay for patient care), administrators at Cape Coral have spent a lot of time looking at ways to survive in the rapidly changing health care business. Long-term planning is difficult, however, because little is certain in the health care industry. In other industries, restructuring usually is spurred by conventional market forces. But when it comes to health care, virtually all the rules about what society is willing to pay are being rewritten. Long-term plans, no matter how carefully devised, might bear little relevance to actual conditions. The only thing that looks like a sure bet in health care is that the pressure to reduce costs will increase.

Cape Coral executives concluded that responding to this uncertainty would probably depend on employee involvement—specifically, on how well employees could balance the demands of delivering a high-quality "product" while adjusting to pressures to control costs and improve efficiency. From everything the executives had read and heard, team-based organizations seemed like the organizational design they were looking for. Yet the health care industry is not particularly suited to reengineering around teams. Stiff regulations, rigid hierarchies, intense specialization, fragmented patient care (few health care workers perform more than one or two tasks), occasionally strained physician/hospital staff relationships—all make such changes inordinately difficult.

Informally, Cape Coral had been trying to resolve the fragmentation of patient services for several years before it embarked on a dramatic restructuring program in 1992. Cape Coral was among a handful of hospitals that began seriously exploring "unbundling" patient care and then "rebundling" tasks to create multiskilled caregiver teams. Cape Coral's administrators were closely following the progress of nearby Lakeland Regional Medical Center, one of several hospitals participating in a pilot program to create multiskilled teams to deliver most patient services.

Cape Coral's decision in 1992 to begin construction of an eighty-bed wing (a major expansion for a hospital of Cape Coral's size) and to renovate the existing facility prompted an extensive restructuring program, one of the most far reaching undertaken by a U.S. hospital, which was called

Care 2000. As part of its restructuring program, Cape Coral set an ambitious goal: to deliver 80 percent of all patient services on patient floors (up from about 50 percent). This move would cut costs, reduce inefficient handoffs, and above all give caregivers time to spend with their patients instead of their paperwork. But accomplishing this goal would require more than continuous improvements—it would demand a whole new design for delivering patient services.

A Team System to Implement Change

Change at Cape Coral began with a steering team composed of most of the hospital's top officers, including the chief operating and chief financial officers, vice presidents, and numerous assistant vice presidents (whose titles changed as the reorganization unfolded). The steering team was chartered to establish values and a mission statement as a framework for the reorganization process—a vision for a dramatically different organization. The values are simple. The Cape Coral of the future is to be guided by, among other things, empowerment ("employees working in teams with ownership and control over their jobs") and productivity (achieved by job and process simplification). The team was to establish goals, milestones, and parameters for the redesign efforts and model new behavior to reflect the new values. For most of the executives on the team, this shift required an introduction to some new concepts, including managing in a team-based environment. Thus the steering team was the first to undergo twenty-five hours of culture change and team skills training.

Within days of its first meeting, the steering team formed the design team. Its mandate included reorganizing Cape Coral's forty-odd departments into a series of care centers and business centers, a process that was to take nearly a year (see Exhibit 1.1). The design team had fifteen members,

Exhibit 1.1. Cape Coral Hospital Design Team Charter.

Purpose:	To organize people to redesign the hospital so that at least 80 percent of all resources and services are focused on patient needs; to create business units of empowered teams that are continuously dedicated to the mission of Cape Coral Hospital.
Completion:	When the business units are effectively operational; after that point the design team continues to maintain Care 2000 through individual work as implementation team members.
Budget:	The design team can make any budgetary requests to the steering team in terms of time allocation to Care 2000; the design team can spend as much time as needed, as long as the operational integrity of their departments is maintained.
Authority:	To research and recommend any changes to the structure and systems of the hospital. The steering and administration teams will actually approve changes before they are implemented or even communicated to the rest of the hospital. The design team has the authority to implement day-to-day operational decisions with the assistance and guidance of the care center administrator.
Meeting and Reporting Status	The design team will meet at least every three weeks and can meet more often if needed.
Success Criteria	• Directors are educated on Care 2000 principles.
	• A communication plan with timely process and content information to the staff.
	• Team member satisfaction with the transition.
Selected Parameters:	The design team may
	• Lead its own meetings
	• Collect its own data for Care 2000
	• Rotate administrative assistants/executive secretaries for design team projects
	• Meet more often than originally planned if necessary
	• Renegotiate roles so that it has time to work on design team projects
	• Borrow or share resources within and from other departments, provided all parties agree and standards are maintained
	The design team must work with the steering team to
	• Remove someone from the design team and select the implementation teams
	• Incur expenses
Responsibilities:	• Assisting with decision making on how data is aggregated
	• Examining data in the analysis phase for accuracy
	• Collecting feedback and other data to measure the success of Care 2000 on the identified targets

Exhibit 1.1. Cape Coral Hospital Design Team Charter, Cont'd.

- Collecting feedback from the staff on steering team/administration team support for Care 2000
- Documenting the Care 2000 process, activities, and results
- Providing a network of information and involvement with other department directors/managers
- Being the primary communicators of Care 2000 updates to the staff
- Providing feedback to the steering and administration teams on their support for Care 2000 and modeling of the Care 2000 values
- Becoming change agents and promoting Care 2000 as part of an overall staff education process
- Relaying problems or dissatisfaction with Care 2000 to the steering team
- Making structured and systems redesign recommendations to the steering team
- Working with the implementation teams to make approved redesign strategies work
- Recommending capital equipment changes on the unit with the implementation teams
- Fixing technical problems at the unit level
- Educating the department heads and implementation teams on the Care 2000 vision, patient-focused care, and empowerment principles
- Educating all team members on the Care 2000 process and the desired results
- Recommending a transition plan (including a cross-training plan) to get units operational
- Assuring people that they are uniquely important

among them nursing heads and department managers from the hospital's three major functional divisions: patient care, ancillary services, and support services. Two physicians volunteered to serve on the team, but after attending two meetings they decided they couldn't afford the time. (Like physicians at most hospitals, those at Cape Coral are private practitioners. While supportive of the reorganization, few felt they could meet patient care demands and serve on the design team.)

Together the design and steering teams explored how work processes and organizational structure would have to change to improve service and reduce costs. Similar approaches were being undertaken by other hospitals at the time, but not on the same scale as Cape Coral. This hospital was determined to revamp not only the way medical care was delivered but also the way all nonmedical areas functioned. Eventually, a radically new organizational framework was proposed. It consisted of four patient care centers (surgical, general medical, specialty medical, and outpatient) and three business centers (accounting, billing, and records; facilities and management; and employee services). The patient care centers would serve as "mini-hospitals" performing most of the patient/administrative services. The business centers would support the four patient care centers.

The design team performed the bulk of the reorganization work. It not only collected and analyzed data from departments throughout the organization but also kept much of the hospital informed on progress in achieving the goals outlined by the steering team. The design team also served as a communication link between the managers and executives on the steering team and other hospital employees, making sure that steering team members were aware of potential problems or dissent among employee groups.

According to its charter, the design team's task was complete once the business centers were operational. At this point the team disbanded, but with a great deal of reluctance—the yearlong process, while grueling at times, had built a great sense of camaraderie and dedication. "The natural tendency would have been to invent new things for teams to do," recalls one member. "But we came to the conclusion that it was time to go on to the next step."

Implementation Teams

After the design team concluded its work, implementation teams were formed to focus on the *how* of Cape Coral's reorganization. These teams, which included many design team members, were chartered to design the work systems for the care and business centers, focusing on revising Cape Coral's entire patient care delivery system.

The first implementation team was formed in the hospital's obstetrics (OB) unit, part of the new general medical care center. OB was chosen because it had only two types of patients—normal and problem deliveries—whereas other units handled as many as fifteen types. Lessons learned here could be applied to tougher challenges in other units. Once the reorganization is complete, each medical center will have at least one implementation team with a structure similar to the OB team and will include at least one member of the disbanded design team because their team experience will undoubtedly prove useful.

The nine-person OB implementation team comprised three nurses from the unit selected by the rest of the OB nursing staff, the OB nursing manager, and several other managers, including the directors of human resources and medical records, both members of the design team. All members took turns as team leader for a month; their chief role was to prepare agendas and facilitate meetings. Dan Edgar, Cape Coral's chief operating officer and executive vice president, was a member of the team, too, but his role was somewhat unusual. As a steering team member, Edgar from the beginning was one of the most active senior executives in the reorganization. On the implementation team, however, he considered himself an observer and resource for the rest of the team. His job was to help the team keep sight of the principles developed by the steering and design teams.

Above all, his presence was a symbol of top management's continued support for the change.

Before the OB team began working, it went through the same training as the steering and design teams plus some additional components: developing a team charter, team interaction dynamics, team decision making, and meeting skills. Then the team began a detailed analysis of how the OB unit operated by identifying all the complex medical, support, housekeeping, and other tasks performed in the unit. The issues facing the OB team may have been simpler than those facing other implementation teams, but they were nonetheless challenging. How would the "span of care" determine the size and makeup of teams? How would teams interact with physicians and with other teams? What training would team members need to become multifunctional? How multifunctional could teams become when many of the medical services required training and certification set by outside licensing agencies?

In the end, the OB implementation team settled on a plan to create three or four extended teams of eleven members in the unit, representing all three shifts and a separate weekend shift. Each team would be responsible for four to eight patients. During each shift, only two team members were present—a registered nurse and another registered nurse or a licensed practicing nurse. During busy periods, teams were designed to "flex up" to accommodate another team member—another nurse or a nurse's aide—so patients would not have to be reassigned to other teams. Providing this flexible team member is one of the issues the implementation team is still working on.

Cape Coral hopes the OB teams and those in other units will become largely self-directed—determining their own schedules and personnel needs, setting their own improvement goals, handling budgets, appraising team members' performance—in short, everything self-directed teams do in manufacturing or service businesses.

Future Team Vision

Cape Coral's team approach will change many aspects of the patient care system, especially the highly compartmentalized way patient services are delivered now. There will be far less need to wheel patients from one specialized treatment or diagnostic unit to another as services are combined and delivered by multifunctional care teams on patient floors. While no employees will do anything for which they are not trained and licensed, nurses in the new teams may find themselves sharing some of the more routine chores once done by lower-paid personnel—for example, drawing blood may be done by all members of a patient care team, not just nurse's aides. (This includes RNs, who typically are paid three times more than nurse's aides.) Cape Coral expects that by requiring higher-paid personnel to share in more routine tasks, overall patient care costs will actually decrease. In hospitals, as in most organizations, the cost of handoffs and rigid job functions has a major impact on the cost of doing business.

Patients will benefit, too. With caregivers sharing more tasks, patients can receive service when it's most convenient for *them* and will no longer have to wait until specialized personnel are available. And by limiting the number of faces that patients will see, the health care system may seem more personal.

Management at Cape Coral is changing as well. The design team's reorganization plan called for the elimination of three of the hospital's seven layers of management. Beneath the president and executive vice president levels, there used to be vice presidents, assistant vice presidents, department managers, assistant department managers, and supervisors.

Once reorganized into care and business centers, the middle layer of managers will be replaced by seven center administrators and one director for every forty patient beds. Patient care teams will report to directors. The director will combine various management positions into one and be responsible for various functional areas such as medical records, environmental services, and engineering.

Cape Coral began its transition to teams by communicating a strong no-layoff policy. Nevertheless, the steering and design teams were open to the possibility that employees attached to their former status as supervisors or managers might find it difficult to adjust to the new team environment. The steering and design teams also knew that nurse specialists might feel anxious about the new system. Would multi-functional patient care teams dilute the value of their specialized training? It's a question that the specialists—and the industry as a whole—will have to answer as the team implementation proceeds. In some instances, nurses will have to brush up on many of the skills they learned in nursing school but have stopped practicing, such as drawing blood and intravenous therapy. Cape Coral hopes team members will be able to cross-train quickly in many types of respiratory and physical therapies. Training in more complex procedures, such as basic chest and extremity X rays, will require changes in Florida's medical licensing requirements as well as national standards set by hospital accreditation organizations. These organizations have been slow to change in the past, but with mounting pressure to control health care costs they are increasingly willing to look at changes to the system.

Results

Cape Coral's restructuring "gets us to about 50 to 60 percent of the gains we have to make," says COO Edgar. "Continuous quality improvement has to get us the rest of it." That task might prove more difficult for hospitals than for other businesses, because hospitals face unique challenges. To survive, let alone thrive, hospitals like Cape Coral will have to deliver cost-effective, high-quality patient care. But quality in health care is an especially complex and changeable factor. Hospitals may no longer have exclusive rights to defining "medical appropriateness" as the demands of the consumer marketplace grow and as hospitals try to match the standards and quality of competing institutions. Meanwhile, hospitals like Cape Coral will continue to be squeezed by those who pay the bills.

Continuous improvement and the team system face major challenges in the health care environment. Thanks to the efforts of its teams, Cape Coral will be among the pioneers to develop solutions to these challenges. Yet many hurdles remain. Developing meaningful ways to reward team performance is a big issue because setting team goals might be easy for some teams and hard for others. Patient types and acuity levels will vary widely from team to team. Wringing out inefficiencies and improving quality might be easier in the OB unit, for instance, than in surgical units that care for many types of patients. The changing financial landscape will influence team goals, too. Achieving these goals without sacrificing the quality of patient care will be among a team's most challenging balancing acts.

Cape Coral Hospital is among the first health care facilities to virtually reinvent itself from the ground up. As an experiment in progress, there are few results to report. But this much is clear: the change process, relying on strong steering, design, and implementation teams, has worked relatively smoothly. When problems arose, they could usually be traced to unclear team responsibilities and ambiguous boundaries. The steering team found itself reining in the design and implementation teams on several occasions because they seemed to exceed their mandates. In retrospect, members of all three teams acknowledge the difficulty of defining clear-cut boundaries when no one could foresee all the issues that would surface. Though disputes may have been inevitable, the general feeling persists that lines of communication, while strong, need to be stronger.

Much of the confusion and anxiety that can accompany a team reorganization has been avoided at Cape Coral, many feel, by the twenty-five hours of culture change training that all employees receive. Even before most areas have begun formally reorganizing around teams, a great deal of natural teamwork has emerged. Often the early training is cited as the catalyst for change. Members of the steering and implementation teams continue to spend a lot of time talking to colleagues in other hospitals undertaking reorganization. Unlike Cape Coral, few of these hospitals seem to emphasize training to prepare employees for change—a mistake, Cape Coral team members feel, that other institutions will end up paying for later.

While no hospital has made the transition to a totally self-directed, team-based environment, Cape Coral has built an impressive foundation. The team effort that is guiding change at Cape Coral provides a good model for other health care facilities facing the same urgency to change—that is, nearly all U.S. hospitals.

2

The Evolving Role of Leadership
in Creating Flexible,
Productive Teams

Development Dimensions International
Pittsburgh, Pennsylvania

Industry	Printing, warehouse, and distribution facility for multination human resource company
Union	None
Type of team implementation	Self-directed work teams created from natural work groups; cross-functional process improvement teams
First teams started	1990
Employees	70
Percentage in teams	100 percent
Team size	2 to 15
Team responsibilities	Identifying and meeting customer requirements; planning and scheduling work; establishing improvement goals and measuring results; helping to select new team members; selecting suppliers; recommending new equipment; sharing fiscal budget accountability; participating in team performance appraisals; identifying team members' training needs and coordinating train-

ing; managing housekeeping and safety plantwide; handling administrative tasks such as tracking attendance and scheduling vacations and overtime.

Organization-wide team responsibilities

Participate on cross-functional product development teams, quality improvement teams, and process improvement teams (customer ordering, project management, MIS development).

Team leadership and governance

In most work groups, former supervisors became permanent team leaders; in work groups that had no supervisors, the facility leader and group leaders selected team leaders. As some of the original team leaders moved on to other positions in the company, team members chose their new leaders. In all eight teams, leaders share responsibilities and activities; in other words, they are "working" team leaders. They facilitate team meetings, help coordinate training, coach team members, and share responsibility for communicating with other teams and support groups.

Leadership outside teams

Group leaders—former managers now responsible for four teams each—are key resources for their teams. They help the teams develop and monitor budgets, set performance and production goals, handle performance evaluations, coach team members and leaders, oversee training, coordinate activities among teams, and lead the process of selecting new team members. Group leaders report to the facility leader.

Team compensation	Although no team-based compensation is used, the team's performance is weighted heavily in determining individual salary increases.
First-year team member training	About 200 hours of training in team interaction skills, problem-solving skills, developing and monitoring performance goals, customer service skills, and technical cross-training.
Subsequent team member training	About 100 hours of training in team meeting skills, giving and receiving feedback, basic budgeting skills, just-in-time, selecting new team members, and business knowledge. Members also receive advanced technical training and ongoing cross-training.
First-year leadership training	About 225 hours of training in the same skills as team members plus training in leading meetings and coaching.
Subsequent leadership training	About 100 hours of training in the same skills as team members plus skills in coaching, selecting new team members, managing and appraising performance, total quality management, communication, encouraging initiative, and workplace redesign.
How team members are selected	Initially teams were created from existing work groups. Today all new team members are selected via a special system focusing on team behavior and motivation.

Associates at all levels participate in the interviewing process; help develop, administer, and score job-specific tests and hands-on simulations; and take part in data integration sessions to determine the best-qualified candidates.

How team performance is evaluated

Guided by group leaders, the teams develop key result areas (KRAs) that are linked to the company's overall critical success factors. KRAs are broken down into objectives (*what* is to be accomplished) and dimensions (*how* objectives are to be accomplished). Teams are responsible for developing self-measurement methods and for monitoring their progress, which is reviewed twice a year with group leaders. Group leaders also meet with all team members to assess individual performance. Each objective and dimension is rated on a five-point scale.

Team impact on organization

Teams have made significant improvements over the past four years. Accuracy has improved dramatically, as evidenced by a 43 percent reduction in client-reported errors. Productivity has increased as well. With only a 12 percent increase in labor costs, employees are handling 86 percent more work. Revenue per employee is up a remarkable 64.5 percent. And the inventory space required for shelf products is down 20 percent, allowing ample space for new products. Moreover, team members report greater job satisfaction, improved collaboration, increased pride and job ownership, and higher self-esteem. They credit cross-training—and the resulting job diversity—with making their work more interesting and enjoyable.

Key lessons

- Technical cross-training can be invaluable, but that doesn't mean every team member has to know how to do every job. The important thing is that the *team* can handle every job.

- In making the transition to teams, it's imperative to focus not only on team members but also on team leaders; otherwise, leaders' needs get lost in the shuffle.

- Frequent, clear communication is a prerequisite for effective team interactions—especially when shift work is involved. Team members need to be in the know if they are to work together effectively.

Background

For nearly twenty-five years Development Dimensions International (DDI) has been providing organizations worldwide with leading-edge training, selection, and assessment programs—many of which include printed learning materials and videos. DDI has always handled much of its printing and distribution in house, and as the company grew the need for increased printing and distribution capacity expanded as well. In the mid-1980s, DDI purchased a printing company and a distribution center.

By the late 1980s, the burgeoning business needed even more printing and distribution capacity. Thus, in 1989, the company made a critical decision: in order to meet current and future demands, it would expand the distribution facility and consolidate all printing, warehousing, distribution, and client service functions under one roof. The 61,000-square-foot facility, which became known as Customer Service Inc. (CSI), also gave DDI a new opportunity to practice what it preached. For years DDI had been helping its clients with their own start-up and expansion projects by designing team-oriented, high-involvement workplaces. With the new facility DDI could further its efforts by instituting its own empowered teams.

CSI organized around the natural work team concept for two reasons: heavy dependence on equipment and technology made physical redesign difficult, and the work flow was already organized efficiently. CSI arranged its work teams around eight production areas—administration, prepress, press, bindery, material control, looseleaf, production (collation), and shipping. Recognizing the importance of experienced leaders and coaches, CSI also decided to work with its current leadership structure: the vice president of distribution and printing became the facility leader; the two managers became group leaders, one responsible for printing and the other for distribution. Most of the work units already had supervisors, who now became the team leaders; if units did not have supervisors, the facility leader and group leaders appointed team leaders.

At first glance it would appear that the leadership role changes were in name only, but that wasn't the case at all. In fact, the changing role of the leaders was one of the greatest challenges facing CSI's team implementation.

The Changing Role of Leaders

With the move to teams, leaders' roles changed in three important ways: in the number of direct reports, in perceived status, and in the level of control and responsibility. Before teams, employees reported directly to their supervisors; after teams, they reported to their group leaders. This adjustment meant that team leaders (formerly supervisors) lost direct reports whereas group leaders (formerly managers) gained direct reports—lots of them. The former press group supervisor, for example, who originally had fifteen direct reports, had no direct reports after becoming a team leader. Under the new system, these fifteen team members reported to the printing group leader who also was responsible for the administration, prepress, press, and bindery teams. Thus a group leader who once had only a few supervisors as direct reports ended up with more than twenty-five direct reports.

Not surprisingly, team leaders and group leaders alike reacted somewhat negatively at first. Team leaders felt they'd lost a much-coveted and hard-earned position as "boss." Group leaders believed they'd been handed a lot more work—hiring, training, coaching, appraising, and listening to some two dozen people. This was progress? Jeff Priano, the press group team leader at the time, admits, "It felt like the rug was being pulled out from under me." When a former direct report said jokingly to him, "I don't have to listen to you anymore—you're not my boss," Priano knew there was more than an element of truth to the remark.

While the facility leader and the group leaders were planning the introduction of teams, they anticipated the supervisors' fears, anxieties, and needs. Yet Mary Hartman, the distribution group leader, says they failed to recognize how much the change would affect their own lives. Three months into the implementation, for example, she realized how dramatically her own role had changed. "We had done so much planning for the team members—their needs, their fears, their training—that we forgot about ourselves!" she says, recalling the adjustment to her new role of coaching twenty-eight team members about their new roles and increased responsibilities. Priano confesses that it was confusing, even a little embarrassing, to move from his job as a supervisor to a team leader. As a team leader he also was a team *member,* which meant running the presses. "When I became a supervisor," explains Priano, "I moved away from working on machines. Now part of my job was operating the equipment again."

Concerns about status weren't the only fears haunting some of the new leaders. With all the hoopla about "flattened organizations" and "eliminating middle management," some of them genuinely feared for their jobs. Although most team leaders readily admitted to thinking their new jobs would be easier without the responsibility of direct reports, they were not sure about how the move to teams might affect their perceived value to the company. If the group leaders *led* and the team members *did,* would there still be a place for the former supervisors? Or would they be let go?

The fear of losing control was another monster to be reckoned with. Priano explains it this way: "When I was a supervisor, I knew where everything was. I knew all the details. But when we started with teams, a lot of the details were left to team members. I felt out of the loop and worried about losing control." Steve Horton, the printing group leader, was a bit more optimistic, although he too acknowledges that he feared losing control. Experience had shown him that some employees would be reluctant to take on additional responsibilities. He also worried that other people would "mess up" what he already knew how to do well. Ray Stich, facility leader, admits that he was concerned initially about team members—especially entry-level employees—

making more decisions, and more difficult decisions, than required in the past.

As CSI's leaders grappled with these issues they were understandably confused and at times discouraged. But they were buoyed by the support they received from DDI's top management. Stich met with DDI's president several times to learn more about the team concept and his vision for its implementation in the new facility. As Stich learned more, he shared his knowledge and enthusiasm with the group leaders, who, in turn, championed the process with the team leaders. It wasn't long before a sense of adventure proved contagious. Soon team leaders began sharing their respect for empowered teams with team members—and anyone else who would listen. Despite their initial doubts about changing roles, CSI's leaders became the key drivers for the team implementation. (Priano recently became an operations leader for a group of sixty permanent and part-time associates. His first decision: the group should become a self-directed team.)

Training Is Job One

No one at DDI expected CSI's leaders to become empowering overnight. No one expected them to know how to lead their teams through all the stages of evolution they were certain to encounter. Rather, it was accepted throughout the organization that the leaders would need to learn new skills to be effective leaders of empowered teams. Similarly, team members would need to learn new skills if they were to solve problems, make decisions, and deal with one another effectively. So, from the outset, training was emphasized—not just in words, but in a commitment of time and resources.

During the first five months of the team implementation, members completed workshops on developing interpersonal and team skills, recognizing opportunities and problems, developing and monitoring performance goals, and developing customer service skills. Cross-training and other technical training needs were addressed, too, as part of the comprehensive team-building approach. Team leaders completed the same workshops as team members plus training in leading meetings. Group leaders were trained as program trainers so they could deliver parts of the programs to others. They also received additional leadership training to support the training they had already received.

Not everyone immediately understood the need for such extensive training. "In anticipation of associates' concerns, we were careful to communicate as clearly as possible exactly what training would take place, emphasizing the benefits to both the individual and the company," Stich explains. "We provided generous amounts of training and coaching to help associates deal with new responsibilities, and we emphasized that teams were a permanent fixture." Although the concentrated training delivered in the first five months led to a more knowledgeable workforce, it had its downside too. "Originally, there was a lot of overtime," says Rick Hamilton, leader of the prepress team, "because we were spending time in training classes and meetings. In production, we work under tight deadlines, and you can't stop production because you have a meeting that lasts all afternoon." DDI dealt with this concern by hiring temporary workers and paying overtime, as necessary, to meet business needs.

In subsequent years, team members completed advanced training in meeting skills, in giving and receiving feedback, and in selecting new team members. As well, team members completed training in technical business knowledge, basic budgeting skills, just-in-time (JIT), advanced technical skills, and cross-training. Subsequent training for team leaders included DDI workshops on giving and receiving feedback, coaching, and selecting new team members; they also completed sessions on basic budgeting skills, JIT, and advanced technical training. Group leaders and the facility leader participated in DDI workshops on managing effective interactions, selecting new team members, encouraging initiative, managing and appraising performance, and workplace redesign.

CSI associates found workshops, supplemental training sessions, and advanced technical training to be essential to their success. But what they're most proud of—perhaps because they were the ones to conceive the idea in the first place—is combining all the components of training into an extensive cross-training program. From the beginning of the team implementation, CSI associates recognized the need to master additional pieces of equipment and to learn new tasks that weren't part of their primary job functions. Cross-training allowed team members to rotate through areas or work on machinery they might not have been exposed to otherwise.

Associates were encouraged to train up and down the supplier-customer chain. Members of the press team, for example, trained with the prepress team to learn what happens to plates before they reach the press. At the other end of the process, they trained in the collating and binding areas so they could understand how printing changes would affect the assembling of large orders. To facilitate cross-training, team members assumed responsibility for their own training and development and set up skill matrices that list all the skills required of a team. Throughout CSI, such charts are displayed prominently. Team members can see at a glance who are the experts for handling different machines or specific tasks—and where they can find help when they need it. The charts also indicate how leaders and team members can reinforce their cross-training programs. The press team's matrix, for example, shows each team member's proficiency in the "soft" skills like screening resumes as well as the "hard" skills like operating different presses.

As team members become cross-trained, they rely on one another to fill in during absences and to handle peaks in production and service demands. In essence, all team members have the opportunity to learn and develop new skills, increase task flexibility, and improve customer service. But Horton is quick to point out the misconception that cross-training means everyone has to know how to do every job. "What works best," he contends, "is to see if it's cost-effective and then to find out which team members want to learn a new skill. We have to remember to value differences among team members. In the end, the *team* has to know how to do everything, not each individual."

Cross-training also helps develop senior team members. After years on the job, for example, many press operators became bored and, because they were at the top of the pay scale, saw only small salary increases. These employees were accustomed to running the most complicated piece of equipment in the shop, so, in a sense, they had nowhere to go and found little challenge in the job. But cross-training allowed them to learn new skills and become even more productive and satisfied with their jobs. Moreover, Priano believes cross-training has made the printing operation more efficient. "Everyone has a better understanding of the work process and how we all fit into the overall job," he explains. "We're light years away from shutting down the presses if someone calls in sick or takes vacation time. Presses that used to sit idle are now breaking production records."

Team members averaged about 200 hours of training—and team and group leaders about 225—in the first year. This time was split fairly evenly between technical and nontechnical training. Each successive year there was less formal training and more informal training and cross-training so that most associates, team members and leaders alike, now spend an average of 100 hours a year in formal training activities. This level probably will remain constant, at least in the near future. Ongoing training will focus on associates learning advanced technical skills or working toward different forms of certification.

A Day in the Life of a Team

Before teams, the managers and supervisors made the decisions and the employees did their jobs. With teams, however, roles became less defined and associates took on increased responsibilities in such areas as technical cross-training and leadership/governance tasks. For example, team members attend meetings to discuss ways to improve processes, how to handle problems, and how to distribute work. They also set goals and monitor progress. They learn how to select new team members, vendors, supplies, and capital equipment. They communicate with other teams about jobs and job-related issues. They indicate training needs and handle administrative tasks. And they constantly look at ways to do their jobs more effectively.

For Andy Betchoski, a member of the administration team, a typical day begins with reviewing what happened on the preceding shift, checking the status of current jobs, and prioritizing the day's work. Then the team develops an action plan—who does what by when—before starting production. The day might also include a demonstration of new equipment. "Before teams," says Betchoski, "the focus was on doing, with a little communication thrown in here and there. But now communication is more important, especially between shifts." Betchoski estimates that about 25 percent of his time is spent communicating. Ken Stetar, a press team member, agrees: "We've always talked. Teams haven't changed that. But now we're learning how to communicate better, and our turnaround time has improved because we've covered all the bases."

Another focus of the teams is continuous improvement of their processes. One team, for example, redesigned the work order envelope to eliminate duplicating information. With the old system, separate forms requiring the same information had to be completed repeatedly. The new envelope captures all relevant information and is filled out only once. According to Betchoski, dozens of team members' ideas have resulted in better, faster processes throughout the facility.

Patrice Andres, a former prepress team member who now is an electronic publishing specialist at DDI's corporate headquarters, still remembers the excitement she felt while learning new jobs. Andres especially enjoyed contacting outside vendors, budgeting, and analyzing quality and production results. She also became adept at communicating with her internal partners in DDI's graphics and editorial departments. To improve communication with graphics and editorial associates, Andres and Rick Hamilton, her team leader, developed a one-day orientation session that covered basic camera exposure, initial film assembly, contacting, mask cutting, contact film assembly, final film assembly, and proofing. Participants at these sessions produce film from artwork and assemble the job as if it were being put on press. Questions start almost as soon as a session begins as editors and designers immediately see areas where they can work better with the prepress team. As they cut rubylith windows and position screens by hand, they begin to understand the painstaking care and attention the prepress team devotes to a job before it can go to the presses. A new respect grows among professionals who are responsible for different phases of production.

Systems Alignment

Whenever an organization introduces a radical culture change—such as teams—systems must be aligned with the new culture. Such was the case at CSI. Almost all systems were affected, especially selection, performance management, compensation, and recognition. These systems changed in two important ways: increased team involvement and an increased emphasis on the team rather than the individual.

The *selection system* relies on assessing the qualifications of candidates against the dimensions that are deemed necessary for success in a job. Tests and simulations are used to determine an incumbent's skills and motivations, too, and then a team of selection-certified interviewers integrates the data and determines the best candidate for the job. None of this technology changed with the move to teams, but Mary Hartman led a major effort to redesign the selection system to accommodate teams. Now team members assist in the process. They interview candidates. They develop, administer, and score job-specific tests and hands-on simulations. They participate in a data-integration session. Indeed, their increased involvement has greatly improved the effectiveness of CSI's selection system, has heightened their understanding of the importance of selecting the right people to work on their teams, and has deepened their commitment to the job success of the people *they* selected.

The *performance management system* was modified to support the team concept too. At CSI, team performance is emphasized. Group leaders meet with individual team members to rate their success on objectives and dimensions. Team performance accounts for 70 percent of each rating and individual performance for 30 percent. CSI's teams also are responsible for developing self-measurement methods for collecting data and monitoring their progress, which the teams review twice a year with the group leaders.

Aligning the *compensation system* with the new focus on teams was a special challenge. At the start of the implementation, team leaders, who had formerly been supervisors, earned considerably more than team members. In the move toward a more egalitarian system, leaders' salaries now increase at a slower rate than team members'; eventually this policy will result in all salaries reaching somewhat equal levels. Another compensation issue involved high-performing team members who were accustomed to receiving higher raises than their lower-performing counterparts. For the high achievers, there was concern that the new system, with its focus on *team* performance, wouldn't reward them as well as in the past. They questioned the decision to weight team performance more heavily than individual performance. Today there is much more acceptance of the value of team-driven compensation, and high-performers act as role models for their fellow team members. They exert peer pressure to keep team performance high—because when the team does well, everyone wins.

The *recognition system* changed as well. Today there is a special Recognition and Rewards Committee made up of team members, and a system has been put in place to encourage team members to recognize one another for outstanding performance. Under the system, team members submit commendations about others to the Recognition and Rewards Committee. The committee reviews the commendations and awards a small bonus to the associates cited. Periodically the names of team members submitting and receiving commendations are placed in a hat and names are drawn for small monetary rewards or gift certificates—thus promoting the continued use of the recognition system. Group leaders also have special budgets for recognizing special efforts with lunches out and other tokens of appreciation. An important lesson has been learned at CSI: focusing on team performance doesn't mean overlooking individual performance. Some people have a strong need for recognition, and it's important to acknowledge it.

Results

In the span of four years, CSI transformed itself from a traditional printing and distribution facility to a model team-based operation. The benefits are fully appreciated by team members who say they like:

- Making more decisions and having influence over their jobs
- Thinking for themselves and wasting less time waiting for others to take action
- Having more variety and challenge in their work
- Becoming more capable and valuable to their team and the organization while feeling a real sense of job security
- Working in an atmosphere of innovation and constant improvement
- Seeing improved collaboration within and among teams—feeling like cohesive work units
- Having more visibility throughout DDI because of their accomplishments and participation on important action teams
- Being recognized for their successes at meeting—and sometimes exceeding—customer needs

These results parallel major improvements in other areas: quality, productivity, revenue per employee, physical space requirements for housing DDI's inventory, and more. One way CSI measures quality, for example, is by tracking customer-reported errors in materials. In the four years since the team implementation, errors have dropped by 43 percent. During the same four years, DDI's material sales increased by 84 percent. CSI's teams handle this significantly greater workload with only a 12 percent increase in staff—attesting to much-improved processes and systems that have resulted in remarkable strides in efficiency and productivity. Akin to improved processes and efficiency, the revenue per employee has increased by 64.5 percent since the inception of teams in 1990. Thanks primarily to a very successful JIT system, the space needed to house shelf materials has been reduced by 20 percent, thus allowing CSI to accommodate new products in the "saved" space. This means that CSI is saving DDI the expense of adding onto the present facility.

One of the key factors in the teams' success has been the focus on technical cross-training, which allows for much greater flexibility in the production process as well as welcome job diversity for team members. Initially teams assumed that in time every team member would master every job—an assumption that turned out to be impractical as well as unnecessary. Instead they learned that while it is critical for more than one person to be able to handle key jobs—like running major pieces of equipment—it isn't necessary for every team member to learn every job as long as the *team* can handle all the jobs. Teams came to recognize the importance of pinpointing customer needs and matching those needs with each team member's style, ability, and motivation.

Another important lesson was that the move to teams meant many different changes for everyone involved. And while it was extremely helpful to anticipate team members' concerns and questions, it was equally important to address leaders' uncertainty about their changing roles. This consideration proved critical in making a successful transition to teams.

Finally, CSI teams discovered the value of frequent, clear communication, especially between shifts. Team leaders and team members have found that the better the communication, the more productive the process because of minimized rework and errors. They also found that by talking with one another, sharing ideas and concerns, they became a more cohesive group and learned to value others' opinions and ideas more than ever before.

DDI is quite proud of its teams at CSI. They offer an outstanding example not only for the entire company but for team-based organizations everywhere.

3

Keeping in Step with a
Rapidly Changing Market

K Shoes, Ltd.
Cumbria, United Kingdom

Industry	Footwear manufacturing and retailing
Union	Footwear, Knitwear, and Allied Trades
Type of team implementation	Redesigned self-directed teams and cross-functional process improvement teams
First teams started	1990
Employees	1,100 in manufacturing (3,000 total)
Percentage in teams	Approximately 40 percent
Team size	5 to 8
Team responsibilities	Managing team resources based on marketplace demand for styles of shoes; performing quality assurance; understanding business and marketplace issues and their impact on demand; handling materials and equipment budgeting; controlling team profit and loss; identifying team training needs; conducting cross-training and problem solving during nonproduction time.

Organization-wide team responsibilities	Various multifunctional groups are formed to analyze work and human resources systems and make recommendations to management, but there is no formal mechanism for team input into organizationwide decision making.
Team leadership and governance	No formal team leaders. Team members meet daily; once a week they meet with team facilitators to discuss quality and performance issues and agree by consensus to make needed changes. Teams can voluntarily disband due to performance or interpersonal problems.
Leadership outside teams	Generally there are two layers of managers above teams in each small facility (100-300 employees): two or more team facilitators (formerly supervisors), who manage and coach ten or more teams, and a plant manager who reports to the corporate head of manufacturing.
Team compensation	Team members are salaried and pay is equalized as much as possible. Team bonuses and other incentives are avoided.
First-year team member training	Forty hours in the classroom and 140 hours on the job: team meeting skills, problem solving, team interaction skills, overall business knowledge and understanding the marketplace, workplace design, cross-training in as many as eight job skills.
Subsequent team member training	Overall business knowledge, supplier partnership development, retail store and customer visits, interviewing, team-building activities.

First-year leadership training	About eighty hours: team meeting skills, problem solving, team interaction skills, overall business knowledge and understanding the marketplace, workplace design, coaching.
Subsequent leadership training	Interviewing, team facilitation and development, supplier partnership development, computerized job analysis, and supervisory training.
How team members are selected	Most teams were created from existing work groups in old operational areas. Some teams are formed using computer-analyzed personality and work profiles to ensure compatibility.
How team performance is evaluated	Teams meet with team leaders frequently to discuss performance, but team and individual appraisals are relatively unstructured. Teams are expected to control costs and are evaluated on "profit and loss." They also are expected to adjust to changing customer demands.
Team impact on organization	Where teams have been well implemented, on-time delivery has risen from 80 to 97 percent and output per employee has increased by 19 percent. Labor costs have declined only by 3 percent because of investments in new training. Quality, as measured by reject rates, has improved dramatically—from 5,000 parts rejected per million to 250.
Key lessons	• It is essential to anticipate and prepare for the effects the new team system can have on former supervisors.

- Management must be prepared for the pace of change and for their new roles.

Background

Shoemaking in the United Kingdom seemed destined for extinction during the 1970s and 1980s—just one more centuries-old industry buffeted by changing consumer tastes and low-cost competition from abroad. In 1955, more than 110,000 Britons were employed in the shoe industry; by 1992, the number had fallen to less than 40,000. During the same period, imports grew from 9 percent of the U.K. market to more than 70 percent. At first, the big overseas competition came from Italian companies, whose advantage was not so much low labor costs as it was style. Then the 1980s saw the emergence of Chinese and Southeast Asian competitors, who were gaining in quality while maintaining an insurmountable labor advantage.

Like other U.K. shoe manufacturers, K Shoes, which also operates retail stores, responded to the threat by squeezing out as much waste as possible from its operations. That meant increasing mechanization, shrinking its payroll, and asking employees to work harder. K Shoes employed more than 3,600 people in manufacturing in 1976. By 1992, the number was down to 1,100. The productivity gains—and the U.K.'s thriving economy in the late 1980s—made K Shoes one of the most profitable units of its parent company, C & J Clark.

But K's productivity gains exacted a very high toll. The 150-year-old company traditionally enjoyed good relations with its employees, but the strain and uncertainty of downsizing and mechanization were starting to show in increasingly contentious employee/management relations. Further-

more, the company's changes provided only a temporary solution to new marketplace demands. By automating and
downsizing, K had positioned itself to be a high-volume producer of a limited number of shoe styles. As a result, employee skills became narrow and specialized. But at the same
time, consumer tastes were becoming increasingly fragmented. Mass production in a business that was rapidly evolving into fast-changing niches no longer seemed like such a
smart strategy. Indeed, limiting the company's flexibility
could one day prove ruinous.

At least that's how three young K Shoes managers saw it.
"We had really come to the end of our particular road," says
Grant Ritchie, change program manager. Ritchie, along with
Robert Perkins, head of manufacturing for the company, and
Martin Kelly, manager of K's Kentside factory, helped spear-
head the movement that is currently transforming K Shoes
into a self-directed, team-based operation. According to Ritchie, "We had exhausted the productivity gains by just getting people to work harder, and by mechanization and
specialization. If we were going to survive in the nineties—
and it wasn't altogether clear that we would—we needed to
do something differently."

All three managers were in their late twenties and hoped
to build a career with K Shoes. One reason they liked the
company so much was the location of its four small shoe
manufacturing facilities in England's Lake District, long cele-
brated by poets and painters for its beauty and idyllic charms.
Apart from tourism, however, career opportunities were limited in this part of England. And although K Shoes had managed to stay profitable through traditional methods (which
the three managers considered somewhat "Dickensian"), a
new formula, as Perkins describes it, was needed to keep
K Shoes one of the Lake District's most attractive employers.

Top management was not indifferent to the need for
change, but there seemed to be little urgency among direc-

tors to tackle the issues that younger middle managers like Ritchie, Perkins, and Kelly deemed critical. All were close to the manufacturing process and aware of its effects on employee motivation and production flexibility. They felt that without change, the company faced the inevitable prospect of moving production to Brazil, China, or Southeast Asia as many other shoe manufacturers had done.

A Different Language

In the United States, a competitor of C & J Clark, the US Shoe Corporation, with manufacturing facilities in Ohio, Kentucky, and several other states, had wrestled with the same problems confronting the young K Shoes managers. It, too, faced an onslaught of low-cost imports and an increasingly noncompetitive domestic manufacturing base. But it largely stemmed the tide by adopting a flexible team-based design that was highly innovative by industry standards.

Robert Perkins attended a seminar sponsored by a trade association in late 1989. He heard Bob Stix, then head of US Shoes' manufacturing division, describe the company's success. Suddenly the "new formula" the K Shoes managers had sought began to take shape. "Stix was using a different language than the one we were using in manufacturing," Perkins recalls. "He was talking about people and teams; we were talking about individuals and individual incentive. He was talking about flexibility and productivity, while we were talking about narrowly defined tasks." Perkins was intrigued enough to invite Stix to the Lake District to meet other K Shoes managers. There the managers quizzed Stix for a day and a half about how US Shoes had restructured its operations and why teams were so important to its survival in the tough U.S. shoe market.

Later, Perkins and other K Shoes managers visited US

Shoes in the United States. The visit revealed numerous parallels between what they felt they needed and what US Shoes had achieved by responding rapidly to market changes through teams. US Shoes was implementing a variation of the Toyota sewing system for making car seats, part of that company's renowned modular production system. As US Shoes demonstrated, the system could be applied to many different kinds of production.

The old way of making shoes involved operators using single machines to perform single functions. There were as many as sixteen different functions. Partly assembled shoes, or work in process, built up next to each operator until it was carted off to the next function in the shoemaking production process. Using the Toyota system, however, US Shoes trained employees to perform five or more functions and move from machine to machine—thus reducing work teams from sixteen members to five or six. Completed work is then relayed to other team members, much as a baton is handed off in a footrace. More work is accomplished with fewer employees, and work in process is nearly eliminated.

Back in the United Kingdom, Perkins asked his directors to let him send a team of ten K Shoes employees to US Shoes for a month. Although the cost was enormous, Perkins, Grant, and Kelly had little difficulty persuading the directors to make the investment—by this time the three managers had emerged as evangelists for change. The ten employees included a union representative, industrial engineers, several factory managers, a personnel manager, and several production employees. When the group returned to the United Kingdom, it served as a steering committee for coordinating the changes that subsequently unfolded. Developing self-directed teams along the lines of US Shoes was the group's biggest priority. A weeklong off-site seminar with a U.K. consulting firm helped the group understand team concepts and their relevance to K Shoes. Later the group would coordinate the work of special teams formed to analyze various systems and processes within the company, including physical layout and rewards and recognition. No formal group, however, was designated to design a new team structure.

Throughout the process, Perkins, Ritchie, Kelly, and other young managers remained the most energetic promoters of change. Through meetings over a six-week period—held after work with attendance voluntary—Perkins and the group met with more than 750 of the company's 1,100 manufacturing employees to explain their vision for the new team-based organization. The managers also made presentations to suppliers, outlining their role in a transformed K Shoes. Initially employees were wary, but most eventually became enthusiastic. After one presentation, a group of employees volunteered to be the pilot team. The group was from the company's Springer plant, K Shoes' most productive and problem-free facility. This was a good place to begin. Perkins and his group understood very well that the odds for initial success were greater in a smooth-running facility.

Teams

The first teams at Springer, and later at K's other plants in Cumbria, ranged in size from five to eight employees. All teams were formed from volunteers. Thanks to the proselytizing of Perkins, Ritchie, Kelly, and others, more than half of K's seven hundred shoemakers volunteered for teams, which assumed varying degrees of responsibility as they matured. Most teams operated with little or no supervision. The change proved wrenching—not to employees but to K's former inspectors, supervisors, and managers, who benefited from a system that rewarded seniority with power and the symbols of power. They had difficulty adjusting to a new system that offers little of either.

Before teams, making, boxing, and shipping shoes at K required as many as 150 separate operations. Using the Toyota production model, K whittled the process to a small number of modular procedures that can be handled by self-directed teams. Meanwhile the number of specific skills team members needed grew from two to as many as twelve. As a result, cross-training became an important team function. When the modularization process is completed from "cut to box," the company hopes to reduce the time it takes to move a pair of shoes through the factory from ten or twelve days to less than half a day. So far, teams have reduced the time required for "uppermaking" from four or five days to thirty minutes. One benefit has been the elimination of huge piles of partly assembled shoes that once littered the factory floor. Space savings have been so great, in fact, that K expects soon to begin consolidating its four factories.

Meetings play an essential role in K's new team system. Teams meet once or twice daily to discuss production demands for new styles—as consumer tastes have become more diverse, the range of styles and colors of shoes K produces during a week can total hundreds. Once a week, teams meet with leaders, who typically oversee ten teams. The leader uses the meeting to review specific team issues (output, quality, costs) and major production and business issues, such as which shoes are selling and which ones are being returned and why. Once a month, all teams meet with the plant manager, who reviews marketplace trends and near-term business forecasts.

Sharing information is important because K's teams—or, more precisely, sets of teams working in modules—are expected to adjust to customer demand. Production targets are no longer set exclusively by upper management. "We feed what's happening in the marketplace directly into the factories," says Grant Ritchie. By monitoring sales, teams are expected to forecast their own staffing and production needs for upcoming weeks. If demand for a particular style is rising, teams will adjust accordingly, often by negotiating with other teams and team leaders for extra resources. If some styles aren't selling, teams will scale down or stop production and set aside time for training needs or problem-solving projects.

Ultimately, says Robert Perkins, the objective is to build up enough business knowledge among teams so that "people will recognize and understand the trends, when sales are going to peak, when they will dip, when to start planning for training needs, when to train, and so forth." None of this would have been possible under K's old compensation system. Employees were paid hourly—and only when there was enough demand to keep them busy. Because sales cycles and seasonal demand in the shoe business are highly irregular, employees often were sent home without pay and frequently worked less than a full week.

K Shoes now puts employees on salary with a guarantee of at least thirty-nine hours a week. When demand is slack, teams consult with facilitators and determine the best way to use their nonproduction time. The move to an all-salaried workforce is part of a process of equalizing pay, a measure that K hopes will strengthen the team system. K's current compensation system is very simple. Three former skill grades, with hourly wage differentials, have been combined into one. (There still are differences in wage rates among K's four plants, however, based on historical differences.) There are no team or individual bonuses and no gain-sharing or profit-sharing plans.

The compensation system represents a deliberate disavowal of some of the incentive-based systems K managers saw in the United States. "We were trying to break a 150-year-old culture that made people focus on their own targeted earning level," says Ritchie. "We are trying to say now that we value you as people, and your contribution to the business is bigger than your ability to make shoes."

Supervisors and Managers

K's team system vastly reduced the company's need for supervisors and eliminated the need for inspectors. While the
rate of progress has varied at different plants, one plant that
employs 130 operates with two management levels—one
plant manager and two team leaders. Other plants are moving in that direction. Former supervisors became team leaders or took on technical, marketing, or retail assignments;
others joined teams. The process of "delayering," as Robert
Perkins calls it, began slowly and was limited to areas in K
Shoes factories where pilot teams operated. As more employees began working in teams, the process accelerated—
mainly because while employees were feeling increasingly
empowered, the remaining layers of management had begun
to put the brakes on continued team development.

So far, forty supervisory and management positions have
been eliminated—more than the company had anticipated
and far more painful than it had feared. "The teams were
making it blatantly obvious to us that this was something we
had to do," says Robert Perkins. "It's like a Pandora's box.
You build these teams, train them, and at some point they are
going to knock on your door and tell you things you don't
want to hear—like, 'We don't think you're being empowering enough. We want more authority, more power, more
input, more communication, more training, and less management.' And we realized that unless we were prepared to face
that challenge, the teams would outgrow us as managers."
The new team environment was especially unfriendly to the
former inspectors, traditionally the oldest and most experienced shoemakers. With their roles eliminated, many of
them were faced with the prospect of making shoes again.
Several quit instead. Others made the transition grudgingly.

One of the biggest new demands of team leaders is training. In the past, training had been a low priority for super-

visors and managers. There was little need for it because the production process was relatively unchanging and the company was shedding employees rather than hiring new ones. Today, however, K's team leaders spend as much as one-half of their time on training. Free of the need to control costs and outputs for various lines of operations, team leaders are also more focused on business issues and long-range planning—much as teams themselves are.

Results

Changing K Shoes' 150-year-old culture didn't happen overnight. The transformation, begun in 1990, continues. No plant is operated entirely by teams and only part of the cut-to-box shoemaking process has been modularized. Thus some of the same 150 steps it used to take to make shoes are still being followed. But when the team redesign is complete, K Shoes expects to reduce the time it takes to make and ship shoes from twelve days to less than one. That will be accomplished by teams trained to handle up to a dozen different process steps, each member cross-trained to fill any job.

So far the effects of transformation are impressive. At Springer, where the first pilot team formed in 1990, on-time delivery has increased from a lackluster 80 percent to 97 percent. There team members perform an average of eight different functions. Productivity per employee has risen by more than 19 percent. Quality—not just at Springer but at all plants with teams—has risen markedly as well. Reject rates were once measured in percentages; 0.5 percent was typical. Now a new parts-per-million measurement is being used to more accurately reflect the sharp drop in rejects. Today the reject figure is 250 parts per million.

Perkins, Ritchie, and other managers feel the company has won back much of the employee loyalty it lost during the

1970s and 1980s, when mechanization cost two out of three manufacturing employees their jobs. "There's a new passion for working here," says Perkins. "People do things they never would have done five years ago. There is a willingness to get involved." Sadly, casualties of the team transformation included employees with many years of loyal service. At the beginning of the process, Perkins, Ritchie, and the other managers hoped that all K Shoes employees would welcome the changes and find new roles in the company. They now acknowledge that they failed to anticipate that inspectors and supervisors might resist the team transformation and that resistance would require "forced redundancies," or layoffs.

The steering committee and Perkins and his group "overestimated the problem," Perkins says, of moving shoemakers beyond their narrow task orientations into teams. And they underestimated the effort it would take to sell this new way of working to inspectors and supervisors. Shoemakers generally needed little encouragement to embrace the changes, but supervisors and inspectors saw redeployment into shoemaking teams as a threat to their status. They also saw it as a threat to their compensation. "We needed to think about it a lot earlier than we did," Perkins says. "We didn't put enough time and effort in getting the staff, the supervisors, and inspectors to a point where they fully understood the change—and where we understood the implications fully enough to be able to tell them what some of the options were."

Also unexpected was the amount of untapped potential released by the team system and how quickly teams took root. The speed of change at times left the management team struggling to keep up with their changing roles in the new environment. Thus moving managers from controlling positions to coaching and facilitating roles became a priority. Fortunately K's teams seem to understand what the new environment demands of them.

4

Building Teams from the Ground Up by Developing New Team Skills

Miller Brewing Company
Trenton, Ohio

Industry	Brewing
Union	United Auto Workers
Type of team implementation	Redesigned self-directed teams based on complete brewing, packaging, and distribution processes; cross-functional teams
First teams started	1991
Employees	410
Percentage in teams	100 percent
Team size	6 to 19
Team responsibilities	Scheduling work assignments and vacations; hiring; conducting peer performance assessments and handling performance problems; assuring safety; maintaining equipment; coordinating with other teams and policy groups.
Organization-wide team responsibilities	An innovative dispute resolution procedure—a policy review board—has replaced the traditional grievance procedure. Team

representatives meet every two weeks to discuss plantwide issues, using consensus decision-making principles to resolve concerns.

Team leadership and governance

Team members rotate coordination of various areas (administration, personnel, safety, quality, productivity, maintenance) according to schedules set by individual teams using a star point system. Star point representatives interface with representatives from other shifts and plantwide policy review groups.

Leadership outside teams

Team managers (formerly supervisors and line managers) provide guidance and serve as resources and training coordinators for up to three shift teams.

Team compensation

Members get a straight hourly wage with annual increases. There are two pay grades within teams (production and maintenance). A pay-for-skills-or-knowledge system, team bonuses, and gain sharing are under evaluation.

First-year team member training

Team concepts (philosophical overview, organizational design, vision and mission, customer satisfaction, roles, and guidelines); world-class manufacturing methods (including total quality management, total productive maintenance, just-in-time, and total employee involvement); safety principles; labor/management (roles, relations, expectations); group dynamics; facilitator training; technical skills.

Subsequent team member training	Conflict resolution, business knowledge, visual controls, interviewing and selection.
First-year leadership training	Team concepts, world-class manufacturing and maintenance methods, continuous improvement principles, team building, developing quality relationships, developing effective team processes, and coaching.
Subsequent leadership training	Team facilitation.
How team members are selected	Applicants undergo an extensive screening and selection process based on job dimensions determined by research to contribute to success in empowered team environments. The hiring process includes tests, job simulations, and targeted behavioral interviews.
How team performance is evaluated	Teams are responsible for meeting production, quality, and safety targets and are given cost and performance data to enable them to make good operational decisions. Consistent with the plant's continuous improvement philosophy, teams strive to perform better than their last shift in all critical areas, including team interaction. To minimize intraplant competition, each team's progress is measured against its own past performance, not against other teams.
Team impact on organization	There has been a 30 percent reduction in labor costs and requirements (and a cor-

responding increase in productivity) in comparison to the company's traditional plants. These improvements are the result of increased flexibility and responsiveness associated with the flatter, team-based organization at Trenton. In 1992, it took about 30 percent fewer labor hours to produce a barrel of beer at Trenton than at other Miller breweries.

Key lessons   Trenton's high-involvement work culture and systems at times conflicted with Miller's corporate policies and procedures, causing some tension. It's helpful to ensure corporate management is "on board" and willing to make the changes needed to support a plant-level team implementation.

Background

Miller Brewing Company, a unit of Philip Morris Companies, sells more than $4 billion worth of beer a year. It is America's second largest brewing company. But being a solid number two doesn't leave Miller much room for complacency: the only real growth the U.S. brewery industry has seen in recent years has been in certain regional specialty brands and local "microbrews," neither of which are among Miller's strengths. Nevertheless, Miller aims to stay competitive by becoming the most productive and flexible brewer in the industry. Its Trenton, Ohio, facility is the proving ground for a team-based approach to brewing. The benefits of this approach, which has cut labor costs roughly by half, are slowly being felt throughout the rest of the organization—slowly because the brewing industry is very traditional. In fact, Miller, which is 140 years old, still operates breweries nearly as old as itself.

Construction on the Trenton plant began in 1981 when Miller was in a race to add capacity to satisfy a growing market. Large, modern breweries typically take three to four years to build and are very expensive. But by the time the $410 million Trenton plant was completed in 1983, beer sales were down industrywide and Miller no longer needed the additional capacity. Even though a new management team already had been selected for Trenton and production facilities had been tested, Miller executives decided to mothball the new brewery until demand picked up. It wasn't an easy decision. The city of Trenton and other Ohio communities saw an anticipated twelve hundred jobs, paying as much as $40,000 a year, vanish in the early 1980s. Local disappointment was intense. And because Trenton and the state of Ohio had offered Miller numerous tax and economic incentives to build the plant, the decision to cancel production presented Miller with a public relations nightmare.

By 1989 Miller had regained its momentum. A new brand, Miller Genuine Draft, had become the fastest-growing beer in the country, overall Miller sales had registered their strongest increase in years, and Miller breweries were operating at nearly 90 percent capacity. The mothballed Trenton facility—called a white elephant by some in the industry—presented Miller with the opportunity to increase capacity relatively quickly. Technically a greenfield site (long built but never staffed), Trenton also presented Miller with the chance to open what executives hoped would be the brewery of the future: one that would give the company the flexibility to expand capacity and embody cutting-edge staffing features to give Miller a sustainable competitive advantage.

Miller executives, determined to avoid disappointing the community once again, decided to keep their plans under wraps until they were certain the decision would not be reversed. Executives chartered a planning and design team for Trenton and gave the team a basic mandate: start from scratch; develop a totally new workplace design for Trenton; abandon all the traditional constraints of brewery operations, some of them decades old. The team faced two limitations, however. Not only did the Trenton facility, already built in the mirror image of other Miller breweries, provide limited opportunity to physically redesign operations but Miller executives asked the design team to work in secret until the opening was officially announced.

The Trenton planning and design team, composed of Miller employees from around the country, met for six months. The team included two plant managers, two plant human resource managers, corporate specialists in accounting, HR, and operations, and plant specialists in operational areas such as brewing, quality assurance, and packaging. Other specialists within the company were invited to join from time to time. They represented all the major functional areas of a brewing plant—brewing, packaging, shipping, water and waste treatment, electrical utilities, and administrative and support groups.

The team drew largely on its own experiences. Benchmarking visits were made to several sites, but the traditional beer industry offered few lessons about innovation. Team-based operations of packaged food companies, such as sister company Kraft/General Foods, provided better insights. The team retained a consultant to provide expertise on empowered team development and help the team plan ways to enlist the support of Miller's union. Union relationships have always been important to Miller—not only to ensure labor peace but also because union members are among the biggest groups of Miller beer drinkers.

The team's work resulted in a comprehensive organization and design document for the Trenton plant. Presented to Miller executives in 1990, the document called for self-directed work teams responsible for whole processes (including brewing, packaging, distribution, and various support processes) and a flattened organizational structure that replaced the six levels of traditional breweries with four. During the presentation, the Trenton design team explained the benefits of self-directed teams to productivity, flexibility, and quality. But what really got the executives' attention was the team's analysis of the effects the new system would have on the brewery's bottom line. The team predicted that the Trenton brewery could produce five million barrels of beer with 52 percent fewer salaried employees and 30 percent fewer hourly employees than a traditional Miller brewery. Because hourly labor costs were so high in the brewing industry (the average yearly income for a Trenton hourly employee exceeded $57,000 in 1992), the figures represented a potential labor savings of millions of dollars per year.

Getting Started

Miller fully staffed the plant with its management team before the first new employees were hired. Several members of the original planning and design team joined the new operation, including the new plant manager, packaging/shipping manager, and human resource manager. A total of seven department heads reported to the plant manager. The plant hired its first nonexempt employee in April 1991, six months after the decision to open, and shipped its first beer three months later. More than 50,000 people applied for the initial 175 positions. The local community's excitement was tempered by the realization that the reborn brewery would require far fewer employees than the 1,200 to 1,400 initially envisioned.

Forty-eight team managers were selected from more than four hundred volunteers from other Miller facilities. They were selected with the help of a comprehensive assessment process to single out those who would thrive in a team-based environment. The assessment process included a team discussion simulation in which applicants worked as a team on "real" problems. This exercise helped the company assess the applicants' team and problem-solving skills. The role of team managers, however, was allowed to evolve as the plant's design developed. As team managers helped shape the new facility, their jobs were to "manage boundaries and work processes," provide training and expertise, and contribute to team development. Day-to-day management of teams, however, was the responsibility of team members. Because only six months elapsed between the decision to open the plant and its official unveiling, and because this was Miller's first attempt to develop teams on a plantwide scale, many questions concerning working relationships between team members and managers were left unanswered.

Teams

By early 1994, Trenton had thirty-one self-directed teams of six to nineteen members each. All operating team members are called production technicians or maintenance technicians. Maintenance technicians must demonstrate advanced electrical or mechanical knowledge. They earn $0.70 an hour more than production technicians. Unlike other companies with multiple pay grades within teams, Miller doesn't prevent production technicians from becoming certified in electrical or mechanical repair even though teams might not need additional maintenance technicians at the time. As part of Trenton's original design document, all technicians are supposed to be "unencumbered by artificial barriers that limit contributions and effectiveness."

Trenton's teams are responsible for an entire process—

not just a step or function within the process, as is typical in traditional breweries. For example, each of the sixteen packaging teams is responsible for can, keg, or bottle filling operations, electrical and mechanical maintenance, and equipment lubrication. Within their process areas, teams are expected to monitor quality, safety, waste, housekeeping, and productivity and make appropriate decisions to optimize team performance in these areas. Trenton teams are involved in most personnel decisions, as well, including selecting new team members, scheduling vacation and overtime, and dealing with performance issues.

There are no permanent team leaders. Instead, teams manage themselves through a star point system similar to those used by many self-directed team-based organizations. Each point of the star symbolizes a different area of responsibility—for example, administration, personnel, productivity/maintenance, quality, and safety. Teams decide by consensus on star point representatives and alternates, who serve for twelve to eighteen months, depending on how frequently each team decides to rotate. Star point representatives monitor areas within their star point and coordinate required team activities.

As in most self-directed team-based environments, communication is essential. At Trenton, electronic mail is one way teams communicate with one another and managers communicate with teams. Every employee has an electronic mailbox and each team has its own local area network terminal. Electronic mail is used so extensively to post communications that team members must use the system to keep up with information in the plant. Moreover, real-time quality and production figures for teams are accessed through the plant's on-line information system.

Trenton's teams work nine-hour days—the hour of overtime is for a daily team meeting. During these daily meetings, teams make shift assignments, decide on the frequency of rotating assignments, and discuss safety, quality, productivity, and performance issues. Each meeting also focuses on one star point area, led by the star point representative. Team representatives from different shifts also meet every two weeks or so to discuss general concerns.

Technicians at Trenton voted in the United Auto Workers (UAW) union six months after the brewery opened. The election was no surprise to Miller, as the brewing industry has always been heavily organized. Relations between the UAW and Miller have been outstanding over the years. In fact, the UAW accepted Trenton's flexible work rules with little objection and forged a labor agreement with Miller that serves as a model for balancing union interests with the requirements of a team-based environment. The agreement includes a summary of the basic understandings between union and management on wages, benefits, and other areas as well as a statement of philosophy rather than a management rights clause. Most notably, provisions for a policy review replace the traditional grievance process. The new procedure involves a policy review board composed of human resources and operations team managers, the vice president of the UAW local, and star point representatives from five different teams. All board members, except the union vice president, rotate duties. The board has hammered out policies on vacations, absenteeism, training reimbursement, and other issues.

Trenton's current compensation system is simple. The starting wage for a technician is $20 an hour. With considerable overtime—much of it because of team and plantwide meetings—Miller technicians earn an average of $57,000 a year. A special task force composed of technicians and managers is currently evaluating a pay-for-skills-or-knowledge system. Gain sharing and other innovative compensation plans might be implemented, too, but the brewery has yet to reach full production capacity so performance and production improvement baselines have been difficult to establish.

Trenton has not established a formal performance appraisal system for team technicians. Indeed it might never establish one, for the peer evaluation system is working effectively. In this system, technicians distribute an evaluation form to five others, either in their own teams or in teams with which they interact. The form asks for a rating in more than fifty areas relating to teamwork, leadership, communication, continuous improvement, and initiative as well as eight open-ended suggestions for improvement. Signatures on completed evaluations are optional. Technicians may share the comments with their team members and managers or withhold it.

Teams also handle performance problems. If peer counseling cannot correct a problem, teams request assistance from team managers. If a problem reaches this point, an "audit trail" is begun to document the problem. Remarkably, few performance problems have led to formal discipline; most have been contained and resolved within the team system. Recently the plant invited a federal mediator and a professional arbitrator to discuss performance management issues with team members, the UAW leadership, and managers. When tough performance challenges do arise, the plant plans to have a system in place to deal with them.

Managers and Leaders

Trenton's team managers serve as resources and training coordinators for as many as three teams. Most have considerable experience in the brewing industry from other Miller facilities. At first their role at Trenton was defined more by what they were not supposed to do than by an active definition of leadership. As many team managers found the situation ambiguous, role clarity for team managers continues to be a priority.

Part of the problem is lack of training. Most of the training during the plant's first months was provided to technicians because they were recruited for team aptitude and few had experience in a brewery or with self-directed teams. Because the time between the decision to open and the start-up was so short, team managers received little team development training. As a result, some team managers felt limited to observing the creation of a self-directed team-based environment rather than actively participating in it. It became clear that more team management training was needed.

Results

The design team's original projection—that the Trenton brewery would produce the same output with half the labor costs of other Miller breweries—turned out to be a realistic target. Despite unanswered questions about managers' roles and the frenzied pace of the opening, Trenton's start-up was remarkably smooth and problem free. Productivity improvements were so impressive that Trenton quickly assumed a pivotal role in Miller's efforts to boost capacity. Originally Trenton was scheduled to brew two or three Miller brands in its first year, but within six months the plant was producing five brands. Headquarters' decision to "load" Trenton was based on economics. Miller assigns increased production to breweries with the lowest cost per barrel; as Trenton's costs steadily fell, the orders flowed in.

Team members and managers at Trenton worked hard to overcome early problems. Because of the rapid start-up pace, for example, training programs to support the new roles of leaders and team members weren't always in place when needed. Training programs at Miller's other breweries taught employees how to perform a limited number of tasks, but the company had little internal expertise to help technicians learn multiple tasks and how to function in self-managing teams. Even more critically, Miller needed methods to help team leaders from its other breweries translate their enthusiasm for this new style of doing business into effective ways to support and lead. Continually loading production—a tribute to Trenton's early successes—made it ever tougher to develop training and support programs. Everyone at Trenton needed time to learn, but time was seldom available.

Similarly, union/management relations were marked by enthusiasm and goodwill on all sides, but many questions remain. The UAW has had to define a new role for itself at Trenton. Even now, relationships between the company and the UAW are sometimes challenging as both sides continue to discover how difficult it can be to define mutual interests and work cooperatively.

Some of the most surprising side effects are seen in the relationships between Trenton and the rest of the company. While Trenton is pioneering new ways of working in the brewing industry, other Miller facilities are changing far more slowly. Not everyone in other parts of the organization understands what Trenton is trying to do, and Trenton's new policies on timekeeping, safety training, and other issues sometimes clash with long-standing corporate procedures. In fact, Trenton's early successes initially attracted more interest from outside the company than from within. Early visitors included managers from breweries in Canada, Chile, the Far East, and elsewhere. Only recently have managers from other Miller breweries come to see Trenton's version of the "brewery of the future."

Trenton has proved to be far more than a bold experiment. With productivity that has vaulted near the top among Miller plants in a very short time, Trenton's lesson will undoubtedly have a profound impact on the company in the years ahead.

5

Streamlining Business Processes to Stay Competitive

Mine Safety Appliances Company
Murrysville, Pennsylvania

Industry	Manufacturing (personal protective equipment)
Union	None
Type of team implementation	Self-directed, natural pilot teams in three areas
First teams started	1992
Employees	Approximately 530 at Murrysville (4,000 worldwide)
Percentage in teams	21 percent of Murrysville's hourly employees
Team size	3 to 18 (most teams have 8)
Team responsibilities	Handling materials, setting continuous improvement production goals, assigning team tasks, tracking labor usage rates, budgeting, monitoring safety and quality control, housekeeping.
Organization-wide team responsibilities	None

Team leadership and governance	Team captains maintain production logs, work with production planning to schedule team production, and update the schedule boards posted in each team area. Teams rotate captains every two weeks to three months.
Leadership outside teams	Traditional supervisory roles are being transformed into coach/facilitator roles.
Team compensation	Compensation systems have not changed, but some employees have acquired new skills, assumed new responsibilities, and moved up the pay scale.
First-year team member training	About forty-five hours of training: working in teams, writing a mission statement, training others, team interaction, consensus management, cause-and-effect diagram analysis, statistical process controls, and other quality tools.
Subsequent team member training	To be determined.
First-year leadership training	Supervisors receive twenty-eight hours of training: principles of empowerment, encouraging initiative, coaching, reinforcing performance, and resolving conflict.
Subsequent leadership training	To be determined.
How team members are selected	Pilot teams exist in natural work groups.

How team performance is evaluated	Team schedule boards show daily and weekly performance in meeting production, quality, and training goals. Team members are evaluated under existing appraisal systems.
Team impact on organization	Murrysville's three pilot teams eliminated chronic backorder problems and increased output for several products by 25 to 65 percent. Scrap and rework were reduced by about 50 percent. Based on the results, MSA hopes to convert most of the Murrysville operation to self-directed work teams within the next two years.
Key lessons	• Feeling an urgent need to improve its competitiveness through teams, MSA launched its teams without changing support systems. As more teams are implemented, other parts of the organization will have to change, too, creating numerous challenges as well as opportunities for improvement.
	• Many Murrysville employees, who have been with the company for decades, have seen programs come and go. Management's support was important in overcoming skepticism and establishing the trust needed to get employees to commit to change.

Background

Generations of workers have relied on Mine Safety Appliances Company (MSA) for their safety and often their lives.

Founded in 1914, MSA pioneered battery-powered electric lights for miner's caps and grew over the decades to become the world's largest producer of personal safety equipment. Headquartered just outside Pittsburgh in O'Hara Township, and with affiliates and subsidiaries throughout the United States and twenty-three other countries, MSA reported sales of about $500 million in 1993.

No other company has capitalized on as many niches in the industry. From mine safety, MSA expanded into respiratory protection, head protection, hearing protection, clothing, safety belts, and hazardous substances monitoring systems. Today there are an astonishing four thousand items in MSA's catalog. While competitors sprang up in certain areas, such as hard hats and respirators, no other company was positioned to serve the full spectrum of protective safety needs. Also fueling MSA's growth were federal regulations—the Occupational Safety and Health Act—which increased job safety awareness. Companies that once might have been lax about worker safety began to take it very seriously.

But during the 1980s this burgeoning market drew the attention of other companies and MSA began to encounter serious rivals. Competitors, from giants like 3M to small specialty manufacturers, began challenging MSA. Not only did they promise immediate availability of products but they undercut MSA's prices. One competitor for battery-operated cap lamps, which are manufactured at MSA's Murrysville, Pennsylvania, plant, even offered to replace MSA's products at no charge to entice customers to switch. Many did—and MSA's market share for cap lamps fell sharply. The story was repeated, if less dramatically, in other product areas. Other problems at Murrysville had grown as well, including absenteeism and accidents. Murrysville's future became increasingly tenuous—MSA could always shift production to another plant. "Our costs were drifting upward and delivery was not reliable," remembers one Murrysville manager. "If we wanted to continue to operate we needed to change quickly."

The Shift to Teams

In 1991 a new plant manager, Frank Gambino, arrived at Murrysville. Gambino and other Murrysville managers knew that in order to address key issues, such as the plant's cost structure and backorders, the production process would have to be dramatically redesigned to drive down costs and increase efficiency. Self-directed work teams seemed the most attractive option—after all, many of Murrysville's four hundred production employees had been working in small groups for years. Thus a foundation was already laid in many parts of the plant for the introduction of self-directed teams. These teams would not be introduced all at once, however. Rather, the goal was to transform the workforce over several years. The first step would be to pilot the concept.

In the first few months of 1992, a ten-person steering committee of managers from human resources, finance, industrial engineering, quality assurance, production, and other areas was formed. The committee—in effect the design and implementation team for the new Murrysville teams—worked quickly. Meeting weekly over a three-month period, the team hashed out such issues as Murrysville's definition of self-directed teams, what the company hoped to accomplish, what training would be needed, what impact teams would have on supervisors and managers, and what systems would have to be changed. The committee made a few site visits, too, including nearby Westinghouse and MSA's Cranberry, Pennsylvania, plant, which had its own pilot team program under way.

The committee settled on three basic objectives for Murrysville's teams:

- They would be responsible for inputs and outputs in an entire process or product line after two or three years.
- They would work faster and more cost effectively than traditional assembly areas.
- They would reduce work in process and eliminate the backorders.

The committee knew it needed to start with a win, so it looked for a team with a high probability for success. The MineSpot™ division, which made cap lamps and batteries, seemed a good candidate. Many MineSpot employees had worked together for years and relationships in the area were relatively harmonious. Moreover, MineSpot employees had seen firsthand the effects of MSA's plummeting market share in an already shrinking market.

The committee unveiled the new team concept during a meeting with MineSpot employees in March 1992. In his presentation, MSA's production manager made it clear that if current trends continued, MineSpot's future was bleak. He then gave employees information they were unaccustomed to hearing from managers. He summarized MSA's perilous market position, explained the trends in market share loss, and compared MSA's labor and cost structure with competitors'. "Every time a cap lamp, spare part, or bulb is sold, eighty-four out of a hundred times the customer buys it from someone other than MSA," the production manager told MineSpot employees. "It may have taken some of us longer than others [to figure it out], but it is clear to all of us that we must improve."

Then the MineSpot employees were asked to participate in Murrysville's first self-directed work team—the prototype for the rest of the plant. A team structure was outlined and training needs were discussed. The committee was prepared for such questions as "What about pay?" "What's in it for me?" and "What if we don't want to join?" Surprisingly, the MineSpot employees raised no such issues. Instead, they responded enthusiastically to the idea and wanted to know how teams could help MSA recapture lost market share, how new team members would be selected, and other work-related issues. Thus the introductory session became Mine-Spot's first working team meeting.

The new MineSpot team adjusted rapidly to the new working style. In some ways it represented only minor changes from the previous pattern, but in other ways it was drastically different. The team's first real challenge was drafting a mission and values statement with the help of MSA's corporate training coordinator, who led the team through a structured brainstorming process. Training was the next priority. During the following two months, the MineSpot team received weekly half-day sessions in team dynamics, statistical quality tools, MSA's budgeting and accounting systems, handling materials, scheduling and tracking production, completing forms such as shipping manifests, and many other areas. Budget training was conducted by plant manager Gambino, who helped the team understand its role as a business unit and explained how its performance would be monitored financially.

The MineSpot team quickly found its footing. In the months that followed the team's formation, team members assumed responsibility for several key tasks: handling materials and writing "issues" and "return" cards for needed parts (formerly done by a materials specialist); setting production goals (formerly done by planning specialists); tracking labor usage rates; inspecting and verifying work quality (formerly done by quality inspectors); even sweeping up their areas (formerly done by janitors). Today the MineSpot team continues to manage itself successfully. Because of the small size of the MineSpot team, team management hasn't been difficult. A team captain (a position that is rotated every two

weeks to three months) handles all the team's reporting requirements, maintains various production logs, meets daily
with planners to schedule production, and updates the
team's "schedule board." (The schedule board is posted in
the team area and gives current information on the team's
production performance, reject rate, safety and absenteeism
record, and cross-training progress.)

The changes in the production process have been dramatic. Once the product assembly process was organized
into as many as fifteen different specialized tasks. Each task
had to be tracked and reported, and many had to be performed or checked by specialized personnel. The MineSpot
team combined all tasks into one "jumbo" reporting requirement—total team production. The change required a vastly
different approach to quality assurance. The old end-item
sampling process was abandoned in favor of in-process testing by team members, the benefits of which are rippling
throughout the organization.

Murrysville's MineSpot team was followed by a team in
the Noisefoe® division—which makes noise-suppressing
headsets for airline crews, construction workers, and others—and in the safety belt assembly operation, which makes
the belts, harnesses, and securing lines worn by telephone
linemen, window washers, and others. A similar implementation pattern was followed for both areas, and progress has
been just as swift. For example, the Noisefoe team sent parts
back to suppliers because of quality problems. That action
might not seem especially dramatic—but consider that under the old task-specialized system, a supervisor would have
discussed the matter with a quality analyst, who would have
taken it up with a quality manager, who would have talked
to the buyer in purchasing, who then might have called the
supplier. Meanwhile, the defective parts would have been
pushed off to the side of the production floor, contributing
to work in process and backorders. Similarly, the belt team

has worked directly with product line managers to create and prototype new products (traditionally done by design engineering). Among other things the belt team has rediscovered a sense of craftsmanship that was long buried under the old work system.

Minimum performance goals for Murrysville's new teams are for the most part still dictated by customer demand. Teams do set their own continuous performance goals, however, which tend to be higher than anything management might have suggested. For example, the MineSpot team set a goal of 450 batteries per week (up from 300) and eventually reached a new performance level of 480. Posting performance data on schedule boards helps teams keep a daily fix on their progress in meeting production, quality, and training goals.

Murrysville's current compensation system dates back to 1974, but undoubtedly it will change as more self-directed teams are formed. Pay grades are determined by a twelve-factor evaluation process. Some team members found themselves automatically bumped up the pay scale because of their new skills and responsibilities. The MineSpot team, which consolidated three functional jobs into one with a new uniform pay grade, represented the first big step in reducing the complex job descriptions. Team members helped draft their new job description.

Managers and Supervisors

As might be expected, the roles of supervisors and managers are changing rapidly at Murrysville. Because the new teams need far less formal supervision, a handful of supervisory positions have been eliminated, all by way of retirement. But for the most part, teams have not yet had a major impact on frontline managers. It's a very different story, though, with

MSA's "task specialists"—materials handlers, quality inspectors, and others who performed specialized functions that teams now do themselves. Many such specialists have been redeployed into direct labor positions.

Supervisors are being prepared for change, however. Anticipating that the team system will be adopted throughout the plant, they are receiving training in coaching and facilitation. Most understand there will be fewer supervisory positions in the future and many current supervisors will be redeployed into technical or special project positions. While that prospect causes some anxiety, supervisors at Murrysville generally have supported the move to teams—they cannot help noting that positive results have been quickly achieved. One supervisor, who works with the Noisefoe team, comments that the old style of supervising mainly entailed "focusing on an endless series of small problems and putting out fires." Working with newly empowered teams who are trying to improve processes, who don't expect to be penalized for mistakes, and who care about what they are doing "makes my job more and more fun," he says.

Results

MSA's team implementation at Murrysville was remarkably swift. Two months after the steering committee met to discuss the idea, the first teams were formed. Within months the new teams appeared to have made great progress in chipping away at some of Murrysville's problems. For one, Murrysville teams succeeded in eliminating the plant's chronic backorder problem—MineSpot, Noisefoe, and belt products are available whenever customers need them. The new teams are substantially more productive, too. MineSpot, for example, increased production of several products by 25 to 60 percent. And all three teams have substantially reduced scrap, rework, and work in process. But numbers don't tell the whole story. Team members say morale and enthusiasm have escalated—even among employees who have been making the same products for decades. "Everyone feels the change," one team member says. "Being listened to, respected, involved in what's going on, has made a huge difference to people who have been doing the same thing for years."

MSA's approach at Murrysville—quickly changing some parts of the organization while not touching others—also created some problems. As one manager puts it, "There is a lot of history here to overcome." That history includes traditional systems and functions that had changed little in decades and inevitably clashed with an empowered team system. MSA's cost accounting system, for example, which was developed years ago, is based on direct labor hours. With fewer direct labor hours because of increased efficiency, on paper the plant's new teams appear to have higher fixed costs than areas organized conventionally. Industrial engineering, quality control, hiring, and promotion are highly traditional, as well, and just beginning to adjust to the team implementation. Changing these areas on a piecemeal basis could delay the plant's timetable for converting most operational areas to teams.

None of these problems will deter the company, however. The recent successes have mapped out a clear path for the future. Besides, says another Murrysville manager, "if we had waited to iron everything out before we started this change, it never would have happened."

6

Making a Commitment
to Involve Everyone
in the Change

Pfizer, Inc.
Terre Haute, Indiana

Industry	Specialty food ingredients
Union	None
Type of team implementation	Self-managed natural teams and cross-functional teams
First teams started	1991
Employees	130 at Terre Haute (40,000 worldwide for Pfizer)
Percentage in teams	100 percent
Team size	4 to 6
Team responsibilities	Monitoring quality and costs, housekeeping, safety, and environmental issues. As teams mature, they will be responsible for peer performance management, scheduling work tasks and production, selecting other team members, choosing supplies and equipment, developing department budgets, scheduling vacations, overtime, and training, and identifying team training needs.

Organization-wide team responsibilities	Teams are represented on their department's "area forum," which resolves problems within the plant's thirteen departments. Each area forum is represented on a "central forum," which meets monthly to forge a plantwide consensus on issues and refer them to area forums for resolution.
Team leadership and governance	A loose team framework ensures that teams evolve with different ways of managing themselves. Some teams are led by facilitators, an exempt staff position. Other teams are headed by nonexempt "lead operators" who had formally headed shift crews. All teams are developing at their own pace. Team members typically volunteer to assume certain responsibilities for indefinite periods of time.
Leadership outside teams	Facilitators coach and assist in team development. Department heads are the only level of management between teams and the plant manager.
Team compensation	Based on individual base pay and standard increases. The organization is implementing a pay-for-skills system.
First-year team member training	Twenty hours: team orientation, team meeting and interaction skills, and business knowledge. Team members also may be crossed-trained in various skills.
Subsequent team member training	Sixteen hours in quality and problem-solving techniques and twelve hours of advanced interaction skills, including training

	others and handling conflict, business knowledge, facilitation, and coaching skills.
First-year leadership training	Sixteen hours: team meeting skills, team interaction skills, business knowledge, team and workplace design, interviewing, facilitation, and coaching skills.
Subsequent leadership training	Quality and problem-solving techniques; business knowledge.
How team members are selected	In each department, teams select interviewing panels of four who interview candidates and make recommendations to the department head.
How team performance is evaluated	Production and business goals are being developed to measure team performance. Pfizer is also benchmarking with other organizations.
Team impact on organization	Steady improvements in productivity and quality are being achieved in most departments. In several areas monthly production records are routinely surpassed.
Key lessons	• Employees need to be prepared for the rapid pace of change and for heavy training demands. The concerns of employees who are skeptical of the team concept should be addressed.
	• The changing role of foreman should be clarified early on.
	• The involvement of employees from all areas of the organization in establishing the team framework contrib-

uted to acceptance of change and enthusiasm for a new way of working. Employee involvement in area forums and the central forum—two mechanisms that are expected to drive the team process forward—is keeping the momentum going.

Background

Many employees at Pfizer Incorporated's Vigo Food Science Group (FSG) plant in Terre Haute, Indiana, thought nothing could ever change them—least of all a trendy concept called empowered teams. For nearly forty-five years as part of what was formerly known as Pfizer's Specialty Chemical Group, the FSG plant was a supplier of bulk ingredients for the food processing industry. Technology at the plant was mainly 1950s and 1960s vintage, which translated into mostly manual operations. Management control was achieved through a hierarchical system—indeed, there were as many as five levels of management control in the plant. Thus employees operated in a highly controlled environment with mostly repetitive job functions. Despite the lack of challenge, the pay and benefits were excellent and turnover was minimal. As long as they felt they were being treated fairly, employees asked little of the company and expected the company to ask little of them.

As in many other companies in the late 1980s, the winds of change reached gale-force velocity at Pfizer, too, which began restructuring its businesses. Although growth had been steady for more than twenty-five years, with an uninterrupted string of dividend hikes, Pfizer's top executives began reformulating the company's long-term strategy. They decided the company needed to tighten its focus on research-based health care operations. Any operations that didn't capitalize on Pfizer's research capabilities or take advantage of emerging health care technologies would be shed.

In line with that strategy, several business operations have been sold or closed since 1988. Others have undergone dramatic changes. Pfizer's Specialty Chemicals Division was one of them. Renamed the Vigo Food Science Group in 1993, the division now focuses on specialty food ingredients that promote a healthy lifestyle. The FSG plant in Terre Haute, with 130 employees, makes, among other things, Chy-Max® (a form of rennin, a milk coagulant) and polydextrose, a low-calorie bulking agent used to replace the sugar and fat removed from low-cal, low-fat foods. The plant also produces animal antibiotics.

As Pfizer started to change, Don Farley, then vice president of the Specialty Chemical Division (and now president of FSG), as well as other senior managers, knew that avoiding the fate of Pfizer's other commodity businesses could be a challenge. Pfizer's corporate objectives focused on high-margin, research-driven business lines. For FSG to remain in step with these goals, a dramatic change had to be made in the management style of the group. In 1988 "employee involvement" became the new theme for the division. Farley saw problem-solving and process improvement teams as a way to align the division with Pfizer's long-term strategy, and teams were initiated throughout the division in 1988. Because Farley felt it was important to decentralize the effort, each facility developed its own initiatives.

Initially the move to teams at the Terre Haute plant was met with resistance. Many employees had been with the company for decades and were within a year or two of retirement. The prevailing attitude was best expressed by one employee, a burly operator in his fifties, who cornered a surprised trainer during a team orientation session. "Look lady," he said, "we just barely tolerate each other here.

You're out of your mind if you think you're going to get us to work in these teams you're talking about."

But before long the resistance was supplanted by enthusiasm. In fact, not too many months later, that same employee was eagerly taking part in a presentation before the division's senior executives, including president Don Kolowsky (retired in 1992), who had flown in from New York headquarters. Once employees laid low when the top brass visited. Their attitude: clean the place up and hide. Now they vie for the chance to conduct tours and deliver reports.

Challenges

Early attempts to use employee involvement to build quality and productivity were only partly successful. At the Terre Haute plant, a consultant was brought in to lead an awareness session for employees, a "climate" survey was developed and administered, and quality improvement project teams were formed throughout 1988. The plant's department managers acted as a steering committee for the efforts. It was a good beginning and it got people thinking, especially the department managers, but little else seemed to change. Employees might have been exposed to new ideas, but they found few opportunities to take initiative or assume responsibility for their work. The situation was similar at other plants. "Many people viewed employee involvement as a one-time program, not a process," recalls one Pfizer manager. "There didn't seem to be an engine to drive it forward."

Meanwhile Terre Haute's department managers, impatient with the slow pace of change, were becoming increasingly interested in work teams. That's why they welcomed the arrival in 1991 of Ramona Rutledge from division headquarters as the plant's training administrator. Her position was created to develop an operator certification training program and coordinate employee involvement programs. At the time, Rutledge knew little about self-managed teams. But she learned quickly. "Basically I was just thrown into it," Rutledge recalls. "We learned together."

Rutledge spent most of the next year researching work teams and educating the organization. Department by department, she provided orientation sessions for teams and later conducted training sessions in such team basics as interpersonal and consensus-building skills. By the end of the year, every employee had received at least twelve hours of training and some as much as twenty-four hours. But before the plant could take the next step forward, Rutledge thought a great deal more education was needed. Talking about teams was only a start; now employees needed to see how they actually worked.

In the meantime, Rutledge was devouring everything she could find on self-managed teams. She spent hours on the phone with organizations whose team systems were featured in business publications and professional journals. Her methodology led her to four successful team-based Midwest organizations with enough similarities to the Terre Haute plant to make site visits worthwhile. Suburu-Isuzu and A. E. Staley in nearby Lafayette, Indiana, were greenfield sites that had operated with self-managed teams from the start. Near Chicago, Johnson & Johnson's personal products plant and Watlow Gordon, a manufacturer, were long-established companies that had applied the self-managed team concept to plants that, like FSG in Terre Haute, were decades old. Rutledge made plans to visit the four plants on two separate trips.

Sixty employees (nearly a fifth of the workforce) volunteered to serve on the site visit team. Six managers would go along on the first site visit, including Rutledge and the plant manager, Matt Cavallo. The rest of the team was picked by lots from among the volunteers, making sure that each department was represented. The employees chosen represented a mixture of the prevailing attitudes in the plant. While everyone had received at least twelve hours of team training, some remained skeptical that the Terre Haute plant could adopt a self-managed team system. Their attitudes, as Rutledge knew, would be very difficult to change.

The site visits were eye-openers. For many of the Terre Haute employees, the notion of work teams still smacked of Japanese-style regimentation, complete with calisthenics in the morning and silly company songs. The visits to the sites showed them quite a different picture. They quickly learned that these places were characterized by a great deal of energy and excitement that comes only from employees having a strong stake in what they are doing. It was plain, from touring facilities and talking to employees, that people enjoyed their work more in team environments. One lesson that especially hit home was the realization that there were different variations on the team concept. Facilities could mix and match team techniques to suit their own needs. Experimentation was allowed. Failure did not have to derail the whole team process. Rutledge realized how fast progress was being made during the trip to Johnson & Johnson, when employees of both companies met to discuss the effects of company culture and history on the pace of change. Months earlier, few at the Terre Haute plant were discussing such sophisticated ideas or speaking so fluently in the new language of teams and empowerment.

According to Rutledge's timetable, the next step would be to form a design team. To start the design process, this team would use the site team's notes on what they liked and didn't like. But soon after the second visit, she realized that the best possible design team already existed—the employees who had learned so much during the site visits. With Cavallo's concurrence, Rutledge suggested the site team put on a design team hat. Everyone readily agreed. The team's objective included developing a loose framework for team development rather than a tight implementation plan. The team was convinced that developing teams would be a lengthy evolutionary process at the Terre Haute plant, as different areas developed at their own rate and in their own style.

But the team's main objective was to draft a mission statement and a set of values to guide team development. Department managers, who had been asked to supply the design team with their own visions of how the team system should evolve, joined in the effort. In the end, the design team came up with something unexpected. Instead of a mission statement and a values statement, the team drafted a series of nine separate statements covering areas critical to team development and specific enough to be measured. Within each area, the design team outlined "growing points" that would help teams advance step by step to true effectiveness. The design team also wanted to make sure that it and management were in complete harmony. The team wanted management to pledge that jobs would not be lost as a result of any efficiencies a new team system would create (apart from any "business" reason for downsizing). The team also wanted management to allow three to five years for the team system to develop, recognizing that progress might be halting, disruptions to plant operations could occur, and setbacks would be inevitable.

A document was drafted spelling out the design team's expectations of plant and corporate management. The team called it a "commitment" to avoid making it sound like a contract. To executives, who had been following the design process closely, the document contained few surprises. After a formal presentation by the design team, the commitment was signed by eighteen plant and corporate executives and the twenty-two design team members. The design team later divided into five smaller teams and made formal presentations to the entire plant.

Teams: A Loose Framework

FSG's team system at Terre Haute is based on existing shifts within each department. Each department has six to eight teams, with four to six members per team. These are natural teams because they are based on existing production processes—a formal redesign of work was not within the design team's original mandate. Instead, the design team formulated boundaries for teams and the "growing points" that would allow teams to gradually expand those boundaries and assume increasing responsibility (see Exhibit 6.1).

As part of the earlier reorganization, the management structure already had changed significantly, at least on paper, by the time teams were formally launched. The number of exempt personnel had been reduced by combining several departments (for example, materials resource planning was created from separate traffic, warehousing, inventory, and purchasing operations) and by eliminating several assistant management levels. The steering committee of department managers changed the title foreman to facilitator.

One of the design team's most concrete proposals was to create "area forums" and a "central forum." A concept adopted from A. E. Staley—a company the design team had visited—the forums help drive the team transition forward. Each of the thirteen departments has its own area forum. Members include a volunteer from each department's natural shift teams and the department manager. A typical area forum has nine members who meet weekly to facilitate communication between shifts and resolve problems within the department. The central forum, by contrast, is a plantwide group with representatives from each area forum, the plant

Exhibit 6.1. Selected Mission Statements and Growing Points.

Customer and Vendor

We are a dependable, fair, and honest supplier, building relationships with external and internal customers through communication, quality, and service. We deal with reliable vendors who provide quality materials and services consistent with our standards. We develop an identity with our customers and vendors and an appreciation of their needs and expectations.

Growing Points

- Involvement in programs that cut lead times, reduce waste, and allow direct communication with customers and vendors.
- Training that fosters business relationships between customers and vendors.
- Participate in the selection of vendors, equipment, and raw materials.
- Direct interaction and decision making with vendors and customers.
- Participate in the standardization and stocking of equipment and supplies.
- Participate in inventory reduction (raw materials, finished goods, mechanical stock).
- Participate in establishing vendor stocking programs.
- Seek and act upon customer feedback to constantly improve.
- Give vendor feedback to ensure constant improvement.

Empowerment

To ensure team efficiency and job satisfaction, team members are empowered with the shared responsibility to respond to the changing needs of our members, our business partners, and our communities. Using continuous and timely training, and innovative ideas, team members will make decisions to monitor and improve safety, environment, quality, cost, and housekeeping within the boundaries of policies and procedures.

Growing Points

- Peer performance management
- Selection of team members
- Equipment selection and supply management
- Budget input
- Production scheduling
- Scheduling vacation, overtime, and training
- Identification of training needs
- Direct customer/vendor contact
- Self-scheduling of work tasks
- Noting and scheduling equipment repairs
- Facility design and improvement
- Contributing innovative ideas
- Taking ownership

Exhibit 6.1. Selected Mission Statements and Growing Points, Cont'd.

Training

Training and development are investments in a continuing process that benefits individual and organization needs essential to consistently improving standards of performance.

Growing Points

- Provide training in communication and interpersonal skills so teams may better interact and respond to team needs.
- Develop a thorough understanding of processes, equipment, and support systems through technical training.
- Deliver business training to promote team participation in budgeting and cost control.
- Educate teams in quality concepts required for continuous improvement.
- Ensure safety, health, and environmental awareness through timely training in procedures, policies, and regulations.

manager, and a representative from a quality control committee and from the steering committee. This forum meets monthly to discuss issues affecting the entire plant and to get updates from the area forum representatives on team developments within departments. The plant manager also updates representatives on the latest business developments affecting the plant. The purpose of the central forum is to forge a plantwide consensus on issues—not decide issues. That's left up to individual departments, primarily through area forum deliberations.

By choice the design team ensured that teams at the Terre Haute plant would all develop a little differently and at their own pace. In some areas facilitators—the old foremen—are considered team members and provide varying degrees of team leadership. Other teams are headed by "lead operators," who in the past had headed shift crews. In both cases, such leadership is nominal because teams quickly developed their own methods of sharing responsibility. Officially Terre Haute's teams are responsible for monitoring quality, costs, housekeeping, and safety and environmental issues as they relate to individual teams and to the entire department. Team members usually volunteer to assume certain responsibilities. Although teams were introduced to the idea of a shared management system that rotates responsibilities among different teams after certain periods, so far most teams have decided to make volunteer positions more or less permanent. Their thinking: if one team member enjoys a particular task, such as monitoring compliance with safety policies, why not let him or her keep doing it? As the number and complexity of team responsibilities grow, however, most teams acknowledge that a more structured system might be necessary, and the growing points address that issue.

The growing points in the team charter envision the day when teams will be responsible for an array of tasks: managing peer performance, scheduling work, selecting other team members, choosing their own supplies and equipment, helping develop department budgets, scheduling production, vacation, overtime, and training, and citing team training needs.

Team training is being conducted on two fronts. In 1992, all employees received a sequential series of basic team training courses spanning twenty hours—including an orientation to self-directed teams, communication skills, working in teams, meeting skills, and consensus building. Follow-up training completed in 1993 included sixteen hours of continuous improvement skills and twelve hours of advanced interaction skills, including training others and handling conflict. Eventually all employees will receive eight hours of training in advanced problem solving and ongoing improvement activities.

Cross-training other team members is the second front. Eventually all employees will receive "train-the-trainer" training. Currently each department is conducting a training needs assessment covering process and job-specific training requirements. Once department job skills are identified, team members proficient in certain skills and qualified to train others will be responsible for meeting their team's training needs in those skill areas. Once team members have mastered a certain number of fundamental skills, they will be eligible for a pay-for-skills system based on team needs.

Supervisors

The biggest change in the way the Terre Haute plant is supervised and managed started before the design team began its work. Foremen, a nonexempt, hourly position, were given the choice of becoming facilitators (a salaried staff position) or being reassigned to a variety of nonexempt roles. Most chose to become facilitators—with the understanding that this role, too, might eventually be phased out as teams matured and took on increasing responsibilities. Downsizing the ranks of facilitators has been accomplished by attrition and redeployment. Because foremen had been nonexempt employees, some faced the prospect of losing considerable overtime pay. To soften the blow, facilitators' salaries during the first year under the new system were based on the previous year's compensation, including overtime, as nonexempt employees.

The transition from foreman to facilitator has been helped by training—including a two-day workshop on coaching work teams conducted by training coordinator Rutledge. Rutledge also had all thirteen department managers clarify their expectations of facilitators in their departments. The goal was to overcome any anxiety and resistance facilitators might feel about the changes and enlist their support as active partners in the team transition.

Results

The transition to teams at Terre Haute is an ongoing process that traces its roots to Pfizer's employee involvement activities of the late 1980s. Although no sharp breakthroughs in productivity and quality have been recorded, improvements have been steady and consistent. Most production records now are routinely surpassed. The biggest gains are invariably seen in areas where work teams have developed the greatest maturity. In antibiotics production, for instance, teams are achieving levels of potency—the chief way to gauge process yields—that would have been extraordinary just a year ago. In fact, surpassing the preceding month's potency levels is becoming the norm.

The plant's results are all the more impressive given that many veteran employees, long used to the old ways of doing things, were initially wary of change. Some employees, however, have complained that too many changes were set in motion at once. Or, as one employee puts it, "We kind of dumped everything onto the plate before making sure the plate was big enough." Training over the last two years has been heavy and work frequently has been interrupted. For some employees, that might have hardened their resistance to change. Ramona Rutledge estimates that as much as 20 percent of the workforce might still feel the team concept won't succeed.

Supervisors and managers experienced the kind of confusion that frequently accompanies the team transformation process. For example, foremen weren't fully apprised of their new responsibilities. Told they were now "facilitators," some sat back and watched teams attempt to handle new responsibilities and establish working relationships—mainly because they didn't know how to support the team development process. Training was later required to alleviate their role confusion—a lesson that the Terre Haute plant, like other organizations, has learned on the road to self-managed teams.

Major problems have been few, however, which might be a tribute to the involvement of employees from all areas of the organization in establishing the team framework. Nearly 15 percent of employees from all departments at the plant were involved in the planning process by serving on the site and design teams or by attending off-site workshops and conferences. And now that teams are being implemented, all employees have a say in shaping their evolution through area forums and the central forum. "It's become clear to employees that this is not a management-driven thing or an HR program," says one Terre Haute manager. "It's a dynamic and changing process that offers little chance for anyone to remain passive."

7

Using Teamwork
to Redesign Core Processes

Sterling Winthrop, Ltd.
Sydney, Australia

Industry	Pharmaceuticals
Union	Shop Distributive and Allied Employees Association; Australian Workers Union; National Union of Workers
Type of team implementation	Redesigned and self-directed pilot teams
First teams started	1992
Employees	500
Percentage in teams	30 percent (all manufacturing employees)
Team size	10 to 12
Team responsibilities	Teams are responsible for all activities "inside the pipe" in the manufacturing of liquid and solid-dose analgesics: planning production, dispensing raw materials, manufacturing, packaging, cleaning and maintaining equipment, handling line changeovers, and collecting and monitoring a series of "right-first-time" quality data. Teams also schedule vacations and overtime and hire temporary labor.

Organization-wide team responsibilities	Teams develop action plans and team goals that are linked to overall strategic business goals.
Team leadership and governance	Teams have no formal leaders and operate largely by consensus. Team responsibilities are assigned informally within the team. There is no system of rotating duties.
Leadership outside teams	"Pipe leaders," or production managers to whom the teams report, are the only official managers in team production areas. Most teams are assigned a facilitator who assists their development, but the position is not supervisory.
Team compensation	No special team compensation.
First-year team member training	Eighty hours of quality and problem-solving techniques, team interaction skills, business awareness, skills in cross-training others.
Subsequent team member training	To be determined.
First-year leadership training	Eighty hours in business awareness, team and workplace design, and interviewing, facilitation, and coaching skills.
Subsequent leadership training	To be determined.
How team members are selected	The first team was composed of volunteers who were evaluated and interviewed by steering committee members. The selection process included psychological evaluations and testing.

*How team
performance
is evaluated*

Teams track performance in six general areas: material and labor variances, various "right-first-time" quality measurements, customer complaints, backorder performance, and line fill rates. Eventually team goals will be tied to the strategic planning process.

*Team impact on
organization*

Teams have simplified a complex production process—reducing the number of process steps from nearly a hundred to fifty and cutting department interfaces from twenty-one to three. Lead time for shipping orders has been cut from fifteen days to five and a chronic backorder problem has been eliminated. During its first year of operation, the initial team handled a 40 percent increase in production with no increase in head count.

Key lessons

- Establish a clear and workable vision of team operation and responsibilities and then stick to it; make sure team accountability is understood and accepted; communicate constantly; be realistic about training and development needs; manage expectations as teams develop.

- Multifunctional design teams can delay progress in the early stages by spending too much time on generic issues and endlessly debating implementation. Eventually, natural work teams will work out team development issues as they encounter them.

- Every change should be accompanied by extensive communication and feedback. Senior managers must take the time to communicate closely with employees.
- Ensure that the right people are recruited for leadership roles and team roles.

Background

With brand-name products such as Panadol, Sterling Winthrop has a commanding share of the market in Australia and New Zealand for liquid and solid-dose nonprescription analgesics. By the 1990s, however, it became clear to Sterling Winthrop's management that several trends threatened the company's position. Its own surveys of retail and distribution customers showed, surprisingly, that brand names, special deals and discounts, and other conventional marketing tools mattered less to wholesale and retail customers than timely delivery and availability—especially during the cold and flu season, when sales of over-the-counter remedies boom. More worrisome, competition in the analgesics market in Australia and New Zealand was heating up and several companies were challenging Sterling Winthrop's lead. Competitors were spending a great deal on advertising. Some of them were getting products into the hands of commercial customers faster than Sterling Winthrop.

Sterling Winthrop began to address these challenges in 1989 through a series of steps designed to rationalize the business and focus on the company's strongest products. Half of Sterling Winthrop's product line was dropped, and the number of backorders filled each month declined from 6,000 to 2,000, dramatically reducing inventory costs. Delivery time also was shortened (although it still averaged fifteen days), and customer complaints were reduced. By 1991, senior managers felt that most of the obvious improvements had been made.

The next steps would involve major changes in work systems—changes the managers weren't quite sure their employees were ready for. That concern led to a "Future Directions" conference involving a cross section of forty-five employees (from managers to shop floor employees). Managers hoped the conference would begin breaking down some barriers to change that the strongly traditional Australian labor system presented—including fairly inflexible work rules and contentious management/union relations. In subsequent months, general manager of manufacturing Peter Martin and his management team decided to address Sterling Winthrop's biggest barriers to customer service: backorders and lead times.

These barriers seemed especially pronounced in liquid analgesics, an area where, as one manager puts it, the company was "running pretty dumb" from a production standpoint. Liquid analgesics production involved nearly a hundred process steps between planning and distribution, with twenty-one different department interfaces. Every interface added time and cost to the production process and presented the potential for a quality glitch. Increasing communication and coordination among departments was difficult because departments traditionally focused on their internal functional needs, not on the entire production process. As a result, materials for production runs would be shuttled from the dispensary to the warehouse to production, back to the warehouse, then off to quality assurance, and so on. The process was simply too complex and inefficient to achieve what Martin and his managers knew had to be done: delivering orders on time and reducing lead time from weeks to days. This would require reducing department interfaces and dramatically cutting the number of process steps. Martin envisioned a simple continuum—a pipeline into which raw materials would go at one end and finished goods would come out the other. All functions and processes that contributed to the production of finished goods would be brought "inside the pipeline."

To achieve this vision, Martin and other manufacturing managers spent two days in a remote farmhouse trying to restructure Sterling Winthrop's manufacturing operations. The managers (from quality assurance, technical services, manufacturing, logistics, and human resources) tried to identify all the barriers to achieving Martin's vision of a simplified production pipeline. The logistics manager helped the group analyze the flow of material through the plant, which was pretty confusing. Areas outside the pipeline included production planning, quality sampling and assurance at various stages in production, warehousing, several staging and inspection processes, and distribution. Areas inside the pipeline included vendor scheduling, material receipt, production scheduling, material dispensing, product blending and packaging, other quality assurance procedures, and final warehousing before distribution. Maintenance and skilled trades functions were so poorly integrated with production that minor equipment repairs or changeovers could halt production for hours.

From the meeting a new initiative emerged—Project Pipe—as well as a detailed seventy-page document that called for, among other things, establishing a pilot work team system in liquid analgesics that would gradually integrate into the pipe all functions and departments that logically belonged there. Ultimately the document outlined a drastically simplified system that would replace the company's twenty-one functional departments with only three—production planning, production itself (composed of teams that handled the entire process from vendor scheduling to finished product warehousing), and distribution. The production pipeline would absorb and consolidate all other functions, reducing the number of process steps from a hundred to fifty. Figure 7.1 illustrates the streamlining process.

The farmhouse meeting also led to the creation of a steering committee for the transition to the new production team system. Members included senior managers representing manufacturing, human resources, logistics, technical services, quality assurance, and the liquid analgesics production area. The steering committee's role included creating a mission statement for a new team system, managing and monitoring the implementation, and assessing results to determine the feasibility of extending the new system to the rest of the manufacturing organization.

A short time later, members of the steering committee met with all employees to apprise them of the changes being considered and to recruit volunteers for a team system in liquid analgesics. Two teams of ten to fifteen members for each of two shifts were planned. Before volunteers were accepted, they were screened through a series of psychological evaluations and interviews with the steering committee. The committee wanted to make sure that the pilot teams were composed of employees with the right aptitude and a strong readiness for change. Ultimately, fifty production operators were selected.

The next step was a three-day off-site conference with the steering committee, the new team volunteers, and other managers who volunteered to serve on Project Pipe. During the conference volunteers were encouraged to discuss their anxieties about abandoning old work systems and their ideas for making a team system successful. The conference ended with the establishment of a cross-functional project team that would do the work of implementing the new team system. Members of the eight-person team included the liquid analgesics production manager, a production scheduler, a human

Figure 7.1. Sterling Winthrop's Project Pipe: Streamlining the Process.

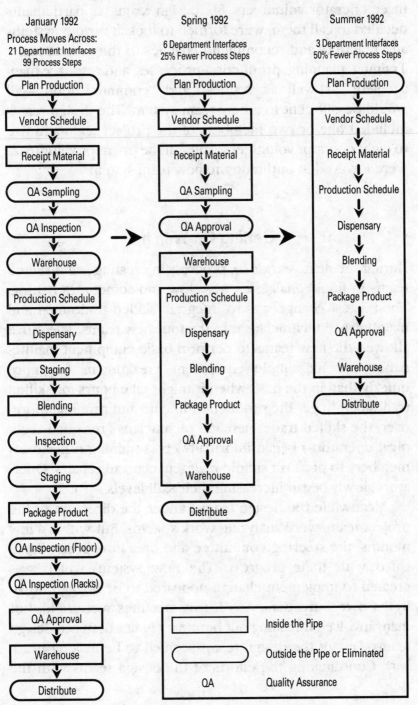

January 1992	Spring 1992	Summer 1992
Process Moves Across: 21 Department Interfaces 99 Process Steps	6 Department Interfaces 25% Fewer Process Steps	3 Department Interfaces 50% Fewer Process Steps

January 1992
- Plan Production
- Vendor Schedule
- Receipt Material
- QA Sampling
- QA Inspection
- Warehouse
- Production Schedule
- Dispensary
- Staging
- Blending
- Inspection
- Staging
- Package Product
- QA Inspection (Floor)
- QA Inspection (Racks)
- QA Approval
- Warehouse
- Distribute

Spring 1992
- Plan Production
- Vendor Schedule
- Receipt Material
- QA Sampling
- QA Approval
- Warehouse
- Production Schedule
- Dispensary
- Blending
- Package Product
- QA Approval
- Warehouse
- Distribute

Summer 1992
- Plan Production
- Vendor Schedule
- Receipt Material
- Production Schedule
- Dispensary
- Blending
- Package Product
- QA Approval
- Warehouse
- Distribute

Legend:
- Inside the Pipe
- Outside the Pipe or Eliminated
- QA — Quality Assurance

resource officer, a purchasing officer, a chemical analyst, and three operator volunteers. Six design teams, as participants decided to call them, were formed to look at various systems and practices and recommend changes to the project team. Training, planning, production processes, and resource management, as well as "values" and "communication"—all would be different in a new team system. The design teams included one or two members of the project team and five to eight operator volunteers. Thus all the operator volunteers were involved in outlining the new team system.

Getting On With It

During the next year or so, progress in creating self-directed teams in liquid analgesics was slow and sometimes halting. The biggest change was to integrate skilled tradesmen and maintenance technicians into the four new teams. The move allowed the new teams to perform basic equipment maintenance and fix simple equipment breakdowns far more quickly than in the past, when it might take hours for skilled tradesmen to get the production line up and running. Moreover, the skilled tradesmen and technicians (renamed technical operators) began informally cross-training other team members to perform simple maintenance and repairs. Operators slowly began increasing their skill levels.

Meanwhile the design teams, under the direction of the project team, were analyzing work systems. But within a few months, the steering committee and operators grew dissatisfied with their progress. The new system, which was created to implement change, appeared to be bogged down by its own bureaucracy. A lot of meetings were held, but many involved thrashing out boundary issues between design teams. Few of the design teams seemed to be making headway. Coordinating the efforts of the design teams with the project team was difficult too. When the steering committee met to discuss the problem, it concluded that the design process was moving too slowly and a more direct, top-down approach was needed. Although the design teams had encouraged participation among operators, the steering committee decided that someone had to be in charge of team development. That person was Stewart Jackson, production manager in liquid analgesics, who was recast as "pipe leader" and directed to accelerate the process of adding functional duties to the existing teams. No longer considered "pilot teams," the teams now were fully functional natural work teams on the road to self-direction.

The accelerated team development coincided with the onset of Australia's cold and flu season. Demand was heavy for Sterling Winthrop products, particularly a new pediatric analgesic. The teams kept up with demand, enabling the company to increase its market share substantially—but only through nonstop overtime and an all-out "blood, sweat, and tears effort," as one manager called it. Before long the stress of the extra work began to exact a toll in terms of conflict among team members. Clearly the steering committee would have to take a second look at training plans—particularly team interaction skills and team dynamics—because the pipe teams lacked the skills to function cohesively during times of stress. What resulted was a comprehensive training plan for each team that included not only interpersonal and problem-solving skills but also diagnosing internal team problems, increasing communication within the team, and working with other teams. A business awareness program also was put together to help teams understand the marketplace and their impact on it. Most important, every second Friday six hours were set aside for team development. Finding the time to focus on development needs had been one of the pilot teams' biggest challenges. Now management was committed to making sure they got what they needed.

Today the original pipe team system has been applied to the remaining production areas in Sterling Winthrop, bringing the total number of employees operating in production teams to 150. Yet progress in team development has been uneven; as one issue or challenge seemed to be resolved, others appeared. Defining the role of leadership, inside and outside teams, has been especially challenging. Several sessions were needed with manufacturing managers to allay their fears about what impact "empowerment" would have on their jobs and to ensure that they understood how the pipe teams were operating. Nonetheless, the original teams have moved steadily toward the company's goal of handling the four main functions inside the pipe. Each team has at least one member who can train other team members in another function, and most team members are trained to perform at least two functions. The teams also handle production planning and scheduling, hiring temporary labor when needed, analyzing customer complaints and providing feedback to management, and working out quality or delivery problems directly with suppliers. The newer teams are basically following the development pattern of the first teams.

Managers and Leaders

One natural consequence of pipe team development has been a decreasing need for traditional supervision—which meant redefining the role of Sterling Winthrop's foremen (forepersons, as the company prefers) and production managers. Coming up with a new role for forepersons turned out to be a thorny problem indeed.

While the foreperson's position survived the implementation of the first teams, some of them had difficulty understanding their new relationship with the teams. Others saw teams as the prelude to eliminating their positions. The steering committee had hoped that with training, forepersons would act as effective team developers. But it became clear that some of them were distancing themselves from teams—"washing their hands of the whole thing," as one manager put it. As a result, the steering committee and project team became convinced that many current forepersons and supervisors were not suited to encouraging team development, either as outside-the-team coaches or as team leaders. This led to the creation of a new position—team coaches for every fifteen to twenty team members—and to advertising internally for the positions. Forepersons were informed they no longer would have "people management" responsibilities. Although their responsibilities were dwindling anyway, the change came as a shock to some. Most, however, joined teams as members or were selected as new team coaches, or facilitators, based on their demonstrated skill in coaching and team development.

Nine new coaches were selected to replace the twenty forepersons. Very quickly the new coaches decided to change their name to facilitators. One facilitator was assigned per team for each shift. The result, at least on paper, was a production system with no layer of management between teams and the pipe leader (production manager). While facilitators still performed certain traditional supervisory functions, their main role was to help teams define their training needs, set up cross-training positions, and encourage teams to assume increasing responsibilities during a two-year period until reaching full maturity.

Meanwhile the role of production managers was redefined. As pipe leaders, managers were expected to relinquish control over day-to-day production and become more like operations managers—linking strategic corporate goals to pipe team goals and assuming more financial planning, management accounting, and problem-solving responsibilities. Pipe leaders still are deeply involved in daily production issues, but as teams mature that involvement should become increasingly unnecessary.

Rewards and Performance Appraisal

Sterling Winthrop's traditional job classifications remain intact, so team members still are considered part of "packaging," "warehousing," or some other function. All are eligible for "skills-acquired" pay raises, but the individual performance measurement system has changed little since the team system was implemented. Team members still receive formal six-month performance appraisals. But now there is a difference: with most of the old supervisors gone, performance appraisals are conducted between individuals and team coaches. Eventually feedback from team members will be incorporated into the performance appraisal process. The biggest change has been a reduction in job classifications—from about thirty to only five. As team members have complained that the old compensation system doesn't reflect expanded job responsibilities, a task force of team members has been created to revise the compensation system. Its main goal is to come up with a new system that reflects both individual and team accomplishments.

Team performance measurement is evolving too. Now teams track performance in six general areas: material and labor variances, various "right-first-time" quality measurements, customer complaints, backorder performance, and line fill rates. For the future, Winthrop hopes to link team performance to compensation and train teams to develop goals that tie into management's strategic planning process.

Results

The steering committee knew the pipe team system entailed several risks. For one, teams challenged traditional labor demarcation issues. For another, team members received accelerated training for which their pay increased more quickly than employees still working under the traditional compensation system. Would other employees resent this "special treatment" and resist or even sabotage the emerging team system? Sterling Winthrop employees, like those in many large companies, had gone through a variety of human resource programs in the 1980s, the effects of which were sometimes short lived. Managers knew the company had only one chance to get a team system off the ground. If teams stumbled badly and were allowed to expire quietly like other management programs, employees might easily shrug off teams as just another work system fad.

Today the first teams, while still not fully mature, have compiled a solid record of achievements. Indeed big improvements have been seen in every area the steering committee initially targeted, including reduction in process steps, lead time, and backorders. One reason productivity has increased so dramatically is a 75 percent reduction in line changeover time. Teams also are far more productive because they now handle many other functions as well—from dispensing and warehousing to cleaning and maintenance.

The first pipe teams and, later, the second and third teams taught Sterling Winthrop a number of lessons that will prove useful if it rolls out teams throughout the organization. In fact, when managers conducted a postmortem of the pipe team experience, about thirty key lessons emerged in five areas: establishing a clear and workable vision and then sticking to it; making sure team accountabilities are understood and accepted; communicating constantly; being realistic about training and development needs; and managing expectations as teams developed.

The steering committee learned that the general manager must be the torchbearer or visionary, gaining the commitment of managers and employees to translate the vision into a workable plan. Equally important, the company discovered, is examining less-risky alternatives for achieving business goals before making a commitment. In short, the most dramatic approach is not necessarily the best approach.

The process of defining accountabilities and roles provided valuable lessons for the steering committee. It found that establishing team accountabilities worked best when employees were grouped in natural work teams, confronting the operational issues that only experience could reveal. Having a plan is necessary, the steering committee concluded, but there's no need to spend a lot of time perfecting it.

Sterling Winthrop also learned that communication helps the team development process to succeed. The steering committee provided ample forums for employees to air concerns and to learn why certain decisions were made. This was especially helpful in preventing rumors from spreading.

Like many companies embarking on team journeys, Sterling Winthrop discovered that training needs—especially in team interaction skills—are often underestimated. Making sure teams get the training time they need is essential.

Perhaps the biggest reason for the first pipe team's success was that all members were volunteers who had been screened for their motivation and aptitude. This relates to one of the biggest lessons Sterling Winthrop learned: a successful team implementation requires the right people. Initial successes, therefore, can be chalked up to sheer hard work and commitment. Teams composed of employees without the same level of enthusiasm might have fractured under the stress. The need for the right people also extended to team coaches and pipe leaders. With the right people, everything else eventually falls into place.

8

Driving Reengineering
Through Empowered Teams

UCAR Carbon
Clarksville, Tennessee

Industry	Manufacturing—graphite and carbon electrodes, graphite specialties, grafoil, and other carbon and graphite products
Union	Three plants are represented by the Operator Engineers and the Union of Oil, Chemical, and Atomic Workers; four plants are nonunion.
Type of team implementation	Teams are at various development stages at seven facilities. Natural and redesigned self-directed teams complement a team approach to management and cross-functional facilitywide project teams.
First teams started	1992
Employees	1,600 in the U.S.; 5,000 worldwide
Percentage in teams	85 to 90 percent
Team size	4 to 20
Team responsibilities	Depending on their maturity and the union status of the facility, UCAR production teams plan work schedules and assign

responsibilities, track key performance indicators (team cycle times, production
yields), determine production rate by
monitoring a just-in-time production system based on current customer product
usage, schedule overtime and vacations,
start and stop production as necessary to
meet production standards. Other levels in
the organization also function as teams, including business unit management.

*Organization-
wide team
responsibilities*

Most decisions on policy changes and human resource issues affecting entire plants
involve a special project team. Project
teams have developed peer appraisal systems and training programs for maintenance specialists. Team leaders meet
regularly to discuss plantwide issues.

*Team leadership
and governance*

For most teams leadership is informal:
members serve as leaders or coordinators
on a rotating basis. Teams at some UCAR
plants use a star point system of rotating
responsibilities for safety and quality issues
and measuring team performance.

*Leadership
outside teams*

Process managers have replaced plant superintendents and foremen and serve as
coaches and facilitators to as many as five
teams.

*Team
compensation*

No special systems so far.

*First-year team
member training*

UCAR made a large investment in training.
Production employees received ten days of
training on empowered teams and their

changing roles in this new environment. Training included team meeting skills, team interaction skills, overall business knowledge, and skills in cross-training others.

Subsequent team member training

Needs are being assessed.

First-year leadership training

All management and professional staff, including process managers, received seven and a half days of training on empowered teams and the changing role of managers in this new environment. Training included team meeting skills, team interaction skills, overall business knowledge, and cross-training skills.

Subsequent leadership training

Needs are being assessed.

How team members are selected

Seniority bidding system

How team performance is evaluated

Teams are responsible for monitoring key performance indicators.

Team impact on organization

UCAR's Project '92 was an organization-wide reengineering process with teams as one key element. Results include a 40 percent reduction in cycle times of most graphite electrode products and a 50 percent reduction in inventories. UCAR hopes that Project '92 changes will reduce its costs by at least $10 million annually.

Key lessons

- The entire organization, including unions, must be involved.
- Essential full-time resources must be committed.
- Necessary personnel changes must be made as quickly as possible.
- Key performance indicators must be established early in the process.
- Teams must be allowed to *implement* learned skills. Implementation, not training, is the goal.
- Line management's commitment is essential for success.

Background

Few companies have acted so decisively and with such a sense of urgency to reinvent themselves as UCAR Carbon. With revenues of $800 million, UCAR is the world leader in carbon and graphite products. But the picture wasn't always so rosy. UCAR's major market—the worldwide steel industry—stumbled mightily in the past decade, and UCAR stumbled right along with it. With little prospect of the steel industry totally reviving itself, and with few opportunities and little time to diversify into other product areas, UCAR realized that change—big change—was the key to its survival.

Once the Carbon Products Division of Union Carbide, UCAR was renamed in 1991 after Union Carbide sold a half-interest to Japan's Mitsubishi Trading Company. (Mitsubishi executives serve on the board and in UCAR's export marketing organization but are not involved in operations.) Today UCAR has three business units. Supplying graphite electrodes for steelmaking is by far the largest, accounting for about 78 percent of UCAR's worldwide sales. Other businesses include a carbon electrode business, which supplies the silicon metal industry, and a graphite specialty business that serves the semiconductor industry. (This business includes UCAR's grafoil unit, which makes flexible gaskets for the automobile and chemical industries.)

Steel companies are only now beginning to emerge from a decade-long slump that sent prices for steel products plummeting and caused UCAR's prices to follow suit. Added to UCAR's predicament was a persistent quality problem: the amount of UCAR's graphite electrodes needed to melt steel in electric arc furnaces was sometimes greater than its competitors'. Because performance is measured by pounds of graphite consumed to melt a ton of steel, the less graphite consumed the better. Compounding this problem, U.S. steelmakers were whittling away at the amount of graphite needed to make steel—in the 1980s most steelmakers required about twelve pounds of graphite electrodes for a ton of steel; today most need six pounds and some need only three.

By the end of the 1980s, UCAR realized there would be no quick fixes. The feeling was especially strong among UCAR's site management personnel at its seven facilities in the South and Midwest. To them there seemed to be little UCAR could do about the industry or the markets it served. UCAR could, however, change nearly everything about the way it did business—a dramatic approach that seemed justified by the dire straits of the graphite electrode business. The result was an organizationwide reengineering program called Project '92, started in mid-1991 and championed by Bill Wiemels, UCAR's vice president and general manager. Self-directed teams were not a foregone conclusion when the project began, but eventually the team approach was adopted at all levels in the company. And Wiemels was one of its most enthusiastic proponents.

Project '92's objectives were not modest. They included eliminating all non-value-added activities in every part of the company, removing all functional barriers to internal and external customer service, and realigning production around processes. Two early groups set the project in motion. A steering committee of senior managers, headed by Wiemels, was created to provide overall direction. At the same time, a core project team was created from middle-level managers in the seven areas pinpointed as targets for change: financial management, pipeline (or production process) manufacturing, raw materials replenishment, research and development, applied technology, customer order management, and sales and marketing. Eventually the core team focused on three main areas:

- Customer order management, which was exceedingly complex—it might take a week for a service rep to tell a customer how long it would take to process an order.

- Operations—which was rife with production bottlenecks.

- Business unit integration—because business units often acted more in self-interest than in the company's interest.

Although eliminating production positions was not anticipated, the core team did plan to streamline management—a process that could eliminate as many as two hundred salaried positions.

Teams

Before UCAR's reengineering process, the company consisted of a corporate-level organization, U.S. operations with seven plants, and an administrative unit (which included R&D and technology specialists). The first change was to take these functionally divided organizations and create self-supporting business units based on UCAR's main products— graphite and carbon electrodes, graphite specialty products, and grafoil gaskets. In the meantime, the core team recommended changes in all seven areas under its review. Within each area, design teams were formed to reengineer the functionally divided structures around either production processes or product areas.

UCAR adopted a team approach from top to bottom. At the senior management level, three business unit teams were formed to operate UCAR's core businesses. Today each business unit team contains senior managers who once headed departments or sites. Each team has a charter and members rotate responsibility for facilitating meetings. While most business unit team members retain many of their former functional responsibilities (for example, finance or managing a UCAR plant), their focus is to reach consensus on the best way to run the overall business—not their individual functions. At the plant level, UCAR's facilities have operated a little differently over the years, depending on whether they are unionized, their age (Clarksville opened in 1980; Columbia is more than fifty years old), and the style and temperament of the plant management team.

When Project '92 was introduced, special project and problem-solving teams, as well as maintenance, engineering, and other single-purpose teams, were nothing new at several facilities, especially at Clarksville. But Project '92 called for something different: multifunctional work teams based on major operational processes, such as making graphite rods from beginning to end. UCAR's new teams schedule their workloads, assign individual job responsibilities within teams, and monitor output and quality.

At Clarksville, where the self-directed work team system

is the most mature, teams begin their shifts with meetings that can last up to fifteen minutes or more. Each meeting has an agenda to assign shift responsibilities, and one team member makes sure the team follows the agenda. As teams plan their work, they may discuss overtime, vacation schedules, and other factors affecting production goals. Usually a daily agenda includes discussion of a production problem or an improvement project. Although several issues might need attention, teams have been trained to avoid overloading agendas—it's better to focus on resolving one challenge at a time. Teams can spend up to $2,000 on equipment maintenance or repair without higher-level authorization.

Operators are expected to learn most of the team's different job stations within several months of joining. The number of jobs can range from four to nine. In the process called graphitizing, for example, team members perform several types of furnace loading and operate cranes and forklifts. Teams in the graphite baking area handle similar processes and operate several additional types of equipment as well. Team members rotate these jobs daily or weekly, and teams publish their schedules every two or three weeks. The team decides when members of other teams are qualified in different job stations. In union facilities, rotating roles and responsibilities remains an unresolved issue. So far, however, UCAR's unions largely support the team transformation process. Steering committees composed of union and management personnel in UCAR's three unionized plants are working to create team structures that both unions and management can support.

Rotating data keeping, safety, quality, and other roles and responsibilities within teams is not mandatory. The design and implementation teams had resolved that certain team "rules" would not be dictated. Rather, they decided, as teams matured they could adopt team management practices that appeared most useful. Most of UCAR's mature teams have adopted some system of rotating key responsibilities within teams—similar to the star point system discussed elsewhere. Teams elect coordinators to track data and monitor issues in such areas as safety, quality, purchasing, and production scheduling. Some teams have designated team leaders who coordinate overall team activity and interface with other teams and plant management. Roles and responsibilities may be rotated as often as monthly. One of the most important roles is tracking and posting the team's key performance indicators: cycle time, yields, downtime, and other team measurements. Each team maintains a log and posts its results on bulletin boards. A low-tech solution, the daily updating and posting of key performance indicators has largely eliminated the need for plant management to pore over monthly financial and production data to determine how well plants are doing.

Production scheduling is perhaps one of UCAR's teams' biggest challenges. Before Project '92, UCAR based production on predicted demand; teams simply received their production orders for the day or the week ahead from plant management. Now UCAR uses a just-in-time pipeline system based on, among other things, consumption of graphite electrodes among big customers who daily fax or transmit their consumption figures to UCAR plants. By triggering decisions to produce more electrodes to meet customers' current production requirements, the figures eliminate purchase orders and keep UCAR's production carefully balanced with what customers are actually using. The pipeline system means that teams must make their own decisions about their production rate based on the flow of material coming to them through the production pipeline. By monitoring inventory, teams decide when to load "green" electrodes (consisting of raw coke and pitch) into furnaces to keep up with changing production demands. If teams fall behind, they can make decisions about scheduling and overtime to pick up their pace.

In UCAR's plants that operate with four continuous shifts, teams might more accurately be called subteams: the teams on all four shifts are considered part of one expanded team. The teams decided to do it this way because in most cases each shift's teams work on the same process. Further, they reasoned, decisions affecting all four shifts should be reached by everyone involved. Each team has a shift coordinator who meets with other shift coordinators, usually weekly, to discuss issues affecting the expanded team. Reaching decisions this way is not easy, however. Because many team members never see one another, maintaining a smooth flow of information is difficult.

The designers of UCAR's team structure resolved that all plantwide decisions require input from every affected group. The leaders of each work team meet regularly to discuss issues affecting all teams. Other special project teams make recommendations on policy changes and human resource issues. At Clarksville, for example, a team of operators and managers developed a new peer appraisal system. A similar team is working on a new overtime policy. Another team developed a training program for maintenance specialists within teams. Still another team, composed of employees and managers from UCAR plants, singled out communication bottlenecks between plants.

Despite the remarkable development of some UCAR teams, the company has not made major adjustments to its compensation system, which is based on job classifications and individual merit increases. "We wanted to be successful as a team-based organization first before we looked at changing compensation," says Jim McKnight, manager of operations. Tying compensation to team performance is complicated, too, by the need to negotiate changes with unions. Although individual and team performance appraisals are largely traditional, Clarksville has instituted a peer evaluation system.

Training

Project '92 was undertaken with a great sense of urgency—and this affected the amount and pace of training received by all 1,600 employees in UCAR's U.S. operations. UCAR wanted managers and hourly employees to be trained simultaneously so that everyone could keep up with the speed of the reengineering process. UCAR was eager to make changes quickly, which meant that an intensive training period was scheduled during peak summer vacation months. Many managers, therefore, were on the job as little as half the time during that period. But disruptive or not, UCAR felt that training was the first big step in a new direction.

Training was designed to help both salaried and hourly employees understand their new roles in a team-based organization. Training for managers, including site managers and business team managers, focused on self-directed teams and the new management and interpersonal skills needed in an empowered team environment. Managers received seven and a half days of training. Salaried personnel in sales, accounting, purchasing, marketing, and other areas went through much of the same training in order to understand their roles as team members and resources to teams.

During the same time period, employees received ten days of team training spread out over several months—a more condensed schedule than the outside developer of the training recommended. Both the pace and the intensity of the training were intended to make sure "people understood that this was different," says Noel Lasure, manager of services for the Columbia, Tennessee, plant. "Any time you do something like this in a large organization, people question whether it's just another program or a new way of life. We wanted to be certain that people understood this wasn't just another program."

Managers and Leaders

No cuts in the number of hourly production operators were envisioned during the planning of Project '92. But UCAR knew that management and other salaried positions might not fare as well. Overall the number of salaried employees was reduced by almost 20 percent—primarily through voluntary separation programs and some layoffs. But greater cuts came in the graphite electrode and carbon production areas, where supervisory and management layers were particularly top heavy. At the Columbia plant, for example, employment dropped from more than 1,110 in 1980 to only 554 in 1993, but five levels of management—including a plant manager, an assistant plant manager, production superintendents, assistant production superintendents, and foremen—had somehow survived.

Overall the number of supervisory and management personnel was reduced by nearly 40 percent in several UCAR plants, eliminating two or three levels of management. Many first-level supervisors and managers went back on the hourly payroll and were redeployed in process teams. The roles of superintendents and foremen were consolidated into one new category—the process manager, who was considered part of an overall process team as well as coach and leader for as many as seven process subteams. Process managers today retain certain supervisory duties—including arbitrating disciplinary actions—and also represent their teams on a site management team.

The team approach currently characterizes all levels of management within the entire UCAR organization. Most managers are responsible for their functional areas and also serve as members of a business team that meets weekly or monthly. Jim McKnight, for example, serves on the graphite electrode and carbon team, which also includes Bill Wiemels. Ron Mitchem, site manager of the Clarksville plant, also serves on a combined plant site managers team. Each team has its own charter and, like all UCAR teams, has developed its own way of operating. Responsibilities typically are rotated and different team members may facilitate team meetings.

"We're doing the same thing at the business team level that we're asking production work teams to do," says McKnight. The purpose, he says, is to eliminate bureaucratic barriers between different UCAR units—making sure that "our primary responsibility is for the business and our secondary responsibility is for specific functions."

Results

One overriding goal of Project '92 was to reduce UCAR's cost structure. Ultimately UCAR hopes the reengineering effort will save at least $10 million a year. UCAR seems well on its way to reaching that goal. Already cycle times for most of its graphite electrode products have been reduced by 40 percent and inventories have been cut in half. And customers are far happier, too, a major focus of Project '92.

How much of this is because of teams is difficult to say. But UCAR has little doubt about the positive effects of the new team system on morale and enthusiasm. Not all operators have jumped on the team bandwagon, but few seem to view teams as just another program—and optimism in the company's future is growing. In fact, last year UCAR earned a profit for the first time in several years.

Above all, Project '92 signaled UCAR's desire to change quickly. New systems were created and implemented with a great sense of urgency. If the pace had been more measured, UCAR managers say now, certain things might have been done differently. "The fast track is not always desirable," says Jim McKnight, but he adds that UCAR probably had little choice. One consequence of the fast pace is that training often occurred well before employees had the chance to practice their new skills on the job. Supervisors and managers, for example, received several concentrated weeks of training. Ideally this training should have been spread out over several months. After each weekly session, managers should have practiced new skills on the job and received comments on their performance before moving on to the next session. Compressing the training into one marathon course limited retention and left many managers lacking confidence once they became immersed in the new team environment. Eventually UCAR had to repeat much of the training.

The fast pace posed problems for teams, too. Most teams began operating before their key performance indicators had been established, depriving them of what might have been a valuable early focus. Teams also suffered from the gap between training and on-the-job performance. Early goals tended to focus more on completing the training than on changing behavior. UCAR is still convinced, however, that an early and massive investment in training was the key to rapidly steering the company in a totally new direction. "We didn't do it by the book," one UCAR manager says, "but it worked."

PART TWO

Experienced and Maturing Stages

9

Teams in Fast-Forward:
Building Commitment Quickly

Ampex Systems
Colorado Springs, Colorado

Industry	Electronics
Union	None
Type of team implementation	Conversion of entire production operation to redesigned self-directed work teams. There are two basic types of teams: *production teams,* which configure complex electronic assemblies, and *work cells,* which manufacture single parts or configure simple subassemblies.
First teams started	1990
Employees	225
Percentage in teams	95 percent
Team size	10 to 12
Team responsibilities	Teams have assumed varying degrees of responsibility for production planning, materials management, scheduling work assignments, scheduling overtime and time off, and meeting production and quality targets. Most quality assurance checks are

performed by teams. Teams also work closely with suppliers and may meet with key suppliers weekly.

Organization-wide team responsibilities

Team members serve on cross-functional problem-solving teams usually led by managers. Team members also serve on teams that advise management on human resource policies.

Team leadership and governance

Production team leaders are former managers and supervisors appointed by business unit managers. Their positions are permanent. They help team members reach consensus on decisions and intercede if necessary. Work cells rotate leadership roles, usually monthly. Work cell leaders coordinate cell meetings and interact with other groups in the plant.

Leadership outside teams

The number of formal managers with direct supervisory roles has been greatly reduced by early retirement and reassignment to teams. Remaining managers act primarily as team coaches helping teams develop training and continuous improvement goals.

Team compensation

No team-based compensation. Team achievements are recognized informally with social events and lunches.

First-year team member training

Twenty hours of team meeting skills, quality and problem-solving techniques, and team design.

Subsequent team member training

Twenty hours of continued training in the same areas plus skills in cross-training other team members and interviewing skills.

First-year leadership training	Twenty hours of team meeting skills, quality and problem-solving techniques, overall business knowledge, and team design.
Subsequent leadership training	Thirty-six hours of continuing training in the same areas plus team interaction skills, interviewing skills, and coaching and facilitation skills.
How team members are selected	Each team has an informal committee that interviews new team members. The committee is composed of two or three team members, the team leader, and a human resource specialist. Team members on the committee rotate, and all receive interview training.
How team performance is evaluated	Team members, team leaders, and business unit managers set team goals relating to continuous improvement, productivity improvement, and safety achievements. Team performance is evaluated informally by management and is not tied to compensation.
Team impact on organization	Since teams were implemented, most measures of productivity have jumped sharply. Inventory costs declined from nearly $80 million to less than $20 million. Scrap and rework costs were cut nearly tenfold. On-time delivery figures reached 98 percent. Team involvement with suppliers has helped the facility reduce its suppliers from more than 2,000 to 135 and eliminate a five-day receiving/inspection period. On-time supplier delivery has risen from 70 percent to 99 percent.

Key lessons

- Any change effort, especially one effected this quickly, can evoke resistance. Some line employees seemed reluctant to accept more responsibility. Some supervisors had difficulty giving up control. Engineers and other professionals believed they were losing status. All these sources of resistance had to be acknowledged and overcome.

- Senior managers' persistent focus on the importance of change was a big plus. They communicated a strong sense of urgency and conveyed a positive outlook.

- Managers took time to listen to employees' concerns and ideas—thus demonstrating that they cared.

Background

When Ampex Corporation introduced the first commercial videotape recorder in the 1950s, it helped make the modern broadcasting industry possible. By the 1960s and early 1970s, Ampex videotape recorders were used in virtually every broadcast production facility in the world, providing a growing source of business for another Ampex product line— magnetic recording tape. Ampex cemented its lock on the industry with many innovations, making video and Ampex virtually synonymous by the end of the 1970s.

During the 1980s, the Ampex success story began to unravel. Ampex held onto its technological edge and managed to survive as the last American-owned videotape equipment manufacturer, but Sony, Matsushita, and other Japanese competitors proved far more adept at manufacturing and marketing, especially when it came to the digital technologies that rapidly replaced the analog formats Ampex pioneered. Ampex's revenues were flat during the later years of the decade but began to plummet, dropping from $700 million in 1990 to $526 million in 1991 to $440 million in 1992. Both customers and employees wondered if the company would survive as several massive rounds of layoffs began, each one supposedly the last—a promise the company could never seem to keep. By 1992, the workforce was reduced to half that of the peak employment year of 1988.

But during the same period, Ampex acquired a new corporate parent—a holding company owned by investor Edward Bramson. Bramson took over personal control of the company in 1991, moving from New York City to Ampex headquarters near San Francisco. Bramson began a process of decentralization that would, he hoped, unleash individual Ampex facilities to develop their own best ways to reduce costs and improve productivity. Bramson also pumped funds into product development to supplement Ampex's aging analog product line. Perhaps most significant, Bramson and other managers went out and started talking to customers. They discovered that while customers still respected Ampex's legendary technology, they felt the company was not responding to their business needs as quickly as competitors. And that dissatisfaction was having a disastrous effect on the company's bottom line.

The Race to Become World Class

With survival at stake, change came swiftly to Ampex's Colorado Springs facility. There Vice President of Operations Kern Hughes and other senior managers were determined to

introduce world-class production concepts to every part of
the facility. Their immediate goal was to reduce overhead
and improve margins. They knew they needed fresh ideas and
would have to move quickly.

The Colorado Springs facility makes video and special
effects equipment for commercial broadcasting and production facilities around the world. It manufactures a basic line
of equipment that is usually customized for individual customers. Acting as a steering committee, Hughes and his
senior management team (which included the controller
and managers in charge of quality, materials, and resources)
set up a series of project teams—"tiger" teams—in five areas
they deemed essential to becoming a low-cost, high-quality
producer. These areas were: total quality management, just-
in-time manufacturing, inventory reduction and storeroom
restructuring, setup time reduction, and cycle time improvement. It was assumed in the beginning that whatever changes
the tiger teams recommended, they would eventually involve
redeploying employees into production teams. Because of
fragmented production areas and sharply separated functional divisions within the plant, it would be nearly impossible to have an impact on these five key areas without
examining work processes and employees' roles.

Each tiger team contained five or six managers and engineers. Their mandate was to analyze various systems and
recommend changes—and do it quickly. While none of the
tiger teams included permanent production employees, they
did make extensive use of "resident experts" (production
employees on the floor) to react to suggested changes and
contribute ideas. The teams also worked closely with several
ongoing product review teams active in all Ampex facilities.
These product review teams coordinated efforts in concur-
rent engineering and design for manufacturability. Meeting
over several months, the tiger teams made recommendations

including new work systems based on self-directed work teams.

The creation of self-directed teams at Colorado Springs was a top-down process: the steering committee acted as a team design committee and made changes by management directive. While the changes greatly affected the way work was done in the facility, the actual transition to teams was fairly simple. The multilevel production operator system was eliminated and replaced with one class of production employee, called processors. Centralized functions, such as engineering, production control, materials support, and quality assurance, were broken up, and personnel in these areas were relocated into production areas—engineers and other professionals joined a single self-directed team or serving several teams. Some supervisors and managers were offered early retirement as part of ongoing efforts to thin management ranks. Others accepted reassignment into the direct nonexempt workforce where they joined newly formed teams. Still others became team leaders—a permanent management-level position. Team leaders, including engineers and former production operators, were responsible for getting the new system off the ground.

Teams

Today several types of teams operate at Colorado Springs. Permanent production work teams of ten to twelve members predominate in most production areas. These teams typically include a team leader, engineers, and processors—all located in common areas. Before the team implementation, engineers had separate office areas and "visited" the production floor when they had questions or felt their assistance was needed. Now they have work cubicles adjacent to their team production areas.

As the production teams usually configure complex electronic assemblies, this means that teams, especially from an engineering standpoint, must be cross-functional. Physical redesign was important to make a linear manufacturing flow possible. Before the redesign, production operators soldered and inserted parts into subassemblies in different areas of the plant—as a result, work in process piled up in operator areas before it was sent to another area. Now products move from workstation to workstation, not department to department. Engineering support is just off the production area, not closeted away in a separate part of the building. As cross-training continues, all team members will be able to perform many if not most of the steps in the process.

Production teams are supported by a second type of team called work cells. These cells operate in areas where single parts are machined or manufactured or simple subassemblies are configured. The name "cell" differentiates these processes from the more complex work done by production teams. Work cells function as teams in most respects—including taking responsibility for meeting output and quality targets, scheduling work and job assignments, and rotating leadership responsibilities among cell members to coordinate cell meetings and interact with other groups in the plant.

Before teams, the environment was tightly controlled. Employees were told how many parts to solder, insert, or assemble each day. If they ended up with time on their hands after completing their assigned tasks, that was fine. Often they just built more product, regardless of how much work in process still had to be cleared off the floor. Like so many other manufacturing facilities, a "check your brains at the door" attitude prevailed. That picture bears little relationship to what visitors find at Colorado Springs today. Teams have helped ensure a high level of communication and cooperation throughout the facility. Almost no work in process can be seen, and the facility has reached a stage where products are virtually built to order for customers, meaning little inventory is amassed. Team members are rarely idle. When team members reach their output target they assist other members or work on individual and team training goals or problem-solving projects.

Most teams begin their shifts with a short stand-up meeting in the team area; some teams hold midmorning meetings to accommodate their suppliers. The team leader presides. Using a flip chart, the leader notes problems from the previous shift, production requirements for the day or week, or the team's most recent quality or production achievements. During the meeting, the team discusses production requirements and assigns tasks and resources. The flip chart is updated throughout the shift and serves as a way to alert the team to developing problems. Often during a shift, the team leader or an engineer might call a short meeting to discuss problems revealed on the flip chart.

Two teams at Colorado Springs are piloting a procedure called "on-error" training in which very short meetings are held with all team members to solve production or quality problems on the spot. When a problem is detected, the entire team meets immediately and attempts to solve it "on line." The first team to use the procedure met 160 times in 1992—but for a total of only ten hours. The team thinks the procedure worked phenomenally well for two reasons. First, the intense focus on fixing problems usually meant faster resolution (and a noticeable reduction in scrap). And second, it improved communication among team members and increased each member's commitment to the team process and the finished output.

Suppliers played a major role in the changes the original tiger teams wanted to make. This was because much of what they hoped to achieve—increasing quality, adopting just-in-time inventory and manufacturing techniques, and giving teams more control over production inputs—depended on reducing the number of suppliers while forging new relationships with those that remained. Because most aspects of the old centralized quality assurance, purchasing, and storeroom functions were reduced or eliminated, production teams and work cells had to work directly with suppliers, ordering many of their parts and raw materials directly. Today many teams at Colorado Springs meet directly with key suppliers as often as once a week.

Officially, Ampex teams are responsible for matching their resources to production requirements, quality, and productivity, for meeting with and responding to the needs of internal customers, and for communicating their team's needs to internal and external suppliers. Quality assurance has become an especially important focus—because quality inspectors have been eliminated, teams can no longer pass on defects to internal or external customers with the assurance that someone will catch the mistake and fix it. Today teams must pay close attention to their internal customers. Often team members sit in on meetings with "upstream" teams to help solve quality problems.

Training

Team training needs are met predominantly through cross-training. The most important is on-the-job cross-training by other team members. Teams—usually working closely with their leaders—identify key skills and establish training goals for team members. For most Ampex teams, the skills are diverse, often complex, and numerous (sometimes amounting to dozens of different skills). Machine shop teams, for example, are required to operate equipment ranging from basics, such as gauges and lathes, to expensive computerized coordinate measurement devices and programmable robotic devices that drill, polish, and deburr at high speeds. Teams in technical areas may be required to build and test specialized audio I/O boards and data interface devices and work with a variety of chemicals. All teams are responsible for their own rework, as well as parts and product-tracking procedures designed to keep inventory and work in process to a minimum.

The complexity of the skill or procedure determines how cross-training is accomplished. Most teams have at least one member who is certified as a cross-trainer in a specific skill or procedure. Becoming certified as a cross-trainer means demonstrating proficiency in the skill and learning coaching and cross-training skills. Depending on the team's priorities, members may be expected to learn some or all of the team's skills. Acquiring a skill requires certification, which can range from demonstrating proficiency to a designated cross-trainer to more rigorous job simulations and testing.

Highly technical training is often shared with facility experts, usually engineers. They work with the training department to teach such skills as soldering and blueprint reading. Finally, the training department conducts ongoing sessions in team building, team interaction, and other areas, including budgeting and business knowledge.

Evaluating and Rewarding Teams

Individual performance appraisals and compensation are largely left over from the old days at Colorado Springs. Both, however, are changing. There are two types of individual assessment, and teams may select the option they prefer. In all cases, team members complete an annual self-assessment. Then they may either review assessments with the business unit manager only or, if the team prefers, participate in a three-way appraisal that includes the team leader. In the first instance, the team leader reviews the employee's self-assessment, the leader may agree or disagree with it, but the business unit manager is in control of the process. In the second instance, the team member, team leader, and business unit manager evaluate the team member's performance separately and meet to discuss how they agree and how they differ. A pay-for-skills system is being contemplated, but currently individual compensation consists of regular merit increases determined by performance appraisals.

Team activity is evaluated too. Team members, team leaders, and business unit managers set team goals related to continuous improvement, productivity improvement, and safety achievements. When management determines that teams have met or exceeded the goals, the teams are rewarded for their accomplishments at informal social events, such as barbecues and catered lunches.

Managers

The development of Ampex's team system coincided with the end of the latest round of layoffs begun several years earlier. The reductions were massive and painful: the Colorado Springs workforce dropped from a high of 1,200 to 330. During the cutbacks, many supervisors and managers took early retirement options; others were reassigned into the direct labor force or resumed previous engineering jobs; others simply lost their jobs. The team system further accelerated supervisor and manager cutbacks with the elimination of line and first-level supervisory layers and several middle-management positions. Some former supervisors were appointed team leaders by business unit managers; others joined teams as processors or engineers. The old supervisory span of control dropped dramatically. Depending on the department, the supervisor/employee ratio changed from one supervisor per fifteen to thirty employees to one supervisor per eighty or more employees.

The remaining managers found themselves recast as "coaches"—working with teams directly or through team leaders to develop team training and continuous improvement goals. Teams needed little day-to-day intervention from managers, however. Several conventional management functions remain, including handling performance and disciplinary problems and evaluating employees' performance.

Results

Ampex felt it had little time to spare in redesigning production systems at Colorado Springs. Instead of a careful and measured team design and rollout, many changes happened virtually overnight. Ideas were gathered by the tiger teams. Then senior management acted quickly, decentralizing production and forming teams without such luxuries as an in-depth team design process and pilot teams. Meanwhile suppliers that couldn't meet new standards for quality and delivery were dropped by the hundreds. The sense of urgency was driven by the fact that sliding sales and seemingly unassailable competition had put the company's very existence in jeopardy.

While these events were dispiriting, they also proved to be remarkably motivating. Today the Colorado Springs facility is a vastly different place—thanks to the team-based production system and employees' efforts to make it work. From 1989 to 1992, most measures of productivity jumped sharply. Inventory and rework costs were drastically reduced. Productivity, as measured by comparing actual throughput to a theoretically ideal throughput, rose by nearly 30 percent—even with a production workforce that is one-third smaller than it was in 1989. Improvements in supplier performance were even more dramatic. Thanks to efforts to make suppliers just-in-time partners, on-time supplier delivery rose to 99 percent.

"Just-in-time, total quality management, total employee involvement, continuous improvement—we did it all at the same time," says one Ampex manager. Somehow it worked. Ampex managed to prevent its overnight transformation from becoming chaotic and demoralizing, always a danger when organizations implement one change after another. Of course, most of the expected problems arose—first-line supervisors resisted giving up control, many production employees didn't want to take on increased decision-making responsibilities, engineers and other professionals resented joining teams in production areas and the attendant "loss of status."

Many credit the persistent focus on immediate change as one of the key elements that made the transformation succeed. Senior managers did a good job of communicating both a sense of urgency and a positive feeling that it was possible to put the facility on a world-class footing, even in the face of tremendous job insecurity and uncertainty about the company's long-term prospects. Senior managers also spent a lot of time on the floor, employees recall, and responded quickly to employees' suggestions. And during monthly "sensing" sessions with cross sections of employees, senior managers gave workers the chance to talk openly about the changes. One employee recalls, "They were relentless in making it clear that once things started to change there was no looking back."

10

Gaining Business Focus
Through Mini-Enterprise Units

Bord na Mona—Peat Energy Division
Leaberg, County Offaly, Ireland

Industry	Peat extraction
Unions	Services, Industrial, Professional Technical Union (SIPTU); Amalgamated Transport and General Workers Union (ATGWU); Amalgamated Engineering Union (AEU); Technical Engineering and Electrical Union (TEEU).
Type of team implementation	"Autonomous enterprise teams" set up to operate as self-managing business units that contract to harvest and deliver peat to Bord na Mona's Peat Energy Division
First teams started	1989
Employees	1,100 permanent, 600 seasonal
Percentage in teams	85 percent of the 1,030 employed in peat production
Team size	Four to five core members (expands to five to seventeen with seasonal workers).
Team responsibilities	Hiring and managing seasonal employees, scheduling work assignments, monitoring quality, achieving production targets, han-

	dling performance and discipline problems, maintaining equipment.
Organization-wide team responsibilities	Teams are partners with management in achieving peat production targets. Teams contract to deliver a fixed amount of peat at a fixed price; management markets and sells it.
Team leadership and governance	No official leaders: responsibilities are shared among team members. Most decisions are reached by consensus.
Leadership outside teams	"Boundary managers" facilitate the team process and help teams achieve production targets.
Team compensation	Teams are paid weekly based on a negotiated production contract with management. Teams receive a minimum guaranteed wage if weather or other factors depress production yields.
First-year team member training	Eight hours of training in general business knowledge and continuing on-the-job skills training.
Subsequent team member training	Sixteen hours of training in general business knowledge and quality and problem-solving techniques; ongoing on-the-job skills training.
First-year leadership training	Sixteen hours of training in understanding financial data, team meeting skills, team interaction skills, and general business knowledge; ongoing coaching from boundary managers.

Subsequent leadership training	Thirty hours on interpretation of financial data, team meeting skills, quality and problem-solving techniques, team interaction skills, general business knowledge; ongoing coaching from boundary managers.
How team members are selected	By works (or site) management following interview.
How team performance is evaluated	Based on ability to meet production contracts and on the team's level of cohesiveness.
Team impact on organization	Bord na Mona's team-based, output-related reward system—along with the investment in new higher-output technology—has created a more flexible cost structure and reduced overall costs. Output per employee has risen by nearly 100 percent. Absenteeism has fallen sharply.
Key lessons	• As the team approach is not static, the new work systems must be continually monitored and modified to achieve the desired effects. • As the role of the first-line supervisor has changed, these employees must be trained in the appropriate skills to operate effectively in their new roles as boundary managers.

Background

Peat—the partially decomposed sedges, reeds, rushes, and moss found in swamps and bogs throughout the temperate zones of the world—is the unlikely raw material for one of Europe's most unusual team success stories. Peat attracts little attention in most places, but in countries where wood, coal, and oil are scarce or expensive, peat has long served as an important energy source. Peat-fueled electricity plants operate in Scandinavia and the former Soviet Union. But no country has maximized peat usage like Ireland has for the past five decades. That's because Ireland is blessed with hundreds of thousands of acres of prime peat-producing bogs but cursed by a deficit of nearly all other natural energy sources.

Bord na Mona (Gaelic for "Irish Peat Corporation") is the state-owned company in charge of utilizing Ireland's bountiful peat supply. Bord na Mona's four divisions sell peat moss to commercial and home gardeners, peat briquettes to consumers for home heating, and most recently peat fiber for pollution abatement systems. But more than half of Bord na Mona's annual £125 million in revenues is generated by its Peat Energy Division, which manages some 85,000 acres of peat bogs in five production centers and sells more than three million tons a year to Ireland's state-run, peat-fueled electricity generating plants. That's enough to meet 14 percent of the nation's electricity needs.

But peat is an expensive energy source because of its labor-intensive harvesting process and a fuel-to-energy conversion ratio that pales next to oil, natural gas, and to a lesser extent coal. Consequently, since the end of World War II, Ireland has been steadily turning to other energy sources, primarily oil and coal. By the mid-1970s, thirty-year-old Bord na Mona was becoming increasingly anachronistic. Peat's demise as a major Irish energy source seemed only a matter of time. Then came OPEC and the oil shocks of the mid-1970s. As the price of oil, and later coal, skyrocketed, Ireland took a second look at its only indigenous energy source.

Ireland became convinced that total dependence on imported energy threatened its national sovereignty. Suddenly peat took on a new importance. That set the stage for an ambitious expansion of Bord na Mona and development of new bogs that once would have been ignored because they were too small and too far from generating plants. The expansion meant floating substantial debt, but Ireland's energy needs were growing and supplies from abroad seemed increasingly uncertain. Thus the risk seemed prudent.

Then the energy-starved 1970s gave way to the energy glut of the 1980s. Oil and coal prices, which once seemed likely to rise forever, plummeted. Now Bord na Mona was saddled with an increasingly noncompetitive product and a mountain of debt. Even the weather refused to cooperate. Peat must be left to dry in the sun before harvesting. But the unending rain and gloom of the summers of 1985 and 1986 severely cut Bord na Mona's production and meant that delivery promises couldn't be met in 1987—another blow to the company's bottom line.

Turning to Teams

In 1988 and 1989, Bord na Mona launched a major restructuring effort to cope with its growing problems. A new managing director, Eddie O'Connor, was appointed. Immediately he saw the need for company reorganization and bottom-line competitiveness, and he pushed for change. High fixed-labor costs meant there was little the company could do when weather reduced the peat harvest. Without some way to make its costs variable, there was little likelihood the company could meet its debt load or make peat cost competitive with other energy sources.

A task force on company reorganization was established. It focused on the company's separate and distinct businesses and how each one could operate effectively and efficiently.

At the same time, a voluntary severance program was introduced to reduce the permanent and seasonal workforce. The task force recommended establishing independent divisions to handle the different markets served by Bord na Mona. Thus was the Peat Energy Division established. Its main focus was reducing costs and improving peat quality. Paddy Hughes, then a group manager and now chief executive officer of the Peat Energy Division, set up an internal working group to focus on these issues.

The working group's biggest challenge, Hughes says, was to develop work and pay systems that allowed the company to "pay for output rather than time." One way to do that would be to compensate employees for production rather than time spent on the job. They would share in the rewards when weather and other factors were good; they would share the financial pain when production couldn't meet delivery commitments. To be fair, employees would need to have some control over decision making at the front line on the bogs if they were to be asked to link their earnings to output.

Creating a team-based approach to peat harvesting was not what the working group initially envisioned. But as the group explored ways to make its costs variable, empowered and highly independent worker teams emerged as the way to do it. Given the risk employees would be asked to shoulder, however, the working group knew it would be a tough sell with Bord na Mona's unions, in particular SIPTU, Ireland's largest trade union. Bord na Mona's old work system was complex, based on high manning levels, and, given the nature of peat harvesting, highly idiosyncratic. Permanent employees spent the May to September production season on the bogs, where they milled, harrowed, ridged, and harvested peat. Seasonal workers were hired during the production season, boosting the workforce to more than 2,500. During the remainder of the year, permanent employees maintained the bogs and equipment. The permanent workforce was highly stratified. Indeed, there were more than thirty-five job classifications, all of them detailing what employees could and could not do. With production spread over 85,000 acres throughout the country and employees given little latitude to make decisions, supervision faced special challenges. Each of Bord na Mona's five production centers had a general works manager, production and maintenance managers, foremen, and supervisors on the sites. In fact, workers were so dispersed that supervisors had to travel by motorcycle from site to site.

The working group made an initial proposition, one they knew would be rejected by employees. It involved eventually taking Bord na Mona out of the peat production business and instead focusing on sales and marketing. Who then would harvest the peat? Using a concept they called "employee enterprise units," the working group proposed asking certain production employees to leave the company (as part of the voluntary severance program), and then form their own small companies to harvest and deliver peat by contract to Bord na Mona. These small companies would share the risks and rewards of peat production and would be far more labor and cost efficient than the company itself, which was saddled with a year-round workforce despite the weather and other factors. Initially the working group proposed employee enterprise units at eight locations covering 10 percent of production operations. If the system worked, it would be implemented everywhere Bord na Mona harvested peat.

The plan was presented as a potential boon to both the company and employees. With smaller, more efficient teams generating increasingly higher peat yields, Bord na Mona would drive down the cost of peat while paying more to the people in the units. If yields dropped because of poor weather, Bord na Mona would pay only for what was delivered—thereby achieving the goal of making its costs variable.

Of course, that meant individual earnings would suffer in poor production years, which was one consequence of the proposed system the company could not minimize.

The idea was rejected immediately by Bord na Mona's unions. They labeled it "contract labor"—a labor system that has always been viewed with suspicion by Ireland's unions. But it got the unions' attention; in fact, the concept served as the first step in the development of Bord na Mona's current innovative team structure. "We were looking for radical change," says Paddy Hughes, "and our view at the time was that we had to make radical proposals to get people thinking sufficiently about the change that was required."

The next several months were a period of intensive discussions between Hughes' working group, management, and the company's unions on restructuring Bord na Mona's production systems. The working group also worked closely with general managers at the five main work sites. During the discussions, the company told the employees and the unions about its desperate financial shape, which generated a spirit of cooperation. Eventually a new framework was developed that preserved much of the autonomy of the employee enterprise concept but satisfied employees' need for job security. This new framework was the "autonomous enterprise team." Each team would essentially manage itself and look after its own bottom line, but it would consist of Bord na Mona employees with a guaranteed minimum wage. The original employee enterprise teams would be piloted, but on a more modest basis. Only new employees would have the option of reverting to direct employment if they desired. Instead of leaving Bord na Mona altogether, they would be considered on leave of absence.

Hughes and Cathal Magee, the group head of human resources, helped hammer out the implementation plan for the company's new team system. They also enlisted other Bord na Mona managers to study systems that would have to be changed to support the new teams. The payment and financial systems would have to be completely revised, for example, and the new teams would have special training needs. One training subject for team members—how to operate as a small business—was targeted as an early priority. The company also knew that as foremen on the bogs would be instrumental in helping the new teams form, they would require training in coaching, facilitating, and team dynamics.

Managing Their Own Turf

Today 85 percent of the Peat Energy Division's production target is achieved by these autonomous enterprise teams. Each team has four or five core members, all considered team "leaders." A typical team might include a former bog supervisor, two skilled craftsmen, and two machine drivers. During the May to September production season, teams hire their own seasonal employees, expanding team sizes to between fourteen and seventeen members. Core teams operate, just as the company had hoped, as small business units. They contract with Bord na Mona to deliver a fixed amount of peat at a fixed price and meet specific quality standards. Teams make decisions about budgeting and allocation of resources—including the crucial decision about how many seasonal employees to hire and when to hire them to maximize critical drying time. Daily decisions about hours worked and team assignments, including who operates which equipment, are made by the team leaders and dictated by the production cycle.

Hughes and other managers had hoped to design a system that ensured all team members would be multifunctional and able to operate all the various machines. This was one of many areas that required hard negotiations with the company's unions, which wanted to preserve specialization within teams. In the end, the decision was left to teams—which quickly realized that flexibility was the key to meeting their production targets. Thus the old specialized job categories that once governed the workforce disappeared on their own as teams matured.

The most urgent training need of Bord na Mona's new teams was in business basics. While the new team system still had certain wage guarantees from the company, most team compensation would be determined by how well teams operated as small businesses. Helping teams understand how to control costs, meet contractual obligations for peat delivery, and ensure that quality standards were achieved (as measured by such things as peat density, moisture, and ash content) were high priorities. But teams also needed to understand team dynamics, which was provided by ongoing coaching from foremen at work sites. While not extensive by most team-based organizations' standards, Bord na Mona's teams received some training in team interaction, decision making, and meeting skills.

Bord na Mona took a hands-off attitude toward evaluating individual performance—another area that was largely a team's own business. Peer pressure is the predominant force that keeps team members performing to one another's expectations. The company's old disciplinary system is largely irrelevant now, because teams are completely self-managing. Indeed, says Paddy Hughes, "we consciously avoid stepping in too quickly to sort out problems." If intervention is needed, foremen at work sites help to resolve conflicts. And a new procedure is in place to resolve grievances quickly and help teams deal with a range of issues that emerge from the new system.

The biggest compromise between the employee enterprise system and the current team system is mostly in the area of wage guarantees. While teams are empowered to act independently in almost all respects, they are still Bord na

Mona employees and receive a basic wage guarantee should weather and other factors depress peat harvest yields. Most members' earnings are based on team output, which is negotiated with management based on such factors as historical standards for tons per acre and equipment capacity. Teams also receive a bonus linked to quality achievement. Wages still are paid weekly. The system requires a constant flow of information from management back to teams. Teams know all the factors influencing what they are paid per ton— enabling them to monitor closely how well they are meeting their production and earnings goals during the harvest season.

Managers

The voluntary severance program that accompanied Bord na Mona's reorganization greatly reduced the number of employees in all categories, including supervisors and managers. A hiring freeze, now in its fifth year, has reduced management ranks as well. This reduction has paralleled the elimination of many things managers were required to do before teams were installed. For example, the elaborate paperwork that once was needed to track hours worked, attendance (absenteeism used to be a big problem on the bogs), equipment breakdowns and maintenance, disciplinary problems, and so on has nearly disappeared. But the need for financial reporting to teams has increased greatly. In fact, Bord na Mona's management has assumed a new role—as business partners with teams and facilitators of their financial objectives.

Out on the bogs, the role of field management has changed with the introduction of teams. Supervisors either joined teams, were redeployed to other duties, or left the company as part of the voluntary severance program. For those supervisors who did join teams, the loss of their previous status was offset by the greater autonomy allowed them as leaders—and by the potential for increased earnings. Foremen, who in the past gave detailed daily instructions to supervisors and served as the main link between the bog and the work site management, found themselves in a new role—"boundary managers." No longer concerned with micromanaging day-to-day bog activities, they have become facilitators, helping teams reach their production objectives and providing coaching, advice, and other support.

Results

Before making its radical proposal for autonomous, self-directed teams, Bord na Mona's management had labored mightily to salvage the peat energy business in Ireland. But nothing seemed to have had more than a temporary effect. Gains were always swallowed up by the seemingly intractable problem at the heart of the business: peat, as it was traditionally harvested, was just too expensive and inefficient to compete with imported coal and other energy sources. The situation was so bad in 1988 and 1989 that Bord na Mona's managers gambled that employees and the unions were ready for a complete departure from the past. Thanks to information sharing and close collaboration with the unions, the managers ultimately were proved to be right.

Under the Peat Energy Division's team system, which now includes approximately 85 percent of production, output has risen during the past five years from 1,700 tons annually per employee to between 3,000 and 3,400 tons. At the same time, the company's costs have fallen sharply—thanks to a smaller company payroll, the ability to make its costs drop during a poor production year, and lower equipment maintenance costs. (Because teams are responsible for meeting their own production targets, they take better care of equipment.) Absenteeism on the bog in the old days ran between 10 and 15 percent; today it is negligible. Like many of the old measures, it's no longer something the company feels compelled to track closely.

As for wages, since 1989 the Peat Energy Division's teams have averaged significantly more than they did before the team system. The exception was 1992, when poor weather again reduced peat yields and, consequently, earnings. These lower earnings, along with certain technical issues involving the payment system, have led to the establishment of a joint management/union review group that examines problems arising from the team-based systems. One major target of the review group is to find a way to offset earnings during poor production years with those achieved in good production years. Although the prospect of reduced team earnings as a result of poor weather was discussed openly before teams were formed, team members didn't fully appreciate its implications until it actually happened.

The improved efficiency and reduced costs under the new team-based system—combined with the improved combustion efficiency of new technology—has prompted Bord na Mona to initiate a feasibility study on building a new peat-fired power station in the midlands of Ireland. As Ireland's peat electricity plants are decades old and facing the end of their useful life, Bord na Mona's future might depend on the new power station. Yet the prospect of a highly efficient cost-competitive Irish peat energy system doesn't seem as far-fetched as it once did, thanks to the remarkable transformation that has occurred among workers given the chance to manage their own turf.

11

The Plant Start-Up
That Became the Model
for High-Performance Teams

Colgate-Palmolive Company
Cambridge, Ohio

Industry	Liquid detergents
Union	None
Type of team implementation	Cross-functional problem-solving and re-designed self-directed teams
First teams started	1988
Employees	200
Percentage in teams	100 percent
Team size	3 to 10
Team responsibilities	Teams handle an entire process: making plastic bottles, filling them with detergent, and packaging product for distribution. Teams are responsible for as many as nine different product lines. Teams make their own work assignments; schedule overtime, time off, and vacations; perform preventive equipment maintenance and handle equipment changeovers; and assure quality control for all phases of production.

Organization-wide team responsibilities	Team representatives serve on various plantwide committees: quality and safety committees, a selection committee that interviews and assesses job applicants; and an issues committee that arbitrates employee complaints.
Team leadership and governance	Teams don't have formal leaders, but one team member is designated as a "point of contact" to communicate among teams, plantwide groups, and managers. Depending on the team, this position is rotated monthly or quarterly.
Leadership outside teams	Area leaders (analogous to foremen and supervisors at other Colgate plants) coach and facilitate operations for several teams.
Team compensation	All team members are salaried and receive annual merit increases. A pay-for-skills system adds a maximum of $1.50 per hour to employees' compensation. All employees share quarterly bonuses based on meeting targets in quality, productivity, safety, and cost per case (of the products they produce).
First-year team member training	The first group of employees received 120 hours of classroom training in team meeting skills, quality tools and problem-solving techniques, team interaction skills, overall business knowledge, and team and workplace design.
Subsequent team member training	Additional training focused on cross-training others, interviewing skills, and ad-

vanced business knowledge, including budgeting and logistics.

First-year leadership training

New area leaders received 80 hours of training in areas that paralleled team member training plus team facilitation and coaching and interviewing skills.

Subsequent leadership training

Eight to sixteen hours in similar areas.

How team members are selected

In its initial round of hiring, Cambridge selected 170 employees from more than 10,000 applicants using an extensive series of tests, interviews, and assessment center job simulations. Subsequent rounds of hiring are conducted by team members and managers who are trained in "targeted" interviewing and assessment center techniques.

How team performance is evaluated

Teams keep statistics on safety, quality, productivity, costs, and schedule adherence. Results help determine plantwide bonuses.

Team impact on organization

The Cambridge plant has set the pace for Colgate in operational efficiency and continuous productivity improvement. Line efficiency generally is at or near the top for similar Colgate operations and often runs 20 to 30 percent higher than sister plants. The plant has run at 82 percent efficiency in meeting scheduled production rates for some quarters; some lines have achieved efficiency rates as high as 92 percent.

Costs per case have been decreasing at Cambridge for several years, and numerous team-inspired improvements are saving hundreds of thousands of dollars annually.

Key lessons

- Morale dipped shortly after the plant opened when advancement opportunities didn't match employees' expectations. Managers had to give employees a more realistic appreciation of what working at the plant would be like in the long term. In a subsequent round of hiring, applicants were given a more realistic job preview. Team members, who now interview and help select applicants, have proved to be good judges of job fit and motivation.

- Management turnover at Cambridge has been very high because Colgate uses the plant to give managers experience in high-performance teams before assigning them to other facilities—thus limiting management's effectiveness in facilitating team development. Teams often have little time to develop working relationships with area leaders and other managers, and new managers have found it hard to establish credibility. While this may benefit Colgate overall, curtailing turnover would allow teams and managers an opportunity to develop better working relations.

- Maintenance employees, hired for electrical and mechanical skills, were formed in teams separate from Cambridge's twenty-one operator technician teams. This created a barrier between the two team systems and limited transfer of skills from maintenance technicians to operator technicians. Promoting cross-training between the two team systems has been a challenge. A more effective team design might have included both types of employees on the same team.

Background

When consumer product giant Colgate-Palmolive opened its Cambridge, Ohio, facility in 1988, it was among the company's first experiments with high-performance work systems. Here the company melded process technology, leading-edge selection systems, and empowered employee work teams to fashion a more productive way to make liquid detergent—a mainstay of Colgate's product line—and to serve as a model for Colgate plants in the decades ahead.

Cambridge makes products—including liquid detergents such as Ajax, Fab, Dynamo, and Palmolive—that are household names in North America and many other parts of the world from Europe to Southeast Asia. Before Cambridge opened, most Colgate detergent for the North American market was produced at plants in Kansas City, Jefferson, Indiana, and Jersey City, New Jersey. All three plants were decades old—the Jersey City plant, in particular, was nearing the end of its useful life. Demand was growing for Colgate detergents, but so too was competition, especially from low-cost generic detergents. When it decided to close the Jersey City plant, Colgate needed a new production facility. Cambridge represented a fresh start—a place where various innovations could be tried without the physical limitations and rigid work rules of the older facilities.

Cambridge was envisioned as a highly automated facility using the latest in computer-controlled process technology. That, in turn, meant that a smaller but far more flexible staff would be needed. Convinced that self-managing teams would be a major component in keeping costs low while reaching new levels of productivity, Colgate invested heavily in leading-edge selection systems. The goal was to find employees "who would not just come in and make the product, but would actively improve the process," as one Colgate manager puts it.

The planning committee for the new Cambridge plant began meeting in 1987. Its members included Walt Golembeski, who was to be the first plant manager at Cambridge; other Colgate managers, who would work at the new plant as managers of engineering, logistics, finance, and other areas; and several senior Colgate executives, including Peter McLeod, vice president of manufacturing, engineering, and technology, one of Colgate's main advocates for "high-commitment work systems." The committee's work led to the creation of a plant start-up team—in addition to the new plant managers, a total of six Colgate supervisors, foremen, and engineers who had been recruited to be team leaders at Cambridge. Their job was to help design the new Cambridge work system, conduct shop tests as construction progressed and equipment was installed, and work with consulting firms that were developing the plant's selection system and the month-long classroom training program for the new employees.

Colgate wanted nothing left to chance when it came to Cambridge's first workforce. Its vision of a high-commitment work system demanded highly motivated employees with strong personal initiative and problem-solving aptitude. Because rural Cambridge, located between Columbus and Pittsburgh, had suffered several plant closings and high unemployment, Colgate anticipated that each job at Cambridge would attract dozens of qualified applicants. Colgate wasn't disappointed. More than 10,000 people applied for the 150 job openings. The handful who earned job offers went through a series of screens that consisted of initial interviews, personality and job aptitude tests, further testing to measure job fit as shown by willingness to work in teams and take initiative, more in-depth interviews, and, finally, assessment center exercises in which applicants performed simulated job tasks in teams and on their own. Once hired, new employees were trained in basic statistical process control and other quality tools and team interaction skills. They also spent considerable time learning how the new plant would operate. In all, new employees received 120 hours of training before the first bottle of detergent rolled down the production line.

Teams

When production first started at Cambridge, the new teams relied on the expertise of team leaders, most of whom had years of experience in detergent production. Colgate was banking on single teams eventually being able to make products from start to finish—blowing the right size polyurethane bottles, delivering filled and labeled bottles to the loading dock, and handling all the quality checks and process adjustments in between. At Colgate's other detergent plants, bottle making was contracted out to a separate company that owned and operated the bottle-making equipment in the plants; filling, packaging, and other steps in the process were all handled by separate departments. At the aging Kansas City plant, different departments were even on separate floors. Cambridge was designed to do it all in one seamless process. The new employees were quick learners—which came as no surprise, given the attention paid to hiring them—and soon teams began living up to Colgate's expectations.

Only two job classifications were created for new employees—operator technicians, who make the product, and maintenance technicians, who maintain and repair equipment. Operator technicians form the production teams. Maintenance technicians, hired for mechanical and electrical skills and paid slightly higher than operator technicians, function in their own teams. All employees are salaried, and there are no formal wage distinctions among operator technicians.

Most of Cambridge's twenty-one operator teams have ten members. Automation means major production steps can be controlled by remarkably few team members. On an average day, one team member may be in charge of the blending area, making sure that hoppers are kept full of polyurethane pellets, which are melted and extruded into a blow molder that blows and labels different size plastic bottles in a few simple steps. Two team members typically work in the bottle-making area. Up to five different lines may run at a time, each producing bottles of different sizes and shapes with different labels. Bottles then are conveyed to another team member in a packaging area, where, among other things, machines blow air into bottles, insert plastic spouts, and pack bottles into cases for filling. From there, the cases are conveyed to the other end of the plant, where one team member operates filling machines, another assembles filled cases onto pallets, and another puts completed pallets on a truck. Two additional team members bring materials to other team members as needed and cover for breaks and lunches. One more team member is in charge of the injection molding area where plastic spouts are created.

Cambridge teams are responsible for most things that

affect their productivity and quality: assigning work, scheduling time off and vacations, determining overtime needs, handling preventive equipment maintenance, changeovers, and repairs (if possible), and conducting quality checks at numerous stages in the production process. (Cambridge has no quality inspectors or quality assurance department.) Usually teams determine what needs to be done for the week during Monday morning meetings. Teams also are responsible for their own cross-training so that all members can fill any role in the production process.

No formal team leaders are designated, but most teams have a "point of contact" (POC) who serves as liaison between the team and area leaders and between the team and various plantwide groups. POCs make sure all team members are informed of changes in policies or communications from management. And when a team's input is needed regarding plantwide changes, the POC delivers that information too. Each team also designates members to serve various roles outside the team—such as a team safety representative (whose duties include conducting a short safety meeting each week and serving on the plant safety team), an attendance representative (there are no time clocks and each team must keep its own attendance records), an overtime representative (who schedules overtime if the team needs it to meet production), and a quality representative (who serves on a plant quality committee and communicates its deliberations back to the team).

Teams also elect representatives to serve on the plant's issues committee, which hears employee complaints about personnel policies and other actions. The issues committee—which includes Cambridge's human resource director and an area leader—is one of several management/employee teams that play a major role in plant operations. A bonus team determines bonus targets and decides which teams and employees are eligible for them. A renewal team plans and coordinates a one-day off-site retreat for all employees and managers.

Cambridge's selection committee is perhaps the most thoroughly developed plantwide team. During the initial round of hiring, the start-up team worked closely with its consulting firm to hire the first group of employees. Subsequent rounds of hiring have been handled by the plant's selection committee, whose members have been trained to interview for the right behavioral characteristics for Cambridge's team environment and to conduct assessment center exercises. Applicants for technician jobs usually are interviewed by a team of two technicians. Potential area leaders may be interviewed by a team of three (at least one technician).

When it comes to interviewing for area leaders, the different perspectives of technicians and managers complement each other well. Technicians are usually interested in the people skills of potential area leaders, reflecting their experiences on the plant floor, while managers often focus on the applicant's technical background and management experience. "What one isn't looking for, the other usually is," says one Cambridge manager.

Training, Compensation, Assessment

Training at Cambridge is grouped into three broad categories: technical skills, primarily a team responsibility; team interaction skills, which mainly are handled by Cambridge's training staff; and business skills, an area of growing importance as teams assume more budgeting and financial planning responsibilities.

Each team demands five major technical skills, mostly determined by the equipment used in the production process. Most team members are trained in at least three areas—

for example, the blending process, the blow molding process, and packaging. A team's training needs are determined when it meets to draft a cross-training plan, which schedules training for individual members and designates experts to provide specific training (or borrows an expert from another team). The plan is reviewed and adjusted quarterly. Each piece of equipment has a self-paced training module, developed with the assistance of team members, that includes written exercises and demonstration procedures to certify a team member's proficiency.

The team interaction component of the training program includes basic team-building and communication skills. Team members learn how to participate in meetings and lead them, how to reach consensus, and how to communicate effectively with other members. Business training includes developing a budgeting process for entire lines of operation (which involves collaboration among three shift teams), inventory management, and materials planning and logistics. Quality training includes ongoing training in statistical process control, total quality management, and most recently in meeting ISO 9000 (international product and service quality) certification standards.

Cambridge's pay-for-skills system plays only a minor role in the plant's training goals. Cambridge's overall compensation scheme was designed to ensure that all technicians fall into the same pay range—a distinct departure from Colgate's other detergent plants, where there are numerous job classifications and as many as six pay levels. All Cambridge operating technicians receive the same base salary as well as annual increases designed to keep salaries in the top quarter percentile for employers in the area. The plant's current pay-for-skills program adds an additional $0.30 an hour when technicians are certified as proficient in a technical skill; the maximum allowable under the system is $1.50. Moreover, quarterly plantwide bonuses can total as much as 20 percent of an employee's annual salary. The bonuses, shared equally by all technicians, are based on reaching targets in safety, quality (as measured by the amount of product returned because of defects), cost per case of detergent, and adherence to schedule.

While the bonuses are applied equally across the board, statistics are compiled for individual teams—which is primarily how team performance is measured. To keep salaries relatively equal, however, individual teams are not rewarded for exceptional performance. But Cambridge is currently developing a "team maturity" model, adopted from another Colgate facility, that may eventually be used to provide its most productive teams with extra compensation.

Area Leaders

The original group of managers and team leaders who formed Cambridge's start-up team in 1988 have been reassigned to other Colgate facilities, where work on high-commitment work systems continues. Cambridge has become an important training ground for Colgate. Indeed, the experiences managers have gained here have helped fashion self-directed team environments at new plants in the United States, Australia, and Eastern Europe.

The growing confidence and maturity of Cambridge's operator teams has smoothed over some (but not all) of the effects of frequent management changes. Cambridge wasn't supposed to need many managers. Today it operates with only two levels of management between teams and the plant manager. Eight area (formerly team) leaders report directly to the plant manager, as do four functional managers. Cambridge's twenty-one teams report to the area leaders, whose roles consist mostly of coaching, providing technical assistance, and furthering team development. Area leaders also coordinate Cambridge's peer review process and counsel individual team members after reviewing self-appraisals and evaluations from other members.

Results

The Cambridge plant has become the pacesetter for Colgate in operational efficiency and continuous productivity improvement—just as Colgate had hoped when it took the chance on this new work system. Line efficiency is commendably high. In one recent quarter, the entire plant ran at 82 percent efficiency in meeting scheduled production rates of cases per hour. Some lines have achieved rates as high as 92 percent. Costs per case have been on a downward slope at Cambridge for several years, too, thanks to team process improvements. In the packaging area, for example, teams decided to tape cases instead of shrink-wrapping them. This simple improvement saves the facility hundreds of thousands of dollars annually. As well, employee turnover has been minimal. A tribute to the original selection process, more than 90 percent of the technicians hired in 1988 are still at work.

From the start, a lot was riding on the Cambridge plant and expectations were high. The first group of technicians was especially enthusiastic about the opportunity Colgate presented—partly because management, excited by the vision, oversold the opportunities. For many technicians, however, expectations surpassed reality. When they found that advancement opportunities might be slower in coming than initially hoped, this led to frustration and a dip in morale. Therefore, efforts were made to give new applicants a more realistic picture of what life would be like in the plant. Today employees play a major role in selecting new employees. With several years on the job behind them, Cambridge's operators look for people who have the potential to contribute to continuous improvement and who can thrive in a team environment. But, as one manager puts it, they're careful not to promise more than Cambridge can deliver. "We're hiring people to be operator technicians, not for their potential to be plant managers," says this manager.

The early decision to create separate teams for maintenance technicians and operator technicians has hindered team development. The design team hoped maintenance technicians, hired for electrical and mechanical knowledge, would transfer their skills to operator technicians, who would be required to maintain and troubleshoot equipment. But this has not happened. With their own specialized teams, maintenance technicians have tended to view themselves as separate from the plant's main production system and have been reluctant to share their expertise with operator technicians. Promoting cross-training between the two separate team systems continues to be a challenge.

Colgate's use of Cambridge as a training ground for managers to gain experience in high-performance teams has hindered team development as well. Only about 14 percent of the original group of managers still are at Cambridge. "Every time a new manager comes in, we have to back up a little," says one employee. As a result, teams often have little time to develop working relationships with area leaders and other managers. In turn, new managers have discovered it can be difficult to establish their credibility, promote initiatives, or suggest changes when teams believe they understand the Cambridge system better than newcomers who may be reassigned in a year or two. But as long as Cambridge continues to post impressive results, Colgate probably will continue to use it as a resource in developing management talent for other facilities. This means the plant will continue trying to balance a stable team system with unstable management—at least until the Cambridge "experiment" becomes a way of life for the entire organization.

12

Making Teams Work
in Union and Nonunion Facilities

Hannaford Brothers Company
Schodack Landing, New York

Industry	Retail supermarket and food distribution
Union	None at Schodack Landing; in-house union at the South Portland, Maine, facility
Type of team implementation	Redesigned self-directed work teams at Schodack Landing greenfield site; similar team conversion under way at South Portland
First teams started	1989
Employees	150
Percentage in teams	100 percent at Schodack Landing
Team size	5 to 25
Team responsibilities	Depending on the maturity of teams, responsibilities include inventory control, developing and delivering training, setting team goals, team budgeting, hiring new team members, safety, quality assurance, scheduling work assignments, peer performance reviews, dealing with misconduct

and performance problems, and most areas that directly affect teams.

Organization-wide team responsibilities

Team members are elected to serve on work groups that advise management on human resource policies or recommend changes in plant operations. One task force helped develop Schodack Landing's pay-for-knowledge-and-skills system, which requires that a peer review panel certify employees in new skills.

Team leadership and governance

Team coordinators are elected by teams and limited to two consecutive six-month terms. Initially they coordinated training needs and facilitated meetings. Now they mainly coordinate interteam activity. On most teams leadership is shared by several coordinators elected for varying time periods to monitor team performance, quality, safety, and other areas.

Leadership outside teams

Operations coordinators have replaced dock supervisors, supervisors, and lead supervisors. Their role is to facilitate the team process. Top leadership at Schodack Landing is exercised by a two-person team eventually to be expanded to four.

Team compensation

Regular compensation includes merit raises and gain sharing. When employees become "team certified" they are eligible for advanced skills training. Certification increases their hourly wage. Teams receive a "team share" based on bottom-line financial results.

First-year team member training	About 15 percent of total hours was spent on training: team meeting skills, quality tools, problem solving, team interaction skills, workplace design, interviewing, coaching and facilitation, and cross-training skills.
Subsequent team member training	About 10 to 15 percent of total hours spent on training: quality tools, problem solving, and overall business knowledge.
First-year leadership training	About two hours a month in: team meeting skills, team interaction skills, workplace design, interviewing, coaching and facilitation, and cross-training skills.
Subsequent leadership training	About two hours a month in overall business knowledge.
How team members are selected	New members are selected and then sponsored by teams as they become team certified from an unassigned pool. New employees are selected by a system that identifies candidates with the desired behavioral dimensions.
How team performance is evaluated	Teams largely set their own development goals. Individuals are primarily evaluated through a peer review process. One measure of team performance is "team share" accomplishments—the certifiable skills achieved by team members.
Team impact on organization	Schodack Landing's operating costs are far lower than similarly sized distribution centers, primarily because of its lean staffing, minor absenteeism, and low employee turn-

over. Low workers' compensation costs—
because of few on-the-job accidents—are
saving the facility more than $500,000 a
year compared to similar facilities. Additional cost savings from team-led operational improvements are substantial.

Key lessons

- Introduce the concept of self-directed
  teams carefully because it can set off
  expectations of immediate and complete team control. Progress must be
  evolutionary: teams assume additional
  responsibilities as they mature.

- Honor the past: don't portray the team
  system as a repudiation of past ways of
  working.

- Don't present the team system as the
  latest revolution in management or it
  might be dismissed as just another HR
  program. Instead, help team members
  understand that building a team-based
  operation is a methodical, evolutionary process.

Background

The transformation of Hannaford Brothers from a food
wholesaler to a regional supermarket powerhouse is one of
the retail food industry's most impressive success stories. In
1977 Hannaford opened its first supermarket in Maine. By
the end of the 1980s Hannaford had pushed into the Massa-
chusetts and New York markets, opening more than a
hundred supermarkets. The company's supermarket revenues doubled during the decade to $2 billion annually. The
reasons for its success have been widely noted (and often

copied) by others in the food industry. Hannaford was one of the first supermarket chains to offer such amenities as fresh-baked goods, a wide selection of fresh fish, fruit, and vegetables, luxurious store surroundings, and careful attention to friendly and attentive customer service. The recipe was just what upscale shoppers wanted during the 1980s, and no one did it better than Hannaford.

But while Hannaford seemed to be doing everything right from the customer's perspective, problems were developing behind the scenes. Hannaford's skyrocketing growth during the 1980s (its stores doubled in number between 1985 and 1990) severely strained its distribution system—particularly its main distribution center at South Portland, Maine. As the volume of food products handled at the South Portland center grew, keeping up became a growing challenge. Overtime became routine. While average hourly rates of $12 were attractive by local standards, turnover increased sharply as employees became worn out by the pace.

The South Portland center was a typical large food warehousing operation. Employees loaded pallets with food based on store orders and delivered them to trucks at the shipping doors. Supervision was tight to ensure that orders were properly filled and waste was minimized. There were few opportunities to allay the tedium at the center by rotating jobs because of the time it took away from day-to-day operations. As a result, employees did the same tasks over and over—often just piling boxes onto wooden pallets. As the fast pace gave managers little chance to respond to problems and employees were not asked to come up with ideas for improvements, productivity suffered.

The extent of the problems at South Portland surfaced in 1988 during an organizing campaign by the Teamsters. During this time, Hannaford was planning a new distribution center in New York to serve its growing Mid-Atlantic market. Although the Teamsters were ultimately unsuccessful in decertifying South Portland's in-house union, the campaign exposed employees' boredom, loss of control, increasing stress, and growing alienation from management. These problems stemmed not only from the pressure to keep pace with Hannaford's growth but also from the growing dissatisfaction with the traditional distribution center environment, which had changed little over the years.

As planning for the new distribution center in New York proceeded, senior executives, including CEO James Moody and president and COO Hugh Farrington, were determined not to recreate the problems of South Portland. The executives had high hopes for the new distribution center to be located in Schodack Landing near Albany. While the new center would add the much-needed distribution capacity, it also was an opportunity to design a model distribution center. Events at South Portland had revealed the problems of the traditional distribution center in the fast-changing and competitive new environment. The system, not the people, was the biggest barrier to meeting new challenges. Schodack Landing was a perfect opportunity to change the system.

A Sociotechnical Systems Approach

Planning for a model distribution center at Schodack Landing began with the creation of a steering committee in the summer of 1989. Members included senior executives in operations, human resources, and newly hired directors of distribution and labor relations. Their mandate: set the parameters of the Schodack Landing design process and develop a charter for the work to be carried out by the design team.

Hannaford hoped that the new design would fit both the greenfield site at Schodack Landing and later the unionized South Portland facility. Because implementation would have to be different at each facility, two separate implementation teams were formed. Schodack Landing would be based on the lessons of South Portland—what didn't work there would be changed from the start at the new facility. The new design would then be implemented on a pilot basis at South Portland, drawing on the valuable lessons learned.

The steering committee met monthly for about a year. Because no one at Hannaford really knew what "model environment" for a distribution center meant, the committee decided to take a clean-slate approach to designing their workplace. Hannaford chose a redesign methodology known as *sociotechnical systems analysis*. This methodology, common to team implementations, focuses on the simultaneous redesign of technical systems (such as work flow and new technologies) and social systems (such as human resource programs and communication patterns). To use this methodology effectively, steering team members attended a ten-day seminar and made site visits to other facilities that used the process. Thus the committee spent much of its time investigating options in both areas. Its goal was to have an effective selection system in place by the time hiring began at Schodack Landing.

Perhaps the steering committee's most important task was to create and support the distribution center design team. Both groups worked closely together over a nine-month period. The fourteen members of the design team were selected from volunteers throughout the South Portland distribution center and represented a cross section of key functions, including nine hourly employees. The design team leader, Andy Westlund, who had been picked to head the new distribution center when it opened, also served on the steering committee.

The design team pored over every facet of the South Portland operation—analyzing Hannaford's business environment and the systems in its facilities, making recommendations to the steering committee on the best possible

distribution system, and working with the steering committee to develop an implementation plan. The team conducted
a social analysis of Hannaford by extensive interviews with
employees and managers. It interviewed retail store personnel (the distribution center's external customers) and Hannaford shoppers. It interviewed Hannaford's senior executives to establish their vision for the company's future. It
conducted a technical analysis of Hannaford's systems—and
identified more than three hundred variances, mistakes, or
poor use of resources. Its recommendations promised to
save $3 million annually.

Throughout the design team communicated its progress
to the rest of Hannaford's workforce and maintained close
links to the steering committee. In fact, communication was
extraordinary in many ways. Design team members sought
comments from employees in small meetings more than sixty
times—resulting in recommended changes in nineteen systems, including compensation and benefits, performance reviews, and gain sharing. After presenting their findings to the
steering committee, another round of meetings with employees was held to gather further comments. Progress was
communicated to employees through memos and bulletin
boards as well.

The steering committee, in addition to reviewing the design team's progress, kept senior management informed, relayed management's concerns back to the design team, made
sure that the rest of the organization understood the purpose
of the design team's work, and stepped in to help the design
team overcome obstacles to getting information or solving
problems. For example, on several occasions the South Portland union raised concerns about the design team's suggestions—such as a proposed peer evaluation system that was
to some a new and somewhat threatening concept. When
conflicts arose, the steering committee helped all sides clarify the issues and reach consensus.

According to Walter Stilphen, Hannaford's director of labor relations and steering committee member, the importance of employees' involvement, control, and leadership in every phase of the design process can't be overstated. "We thought that part of the process of getting there was *being* there," Stilphen says. In other words, the principles that guided the design process would be the same principles that governed the workplace at the new facility—and eventually at all Hannaford distribution centers. Thus, Stilphen says, it was essential to "mirror the behavior we were trying to create in the future." That behavior consisted of symbolic gestures (for the first time hourly associates on the design team found themselves off the time clock) and management's willingness to share authority and recognize hourly associates as experts on workplace redesign.

Teams

The implementation team at Schodack Landing worked out of two trailers in the spring of 1991 as the new distribution center was being built. The team consisted of Andy Westlund, the center's first director, and ten hourly employees from South Portland who were reassigned to the new distribution center. A similar team was at work at South Portland.

The operation of a traditional food warehouse is complex because of its size and volume. Employees, called selectors, pull products from inventory, load them onto pallets, and deposit the pallets at the loading dock. Selectors usually lose all sight of what happens to their handiwork beyond the loading dock door. Duties are highly functional: inventory controllers make sure shelves are properly stocked; selectors pull cartons from shelves and build pallets; forklift operators take the pallets to waiting trucks; supervisors schedule assignments and make sure everyone follows procedures. At

Schodack Landing, however, the old functional divisions—
selectors, forklift operators, and inventory controllers—were
eliminated. Instead teams became responsible for all duties
related to filling and delivering orders to the shipping dock.

Associates, as new team members were called, were
hired using an innovative selection, assessment, and simulation process that evaluated applicants for their ability to
learn, work in teams with little supervision, solve problems,
and function in a high-involvement environment. All were
important qualities. As teams matured, more complex functions would be assumed by team members, including hiring,
developing and delivering training and discipline, budgeting,
and maintaining inventory control. Hannaford's goal was to
make all tasks a team responsibility once team members had
gained the appropriate training and experience. This meant
that while some specialists would be needed early on, their
roles would be phased out as teams evolved.

Each team focused on specific customers—up to three
supermarkets—that it directly supplied. In fact, part of the
team charter was to maintain regular contact with these customers through surveys, store visits, and riding along with
trucks to see how deliveries were handled at the store. Currently the Schodack Landing distribution center is divided
into seven teams ranging from five to twenty-five members.
Six teams serve Hannaford supermarkets and are specialized
only in that different teams handle different categories of
food, such as frozen foods or perishables. The seventh team,
with ten members, provides specialized resources to other
teams.

Within each team, leadership is based on a star point
system. Some star point positions require certifiable skills,
which can be achieved through the center's pay-for-knowledge-and-skills system. Team coordinators, an elective and
rotating position (limited to two consecutive six-month
terms), initially played an important role as they helped

members acquire the basic cross-functional skills the team needed. Their importance diminished as teams matured, however, and now coordinators serve mainly to coordinate activities among teams. Within teams, most decisions are reached by consensus.

One striking characteristic of team life at Schodack Landing is the amount of meeting and training time members receive. In the facility's first year, as much as 20 percent of associates' time was devoted to development (as opposed to production); today 15 percent of their time is spent on meetings and training. This is because in addition to scheduling work assignments, overtime, and vacations, teams are responsible for peer reviews, dealing with performance problems, and identifying individual and team training needs. While the time commitment remains heavy, productivity is not hampered. All team members receive training in conducting effective meetings, so time is not wasted on items that aren't on the agenda.

Compensation and Pay

Schodack Landing opened with several questions deliberately left unanswered in order to give team associates a major role in designing their own compensation system. The design team had recommended a pay-for-knowledge-and-skills system and drafted some broad outlines, but the implementation team decided not to fill in the details until the new facility was staffed and running.

Today the starting wage at Schodack Landing is approximately $10 an hour and increases to a little more than $12 an hour after eighteen months. By then associates are expected to be "team qualified" (which takes four to nine months) and "team certified" (which takes six to eighteen months). Being team qualified means associates show they understand the basic team duties and processes. Being team certified means associates demonstrate strong team interaction and problem-solving skills. To pass this threshold, team members apply to a peer review board that evaluates candidates based on demonstrated performance. Team-certified associates can then participate in a pay-for-knowledge-and-skills program that can add another $2.50 to their hourly wage. The program is divided into four skill tracks. The decision to complete a skill track is made by the associate and the team itself, both of which benefit. Team members who complete the training receive an hourly increase. If the new skill adds to the team's productivity, all team members receive an hourly "team share" increase.

Results

Hannaford's effort to create a new design for the Schodack Landing distribution center and its old center in Maine has yielded mixed results. By almost all measures Schodack Landing turned out to be everything the company envisioned. Retrofitting South Portland has proved to be a bigger challenge. There both the union and the supervisors and managers have struggled with redefining their roles in an evolving team-based environment. The prospects of a supervision-free work environment and such innovations as peer reviews have clashed with long-standing union practices. Innovations practiced at Schodack Landing—such as the way teams handle performance problems—are proscribed by South Portland's union contract.

Even so, pilot team implementations at South Portland have produced some major productivity and cost savings. According to Hannaford, the South Portland facility is among the industry's most cost-efficient distribution centers. In its first year of operation, Schodack Landing matched South Portland's productivity rate—despite employees spending 20 percent of their time on nonproduction activities. Factors contributing to that record include low absenteeism and low employee turnover (in an industry that traditionally suffers from high absenteeism and high turnover). Perhaps the biggest contributor to Schodack Landing's productivity is labor savings—the facility operates with fewer than half the specialized or supervisory roles needed at South Portland, including high-paid senior plant managers.

Workers' compensation costs at Schodack Landing tell another significant story. In its first year of operation, the facility reported dramatically fewer on-the-job injuries than Hannaford's facility in Maine. Hannaford has calculated that workers' compensation savings alone result in a savings advantage of $0.79 per employee per hour of operation. And in an industry in which profit margins rarely exceed one cent on the dollar, the money not spent on workers' compensation has a significant impact.

Because one important role of the new facility is to give the company a competitive advantage in a tough, low-margin business, Hannaford is reluctant to say much publicly about other ways in which savings have been achieved at Schodack Landing. But it will say that in all the ways that count, Schodack Landing substantially outperforms other facilities. Hannaford appears to have created the model that will indeed lead it into the future.

13

Project-Based Teams: Creating Flexibility and Focus in a Matrix Environment

Harris Corporation
Melbourne, Florida

Industry	Electronics
Union	None
Type of team implementation	Employee involvement teams (for process improvement) and cross-functional project teams (for specific programs)
First teams started	1984
Employees	8,000
Percentage in teams	65 percent
Team size	6 to 10 (employee involvement teams)
Team responsibilities	Employee involvement teams are responsible for meeting process improvement or other goals, usually suggested by teams and approved by management.
Organization-wide team responsibilities	Several types of teams in Harris's system work on projects that span functional areas: cross-functional project teams draw members from a variety of work cells to work on systemwide improvement proj-

ects; system improvement teams tackle systemwide projects but disband when projects are complete; commodity teams are collocated from a variety of functional areas to complete contracts. Teams have advised management on HR policies such as peer evaluation and rewards and recognition programs.

Team leadership and governance	Team leaders usually are selected by managers and required to receive team leadership training. Leaders don't rotate, but they may step down or teams may select new leaders by consensus, subject to management agreement.
Leadership outside teams	Employee involvement teams report to management teams once a month on progress toward meeting goals.
Team compensation	Team compensation is largely symbolic or honorary. Team members receive $100 bonuses twice a year if teams exceed baseline performance expectations. Teams also vie for division and corporate awards.
First-year team member training	Twenty to forty hours training in team meeting skills, quality/problem-solving techniques, team interaction skills, business knowledge.
Subsequent team member training	Same as above depending on team needs.
First-year leadership training	Same as first-year team member training plus training in workplace design and facilitation and coaching skills.

Subsequent leadership training	Same as above depending on team needs.
How team members are selected	Members are selected by management teams.
How team performance is evaluated	Teams are assigned goals (or suggest their own goals) and report to management teams on monthly progress. They also file monthly reports and wrap-up reports with the TQM office, which maintains a database of team projects and results. Twice a year, teams and management teams evaluate each team's performance on goals, schedules, and the effectiveness of the team process.
Team impact on organization	Harris estimates that teams save $4 to $5 for every dollar invested in the team system. Currently seventy-eight teams are active in the Palm Bay Operations of the Electronic Systems Sector, working on improvement goals that affect all aspects of the operation. Cycle time and costs for most systems contracts have fallen steadily since the team system was expanded in the early 1990s.
Key lessons	• Enthusiasm for teams sometimes led to the creation of EITs that made little business sense. Today the organization ensures that teams have clear charters and are aligned with specific business goals.

- It was sometimes hard to establish truly challenging team goals. Today the TQM staff works closely with teams to set ongoing goals.
- Lack of attention to training supervisors and middle managers led to anxieties about ambiguous roles and confusion about management responsibilities. Today they receive training to help them adjust to the changes.

Background

Harris Corporation occupies an unusual position among electronics manufacturers. With its collection of seemingly disparate businesses (office equipment, semiconductors, broadcast transmission equipment, defense and commercial electronics), Harris has grown into a $3 billion business with a strong reputation for innovation and technological excellence.

Harris has been farsighted. Since the first hints of cutbacks in defense spending surfaced in the 1980s, Harris's Electronic Systems Sector (ESS), which employs more than nine thousand and has sales topping $1 billion, has steadily reduced its reliance on defense work. While it still does more than 25 percent of its business on specialized communication, navigation, and testing systems for the military, Harris hasn't suffered the blows other defense contractors have. Harris's ESS successfully targeted new niches—primarily nonmilitary government agencies, including NASA and the FAA, which in 1991 awarded Harris a $1.7 billion contract to upgrade its air traffic control voice communication system.

Teamwork in various forms has had a long history at Harris, beginning with quality circles in the early and mid-1980s.

The current team system at ESS includes cross-functional program teams assembled for major projects like the FAA contract and process improvement teams, called employee involvement teams (EITs), that have literally reshaped the way ESS operates. Unlike most organizations profiled in this book, ESS does not operate with a system of permanent self-directed work teams—the division does little actual manufacturing (a major production run might reach sixty units) and the nature of its work requires continually changing team assignments. Still, few U.S. companies are as influenced by teams. And few seem to profit as much from the team experience.

Two things occurred in the mid-1980s to spur Harris's team systems. First, in 1984 Harris was awarded a major electronic systems contract for the B-1 bomber program; this required a new production facility and a rethinking of traditional work systems. Second, Harris's senior executives were adopting a change of philosophy; they were seeking breakthroughs in innovation and productivity as part of a long-term strategy to become less dependent on defense business. They looked to companies such as Motorola (with its zero-defects culture) and nearby Florida Power and Light (a Deming Award winner) that were achieving success with new techniques. But Harris's executive team was determined to find an approach consistent with its own company values, which had always focused on empowerment (although the company didn't call it that at the time) and individual responsibility among its largely professional workforce.

The result was the implementation of the "Quality First" program. This program focused on three areas senior executives felt needed the most attention:

- Customer satisfaction. (Harris's engineering culture, convinced of its technological superiority, could sometimes strike customers as arrogant.)

- Accelerated growth in new products and new contracts. (Harris's technological smugness lead to a "not invented here" syndrome that could close the company off from good ideas from the outside.)
- Continuous quality and productivity improvement.

ESS soon developed its own version of the Quality First initiative, spearheaded by Jack Johnson, then program vice president for the B-1 project. At the time, a new facility was being planned for the B-1 contract and other projects. Malabar Production, as it was called, was intended to be a world-class manufacturing facility. The facility was designed with input from manufacturing engineers and product assemblers to support a free flow of materials and communication among both project teams and work cells—which meant it had few of the assembly lines and isolated office areas of traditional facilities. The first work cells at Malabar were trained in statistical process control and other quality tools. While these teams still had formal leaders, process and quality improvement activities became a strong team responsibility. The first improvement team at Malabar still exists today. Calling itself the "Masking Bandits," this work cell team in the facility's coating room has completed more than thirteen improvement projects.

Around the same time, ESS consolidated all its manufacturing and material operations under Jack Johnson in an organization called Palm Bay Operations Manufacturing. Formal efforts soon began to develop a framework to support the creation of teams with a campaign Johnson called "Performance Excellence: Our People Lead the Effort," or PEOPLE. Johnson assigned someone on his staff the full-time job of coordinating and supporting process improvement team activities and training employees to be roving facilitators of team development. Johnson also created a PEOPLE Steering

Committee for Manufacturing, which still meets today and serves as a quality council. At first members included heads, or directors, of Palm Bay's various manufacturing units and functional departments, such as quality assurance and human resources. Eventually directors were appointed to chair four subcommittees that designed a framework for Palm Bay's team system. And given the complexity of operations within the division, this team system became quite elaborate.

Improvement Teams

Today more than 65 percent of Palm Bay's employees participate in teams. There are two main types: *employee involvement teams* are relatively permanent and work on process improvement goals assigned by managers or suggested by team members; *program teams* are temporary cross-functional teams of engineers, materials and procurement personnel, and manufacturing specialists brought together to work on commercial and defense contracts.

The Masking Bandits and other early teams served as models for Palm Bay's employee involvement teams. Most EITs consist of six to ten employees who do similar work and share the same suppliers and internal or external customers. These ongoing teams may form on their own or be appointed by managers. EITs focus on process improvements affecting their work area and specific improvement goals suggested to the team by managers or team members. Usually EITs meet for an hour a week. When an EIT is created, its leader is selected by a management team because Harris believes strong leadership is essential to keeping teams focused on goals. Although the decision to become a leader is voluntary, most accept the offer. In addition to keeping teams focused on goals, team leaders keep minutes for team meetings, request help from process experts if needed, bring in a facilitator from Palm Bay's special team facilitation department if the team is experiencing problems, and brief the EIT's management team once a month. Leadership changes if a leader decides to step down or the team decides it's time for a change. Usually the management team must approve the change. All team leaders must be trained as a team facilitator.

A variation of the EIT is the system employee involvement team (SEIT), which tends to be more cross-functional than EITs. With six to twelve members selected from different work cells, SEITs focus on system improvements. Like EITs, SEITs meet weekly and report to a management team regularly. A system improvement project (SIP) team tackles a systemwide problem (usually selected by management) and disbands when the project is completed. SIP members are selected for their specialized skills and work on projects such as developing enhancements to ESS's critical Integrated Supplier System and benchmarking various manufacturing processes among other electronics systems companies.

There are dozens of EITs and SEITs in Palm Bay and a much smaller number of SIPs. Their work affects all aspects of the operation. Examples of EITs include the LASS team (Land, Air, and Sea Specialists)—eight administrative personnel in the transportation and shipping department (and all women, hence the tongue-in-cheek name) who have completed a dozen projects that have dramatically improved shipping efficiency and lowered costs—and the Pro-Testers in ESS's test center, whose twelve completed projects include developing a cross-training system for test center technicians and a preventive maintenance system.

SEITs include the Performance Plus team, which in 1993 won the top award at a national team competition sponsored by the Association for Quality and Participation. The eleven-person team, formed in 1988, is composed mostly of employees involved in taking contract specifications and creating proposals. It includes a quality assurance administrator, a test manager, a production scheduler, quality and process engineers, and administrative personnel. The team has greatly streamlined the proposal process, which can be quite complicated, by developing two reference manuals that reduce the costs of developing proposals and improve accuracy and quality.

Commodity teams, the final type of employee involvement team, also play a major role at Palm Bay. These teams select preferred suppliers—identifying "best in class" from among Harris's five thousand suppliers—as part of an ongoing effort to develop strong supplier relationships. Palm Bay's fifteen commodity teams, each focused on a major component area, typically include a buyer from one of ESS's divisions, a quality assurance inspector, and component, quality, and design engineers.

Program Teams

Less permanent, though equally vital to Harris, are the program teams. ESS depends on a steady source of big commercial and defense projects, many of them one-time-only projects in which both technology skills and the ability to meet deadlines at fixed costs make the competitive difference. ESS senior managers or executives in charge of a project can pull together team members from nearly any functional area to work on the project. Once a month they return to their "center of excellence," or functional area, to brief colleagues on the project's progress and discuss challenges the program team is encountering.

On projects of longer duration, it's especially important that team members maintain regular contact with their functional areas to keep up with changes in technology. For example, engineers on the team that helped Harris win the FAA contract spent many years focused almost solely on that effort. Unless they kept up with fast-moving trends in telecommunication technologies, they might have been severely disadvantaged once they were reassigned to their functional areas or to another project. Links between the ESS and academia also help engineers update their skills so that they aren't "punished," as one manager puts it, for making a total commitment to their project.

Managers are closely involved in many aspects of team life at Palm Bay. Not only do they model appropriate team behavior and demonstrate commitment to the company's values, but managers and executive leaders play a strong role in employee involvement and project teams. All teams report to a "C team" of middle managers, for example, whose responsibility, according to their charter, is to assign team goals or help teams form their own goals, select team members and leaders, and establish a goal completion date. Management team members also are expected to attend 25 to 50 percent of team meetings in their areas. At Palm Bay there are seven C teams, and each includes representatives from several functional areas.

Team Support

The first-year goal of the PEOPLE initiative was twelve employee involvement teams, each mature enough to function without an outside facilitator. To get there Johnson hired a full-time coordinator who looked to existing teams for good facilitators as more teams got going. Teams like the Masking Bandits and others, who by the early 1990s had several years of experience, proved to be a good source of natural facilitators. This cadre of facilitators trained new teams and attended the initial team meetings. As teams became mature enough to work on their own, facilitators moved on to other teams.

By 1992, with eighty-five teams operating at Palm Bay, the facilitation staff was reorganized into a TQM office to support team activity throughout ESS and Harris. The name change reflected the change in responsibilities. The need to provide close support for most teams at Palm Bay had disappeared, but other functions in ESS began clamoring for help. Facilitators also helped program teams get off to a good start by coordinating team "kickoffs" that included one- or two-day sessions to help teams and their internal customers define team missions and goals, clarify the roles and responsibilities of diverse team members, and discuss ways to resolve conflicts.

As the TQM program has spread throughout the corporation, the facilitation staff has continued to expand its own skills and now serves as a partner to internal TQM consultants. The TQM office also serves as a central clearinghouse for team activity. Teams are required to document their activities and submit brief monthly reports and project summaries to both their C team and the TQM office. The TQM office uses the reports to monitor team progress, making sure teams are headed in the right direction and stay focused on their goal. The office also uses the reports to maintain a database of all team activity. New team goals are compared against projects in the database to avoid overlaps in team activity. If a team wants to work on improvements to circuit board "solderability," for example, the TQM office queries its database to make sure the task is not already being done by another team.

Training

Teams have been so thoroughly integrated into the fabric of life at Palm Bay that there is not much "special" team training. The only hard and fast training requirement for EITs is that all team leaders must be trained in empowered, interactive management and team interaction skills. Team leaders are trained in group dynamics and individual problem-solving styles, as well. Team leaders and members alike receive training in quantitative problem-solving techniques. Recently team members have been trained in providing performance feedback to other members. Program teams, which work together on the job daily instead of just during weekly team meetings, also receive an intensive team-building kick-off at the start of a program—usually an eight-hour session of setting goals and clarifying roles. Most program team members also receive training in cross-training others. (Teams usually meet their own cross-training needs.)

Performance and Rewards

Palm Bay's EIT system is somewhat separate from the organization's primary performance management and compensation systems. Teams must report regularly to their C team management and file monthly status reports with the TQM office. They also file reports upon goal completion.

Twice a year the teams and their C team management evaluate the teams on four areas: full performance, schedule performance, team cooperation with other groups, and how well the team process is working. Teams significantly exceeding standards receive a $100 bonus. But this is far from the most important part of Palm Bay's award system—recognition holds that honor. Every year, an employee committee coordinates an annual awards celebration during which all Palm Bay employees are thanked for their contributions. High-performing employees and teams receive awards.

Early Mistakes

During the first days of the PEOPLE campaign, enthusiasm ran high for creating teams. In fact, the success of early teams led to a headlong rush into assigning employees to teams even when it made little sense to do so. Employees in certain areas were assigned to teams without consideration of how those teams were aligned with business objectives or what goals they would be able to achieve. Quotas were set for establishing a certain number of teams by certain dates. Entire areas were divided into as many as forty teams—sometimes consisting of only two or three employees who shared proximity but little else. The result was a lot of wasted hours in team meetings and team training. Important lessons were learned, however. When things settled down, Palm Bay stopped playing a numbers game and began to make sure teams had clear charters and were aligned with meeting specific business goals.

Moreover, managers had trouble establishing challenging goals for many teams in the early days. The project team that won the FAA business had a simple and highly elevating goal: Do what it takes to win the contract. Employee involvement teams had goals as well, but managers discovered it was tough to advance beyond 10 percent improvements in costs or cycle times—often easily achievable—to goals that kept teams motivated and committed to the team system. After meeting their goals, some teams asked: What's next? Some still do, and the TQM staff continues to work closely with them on setting goals. Many teams, however, with time and experience, have mastered the challenge—indeed, an "annual report" on team results published by Palm Bay describes teams working on their tenth goal. The close interaction between C teams and EITs helps teams stay on track. And the seven-person TQM office is there when intervention is needed.

In the push to build EITs, the roles and responsibilities of middle managers and supervisors were overlooked in favor of senior managers and team members. Many supervisors and middle managers received only a cursory orientation to the new employee involvement system. Assemblers and technicians learned statistical process control and other quality and problem-solving techniques, for instance, but their supervisors and managers didn't. The result was empowered and enthusiastic employees at one level, senior managers committed to change at the top level, and between them a stratum of middle managers confused and anxious about what they saw happening. In some cases, supervisors and managers withheld data from teams or attempted to assume team reporting functions themselves. Eventually they received training to help them adjust to the changes and learn to trust employee involvement teams.

Results

Although quantifying the effects of hundreds of process and other changes generated by the team system is difficult, Palm Bay is satisfied. In 1992, for example, when twenty-four goals were successfully completed, EIT activity cost an estimated $950,000. Documented savings for that same year totaled nearly $4.5 million. Work on the B-1 bomber project, which inspired the current EIT system, has benefited greatly from the changes. The hundredth communication set shipped by Harris cost 18 percent of the first set shipped—while reliability has steadily increased and defects decreased throughout the life of the project.

One of the first hurdles the EIT system had to overcome confirmed how well the system was working. Many management systems and other processes were changed by the team initiative—but none more fundamentally than Palm Bay's accounting system, which had been set to recognize time charged out to jobs as revenue and everything else as overhead. As teams helped Palm Bay become progressively more efficient, time charged out to jobs soon began to decline while the corresponding time charged to overhead increased. This meant that over the long run Palm Bay's team system would require that more work be brought into the organization because employees were able to complete jobs faster and more efficiently—an unexpected but perhaps predictable challenge in an organization where teams have become so pervasive.

14

Achieving Customer Satisfaction by Managing the *Whole* Business with Teams

Kodak Customer Assistance Center
Rochester, New York

Industry	Customer service
Union	None
Type of team implementation	Phased-in consolidation of two separate customer service "call centers" into redesigned, self-directed work teams. Various cross-functional, multilevel teams (called councils) serve as links with business units and work on improving and managing key processes.
First teams started	1990
Employees	300
Percentage in teams	50 percent
Team size	3 to 20
Team responsibilities	Teams are based on customer regions, specialized product areas, or unique customer groups. Responsibilities include scheduling shift and work assignments, training and coaching other team members, evaluating how well team members handle

customer assistance calls, monitoring customer satisfaction, and making ongoing process improvements.

Organization-wide team responsibilities

The team-based management system includes business councils (responsible for determining the needs of specific Kodak business units) and process councils that oversee internal operations. Business councils consist of one or more of the KCAC's twelve business managers and an equal or greater number of elected team representatives. Managers serve on some but not all process councils. The oversight group is a leadership council of all managers and two employees, the latter serving for three months at a time.

Team leadership and governance

No designated team leaders; teams make internal decisions by a loose form of consensus.

Leadership outside teams

Twelve business managers provide coaching and team facilitation and work with teams through business and process councils.

Team compensation

Currently based on Kodak's standard compensation policies with regular merit increases. A "team share" system provides equal bonuses to all KCAC employees based on process improvement savings. A new pay-for-skills program is now being implemented.

First-year team member training

150 hours: team meeting skills, quality tools, problem-solving techniques, team

interaction skills, team and workplace design, interviewing skills, team facilitation and coaching skills, and cross-training others.

Subsequent team member training	120 hours in the areas cited above plus business and financial skills training.
First-year leadership training	150 hours: team meeting skills, quality tools, problem-solving techniques, team interaction skills, and team facilitation and coaching.
Subsequent leadership training	120 hours in the areas cited above.
How team members are selected	Team representatives serve on a selection committee that interviews new employees.
How team performance is evaluated	The KCAC's leadership council establishes—using team feedback—annual key result areas (KRAs) and key result measurements (KRMs) for the entire organization. Teams then establish their own KRAs and KRMs based on their own team's goals and the organization's goals. Teams receive two interim performance assessments and one formal assessment during the year by a process council set up to review team performance. Teams are responsible for monitoring and collecting data on meeting performance targets.
Team impact on organization	Employee productivity (as measured by calls handled per hour) has doubled—as have first-time accuracy levels in helping

customers find the right solutions to their problems. Employee turnover, traditionally a problem in call centers, has fallen to about half the industry average.

Key lessons

- The design team met regularly with employees—soliciting feedback and introducing them to working in small problem-solving teams—which helped the transition to teams once the organization was reorganized.

- As the hectic daily workload makes it hard for employees to look ahead and develop a continuous process improvement perspective, managers must model new behavior and expect a temporary dip in productivity.

- Training needs can be enormous when the transition to teams is accompanied by an ambitious new mandate that greatly expands employees' responsibilities.

Background

The Kodak Customer Assistance Center (KCAC) is a comprehensive presale and postsale customer support organization for all of Eastman Kodak's "imaging" products. In Kodak's case, imaging is a vast category and it's getting bigger all the time. It includes film, cameras and home projectors for consumers, equipment and supplies for professional photographers and commercial film developers, and a variety of products for the printing, publishing, and graphic arts industries—plus office equipment such as copiers, microfilm read-ers, and the newest generation of "hybrid" devices that often combine computers, scanners, copiers, and communicators into one. The rapid pace of development in digital information processing means Kodak's imaging product line will undoubtedly get even more complex in the years ahead.

The KCAC's presale activities include providing technical information to potential buyers and helping Kodak's sales and marketing organizations qualify potential sales. Postsale activities include answering thousands of questions a day about Kodak products from customers ranging from home photography buffs to professional users of sophisticated equipment. To make life even more complicated inside the KCAC, it also provides a range of services for many Kodak business units, including order processing, tracking credits and adjustments, and verifying proof of delivery.

The KCAC is actually the new name for two organizations that were recently merged. Kodak's Copy Products Information Center (CPIC) was formed in 1989 after Kodak bought IBM's copier business and combined it with Kodak's own office products business. Since then, Kodak slowly has been integrating that unit with what used to be known as the Kodak Information Center, which provided telephone customer support for the rest of Kodak's imaging products. Although the combined Kodak Customer Assistance Center was formally created in 1991, complete integration of the two units has yet to be achieved and they are housed in separate buildings. As the Copy Products Information Center has had a big head start on implementing a team system, most of this team story concerns changes that have been made there.

When Roger Michaelsen was appointed to direct the new Copy Products Information Center and, later, to create a comprehensive Kodak customer support center, he had a choice to make: put together a typical call center operation, where customer service representatives (CSRs) sit glued to a telephone headset for eight hours a shift answering as many questions as possible, or create a high-performance work environment based on teams. Typical call centers tend to be monotonous, closely supervised environments. Employees usually must meet hourly call quotas and supervisors frequently listen in. The pace can be grueling and employee turnover is high. Michaelsen knew that such a traditional environment might serve Kodak poorly in the coming years. Kodak wanted to create a single customer point of contact for a huge range of products—and no handoffs from one representative to another because questions couldn't be answered. On-line databases could solve part of the problem. But the call center model of the past, with its high employee turnover and narrowly specialized CSRs, would be inadequate, Michaelsen felt, to provide a high level of customer support for Kodak's growing product line. Instead, Michaelsen envisioned a team-based work environment with team members trained to support dozens, if not hundreds, of products and everyone intimately involved in continuous process improvement. Most of all, Michaelsen said he didn't want to "get a traditional organization in place and then have to figure out how to disassemble it later."

In 1988 when the newly expanded support center was being planned, Michaelsen turned to M. K. Farukhi, an organization development specialist at Kodak, for some answers to his questions about high-performance work systems. Farukhi and Michaelsen have worked closely on the center's team system ever since. Their initial goals included enlisting the support of other managers in the new center—which Michaelsen soon began calling his leadership team (later changed to leadership council)—and developing a vision and charter for a design team.

Both Michaelsen and Farukhi were convinced that successfully introducing a self-managing team system required first a change in management behavior and then a way to ensure that changes were visible and consistent. They hoped that managers would serve as models for employees as the team system was planned and implemented.

The design team first met in 1989. Its six members, nominated by the 150 employees of the Copy Products Information Center, included five customer service representatives and one manager. The team met for one or two days a week for nine months, depending on the center's workload. Michaelsen served on the team for the first three months. The design team's mandate included defining the behavior and roles for both managers and team members. Meanwhile the leadership team was defining its own behavior and roles, and both teams met to compare differences and hammer out compromises. The design team relied on consulting support from Kodak's Management Services Division. During the team's nine-month existence, it studied, printed, and videotaped material on customer service, work design, and team building.

Ultimately the design team served several purposes—some not anticipated when it was created. Operating in "experiential mode," the team initially met without rules for developing agendas, conducting meetings, reaching decisions, or doing any of the things that characterize a smoothly running team. As a result, the early months often were marked by wrangling over procedural matters and the team suffered from spells of gridlock and role confusion. At times, days would go by with little progress. Out of the "depths of despair," as one team member put it, valuable lessons were learned about what makes teams fail as well as succeed. Most important, the design team learned that a good team *process* is essential. Later, some of the problems faced by operating teams seemed trivial compared to what the design team had experienced.

These lessons came in handy later when design team members held a series of update meetings with the rest of the Copy Products Information Center staff to go over the team's progress, answer questions, and solicit comments. The meetings had another agenda, too, unstated but no less important: to make staff members familiar with working in teams by having them break up into small groups and conduct brainstorming and problem-solving activities. Over the months, employees were encouraged to build on each session by analyzing how and why their small groups worked effectively and, in the process, learning about such team skills as consensus decision making, providing feedback, and managing conflict. By the time the new team system was unveiled in the spring of 1990, all employees already had many hours of working in teams under their belts.

The New Organization

Before the launch, each CPIC customer service representative was responsible for handling two or three of the dozens of different functions or product areas—from answering questions about copiers, printers, and other products to various sales-related activities such as entering orders, credits, and adjustments and tracking proof of delivery. Employees were highly dedicated to taking care of customers. Once they received their daily instructions, they needed little incentive to focus intently on the day's primary business—answering the phone. Thinking ahead, however, involved adjustments that many employees found difficult. "How can we afford to spend time away from the phone in training classes or team activities?" many wondered. "Our job is to help customers who need information, and there's always another customer on the line."

Today the CPIC has a new name—the Kodak Customer Assistance Center—and a new structure that combines permanent operating teams with organizationwide "councils" that oversee internal operations and relations with Kodak's business units. Eight operating teams form the backbone of the organization: three teams of about twenty members each provide product support and presale and postsale assistance based on geographic territories (North, Central, South); three smaller teams focus on two specialized segments of Kodak customers, scientific and corporate users; and two teams provide support to the rest of the organization. There are three different councils under the new system: the leadership council, made up of all business managers and several employee representatives, sets overall direction and policy; seven business councils, composed of business managers and elected team representatives, interface with key Kodak business units to understand their requirements for support and assistance and translate those requirements into team procedures; and eight process councils, mainly staffed with elected team representatives, help shape the KCAC's internal processes. For example, process councils determine internal staffing needs and interview and select new employees as well as set KCAC's policies on team and individual rewards and recognition for outstanding performance. They have helped develop a new skills certification system, as well.

The KCAC's operating teams, especially the large regional teams, are expected to handle all twenty product and sales support functions of the old Copy Products Information Center—making on-the-job training and coaching one of the biggest responsibilities of teams. There are other responsibilities too: scheduling shift and work assignments; "call evaluation," in which team members assess how team members handle calls; and customer callbacks (calling customers to determine their satisfaction with the way their transaction was handled). In addition, several separate resource teams provide technical and training support to the operating teams—including a four-person training team and an information technology team that maintains the on-line databases that are essential for answering many types of customer questions.

One of the most important roles of the operating teams is to provide representation on KCAC's council-based management system. The councils aren't called teams because, in the KCAC framework, teams are considered to be permanent. The councils are rotational—while some managers might be permanent, associates rotate in and out according to schedules established by individual councils. The business councils, composed of one or several of the center's twelve business managers and an equal or greater number of elected team representatives, are especially crucial to meeting the needs of internal Kodak customers. It is their job to translate the marketing and product support requirements of specific businesses—from office, consumer, and professional imaging to newer categories such as photo compact disc imaging— into procedures and performance measures for KCAC teams. The business councils also establish the skill levels the KCAC needs to support the organization and, working with operating teams, reallocate resources to meet changes in demand. The seven business councils also elect representatives to serve on an operations coordination council, which looks at the effect of specific business council issues on the entire organization. The eight process councils are similarly staffed with elected team representatives. Managers may serve on process councils as well.

Both the councils and KCAC's operating teams look to the leadership council for overall direction and guidance. The leadership council consists of the KCAC's twelve business managers, director Michaelsen, and two at-large members, drawn from associates, who serve a three-month term. The associates may be asked to excuse themselves from meetings at Michaelsen's discretion, but this is very rare. Otherwise they are expected to participate fully. One chief role of the leadership council is establishing the boundaries within which the business and process councils and operating teams work. If councils and teams make decisions consistent with these boundaries, the leadership council seldom interferes. As a result, the KCAC is run largely by councils and teams. If the leadership team questions a decision, it does not overrule it. Rather, it attempts to provide better direction by adjusting the council's or team's boundaries.

Meeting a Growing Challenge

As the KCAC moves toward its vision of providing one focal point for customer transactions for all of Kodak's product lines, the knowledge required of team members has grown tremendously. Multifunctional once meant that teams would be able to support twelve different product areas. Now the KCAC's goal is giving teams the training and resources to support as many as a hundred different products or transactions for internal and external customers.

It's an ongoing challenge for business councils, through their interactions with Kodak's business and marketing units, to define the evolving skill requirements of teams. And it's an ongoing challenge for process councils to develop the cross-training and certification systems needed to meet these changing requirements. In addition, a special four-person training team helps coordinate cross-training within teams and organizationwide training needs, delivering training on its own or turning to outside resources when needed.

The KCAC is slowly developing a pay-for-skills program and is on the verge of piloting a new system developed by a process council. Progress has been slow because the KCAC, by Kodak standards, is a small operation that is expected to handle many different functions and products. The process council's task meant establishing a multilevel certification procedure—user, resource, instructor—for more than a hundred areas by using experts from operating teams and business councils. Certification (through testing and demonstrated proficiency) will eventually affect individual compensation. For now, compensation is based on regular merit increases and a "team share" system that rewards the entire organization for process improvements that result in demonstrable savings. While team members will be encouraged to achieve certification in many areas, business councils will be the ultimate judge of the skills each team needs.

Much time and attention were spent on the KCAC's performance appraisal process, which consists of several parallel systems that touch the lives of everyone in the organization. Both a design team and later a process council helped develop the framework for teams and employees, which closely resembles the performance appraisal system managers adopted for themselves at the start of the team implementation. Greatly simplified, the annual cycle for the system begins in midyear when the leadership council establishes performance targets called key result areas (KRAs) and key result measurements (KRMs) for the entire KCAC based on the requirements of each Kodak business unit. The leadership council also establishes its own KRAs and KRMs.

Business councils then review overall KRAs and KRMs for the KCAC with teams and ask for comments. Teams often request changes—frequently by making KRAs even more challenging—but changes are accepted only when backed by solid data. Teams then establish their KRAs and KRMs; team members follow suit with individual plans. The leadership council then reviews team performance goals and uses them to revise a preliminary annual operating plan. Teams and individuals have two interim performance assessments in the spring and the fall. Individuals meet with subteams from a performance appraisal review process council, while entire teams meet with a member of the leadership council. Both teams and individuals are responsible for monitoring and collecting information and comparing it against performance objectives. For individuals, as targets for improvement are worked into a personal development plan.

Finally, teams and individuals undergo formal performance appraisals at the end of the year. Individual appraisals include peer evaluations as well as key team results to arrive at an overall assessment that influences merit increases largely along the lines of Kodak's traditional compensation policies.

Results

As a nontraditional call center, the KCAC has posted some very nontraditional results. Within a year of the big team launch, employee productivity (as measured by calls handled per hour) has doubled. Accuracy levels in helping customers find the right solution have doubled as well. Productivity levels, in fact, are so high that further incremental gains will be difficult. Above all, new employees reach high levels of productivity far more quickly than in traditional call centers, thanks to the support the team gives new members. Employee turnover has fallen as well and now stands at about 7.5 percent—around half the industry average.

KCAC managers draw special satisfaction from changes in employees' perceptions of leadership effectiveness. As part of the leadership council's performance appraisal, employees evaluate the council using a thirty-question survey that rates management performance in five dimensions. Scores are compared against a database of responses from hundreds of U.S. organizations. The first time the leadership council was evaluated, its percentile rankings were average. While the leadership council did respectably on "challenging others" and "inspiring a shared vision," it ranked in the bottom third on "enabling others to act." A year later, the leadership council was near the top in all dimensions.

Management's true test, however, may come when both halves of KCAC are finally integrated. Most of the progress so far has been made in the former Copy Products Information Center. The old Kodak Information Center, the other half of the KCAC, still suffers from high employee turnover and its team system is still in its infancy. Some of the problems the CPIC overcame will undoubtedly arise again—especially the difficulty of balancing the need for a high-volume call center with the need for continuous improvement. Focusing on the next customer's call makes it very hard indeed for employees to contemplate long-term improvements. It was a challenge to break through that way of thinking, Michaelsen and Farukhi say, because it was such an ingrained part of call center culture. As part of the culture change effort, managers tried to lead by example—by taking training themselves, by modeling new behavior, and, perhaps most important, by relaxing performance standards so that no one was penalized for being less productive.

Indeed, the CPIC did suffer an initial dip in productivity and quality when the team system was introduced—the same productivity dip that other organizations have experienced as they made the transition to teams. The drop in productivity came about not only because so many things were new, but also because expectations had to be relaxed due to extra demands on employees' time. Although performance levels did rebound and eventually surpassed previous levels, the transition to teams meant learning many new skills and providing customer support for dozens of Kodak products, services, or business functions. "I couldn't have imagined how massive this undertaking would be five years ago," says Michaelsen. While progress has been impressive, the KCAC can't afford to rest on its laurels.

15

Using Total Quality Management as the Foundation for Teams

Milwaukee Mutual Insurance Company
Milwaukee, Wisconsin

Industry	Insurance
Union	None
Type of team implementation	Cross-functional and problem-solving teams and natural self-directed work teams. Some redesigned self-directed teams; employees went from functionally divided operations to teams that handle all policy rating, underwriting, and processing for geographic areas.
First teams started	1990
Employees	750
Percentage in teams	100 percent (of 500 headquarter employees)
Team size	8 to 10
Team responsibilities	Scheduling work assignments and vacations, evaluating peer performance, monitoring quality and productivity, improving the process, making business decisions in geographic territories served, hiring new

221

team members, representing teams in companywide policymaking bodies.

Organization-wide team responsibilities	Employee teams advise management on all human resource policies and many major business decisions.
Team leadership and governance	Most teams don't have formal leaders. Teams rotate important record keeping, measurement, and training functions. Most organizationwide personnel decisions are reached through ad hoc employee/management groups.
Leadership outside teams	Managers and supervisors have ceded many managerial duties to teams and now facilitate the team process, provide coaching, coordinate performance reviews, and handle disciplinary problems.
Team compensation	Base compensation is determined by a skill-based system with eight pay grades. Team bonuses are based on quality and performance measurements compiled by teams and corporate financial results. Individual merit increases are based on a peer performance review.
First-year team member training	Includes team meeting skills, quality and problem-solving techniques, team interaction skills, team and workplace design, business knowledge, cross-training.
Subsequent team member training	In the same areas.
First-year leadership training	In the same areas plus facilitation and coaching skills.

Subsequent leadership training	In the same areas.
How team members are selected	Job applicants are evaluated by the HR department, using job requirement and corporate culture profiles, and referred to area managers. Applicants are then interviewed separately or together by team and manager.
How team performance is evaluated	Each team has statistical baselines that cover operational efficiency, customer satisfaction, cost control, and team effectiveness. Team performance is evaluated against these measurements.
Team impact on organization	Teams contributed to a drop in loss ratios resulting in substantial savings, a 20 percent decrease in policy processing time, and vastly reduced operating costs. Employee turnover—once as high as 36 percent—has dropped significantly.
Key lessons	• Managers felt unprepared to assume coaching and facilitation roles because of lack of training. Many needed support systems to enable them to facilitate the team process. Concerns about employees' judgment made some managers anxious about "letting go."
	• Numerous changes introduced simultaneously can overwhelm employees. A measured rollout improves the efficiency of the team transformation process.

- Teams need realistic performance baselines. Unrealistic targets can unfairly penalize teams and hamper their development.

Background

Milwaukee Mutual Insurance, like many other regional independent insurance companies, faced a changing marketplace in the 1980s. Until that time, independent insurers like Milwaukee sold policies through local independent agencies. These agencies often handled insurance lines from several companies and directly serviced policyholders. This was how most Americans bought insurance until the 1980s when companies such as Allstate, Prudential, and State Farm began selling directly to consumers. These companies enjoyed many advantages—lower costs, larger marketing budgets, better control over customer service—and began winning a larger market share. As these giants dueled for market share, consumers learned to shop around for price and service. This required smaller independent firms, like Milwaukee Mutual Insurance, to adjust to the new demands of the insurance marketplace.

Change was not easy for 75-year-old Milwaukee, long used to slow, comfortable growth in its safe Midwestern market. The company decided to face the changes head on.

A management committee was formed in 1987 to devise a plan to strip away everything that didn't provide value to internal and external customers (its independent agencies) and didn't increase productivity and profitability. The committee cited four broad areas that needed improvement: operational efficiency, customer satisfaction, cost containment, and the technical proficiency of employees. From the start, the concept of the self-directed work team was seen as the engine that would drive improvements in the company. It was felt that empowerment and job ownership offered the greatest hope for meeting ambitious productivity and quality improvement objectives.

Teams

The four thrusts for improvement were called the TCCP process—for *Teams* (meeting goals and milestones through team efficiency), *CATS* (customer answers to surveys), *CURE* (containing unit/loss ratio expenses), and *Proficiency* (achieving operational excellence). Establishing measures to track improvements in each area became the responsibility of employees in all departments (thirty departments at the time). The TCCP process has remained at the heart of Milwaukee's continuous improvement efforts. TCCP measurements are compiled and posted monthly in each department and team area. They serve as the basis for team performance evaluations and several types of team bonuses.

The reorganization of Milwaukee's core insurance operations is the best example of how the TCCP process transformed the company. Traditionally insurance companies organized the process of selling and servicing policies around three major steps: policy rating, underwriting, and processing. As a result of this compartmentalization, employees in one department knew little about the concerns and realities of another. Once employees in one department provided their input, policies were shuttled off to the next department for further action. Frequently policies were sent back to a department for changes or additional information. This was the case at Milwaukee, too. And because policies often were in transit from one department to another, policies could not be found when an agent called with a question.

As a result, processing could drag on endlessly. Employees passed the buck or the blame on to others. Commercial raters complained about the quality of underwriting. Underwriters questioned the judgment of commercial raters. Everyone complained about the slow pace of the claims process. The biggest casualties were the customers—both the company's independent agents and the policyholders—because no one was completely in charge of meeting their needs.

Because of such drawbacks the company chartered insurance operations employees to design and install design teams at Milwaukee. The initial step was a meeting with representatives from each area in insurance operations—a human resource manager, who summarized changes being made in other insurance companies, and independent agents, who were invited to share their impressions on the quality and responsiveness of Milwaukee's service. Employees were given just one instruction: ignore the way the insurance operations were currently run and come up with a new approach.

An obvious but dramatic solution was found. Finding compartmentalization to be an insurmountable barrier to efficiency and customer service, structure was abandoned. The division was separated into a series of teams that provided complete service from underwriting policies to processing claims for customers in specific geographic areas. One team would serve agents in the northern half of Wisconsin, for example, another in the southern half of the state. Similar teams were created for other regions.

The change meant physically redesigning the way the unit worked. Separate departments were erased. Teams consisting of underwriters, raters, and processors were brought together into common work areas. The centralized filing system was eliminated; teams maintained their own customer files instead. Questions that once took so long to answer could be answered almost immediately. Policies no longer had to be shuttled back and forth between departments. And as the original departments were highly stratified, this required another big change. For instance, there were four levels of commercial raters. Under the new team structure, each commercial rater had to be able to handle all aspects of rating. Throughout the entire insurance operation, twelve levels of jobs were reduced to four.

Because self-management was one of the original goals of transformation, the six-to-eight-person teams assumed many managerial and administrative duties. For example, teams became responsible for scheduling work and vacations, timekeeping, maintaining relations with the agency's various territories, measuring and compiling the all-important TCCP indicators, and making decisions on many pricing and product mix policies in their territories (once the exclusive domain of senior management). In addition, mid-level management positions were reduced by about two-thirds as employees who directly supervised others were redeployed into team-based technical or marketing positions. The remnants of management were involved mainly in coordinating the performance review process, handling disciplinary problems, facilitating the team process, and coaching. Although morale problems eventually arose among these remaining managers—problems about their roles and usefulness to the organization—the process was not as wrenching at Milwaukee as at some companies.

Other departments, including human resources (HR) and MIS, adopted a similar cross-functional, internal customer focus. Hiring an employee, for example, once required managers to consult with an employment specialist, a compensation specialist, a training and development specialist, and often a benefits specialist. As part of Milwaukee's transformation, the HR department eliminated the specialist approach. Now each employee is assigned to an HR representative who serves as a single source of information and assistance on all HR questions, including hiring, benefits, and employee relations. The HR department still maintains a high degree of internal specialization, however, when it comes to complex questions about medical benefits, taxes, and other areas.

The MIS department became more efficient, too. Before the changes, only a handful of MIS personnel worked with end users to define application needs. This approach typically resulted in the need for extensive revisions once the new program was installed. Now MIS personnel are organized into teams based on functional projects. The teams include the end users of new systems, who work closely with the MIS personnel team to define specifications and develop an implementation plan. This approach demystifies the development process and produces results that are much closer to actual user needs.

A unique aspect of Milwaukee's transformation is the role employees play in making key decisions that affect everyone in the company. Employee teams have reshaped virtually every aspect of the company, and employees continue to have a dominant voice. Employee teams have simplified job grades and evaluations, eliminated most job titles, and devised new compensation and benefits plans. Similarly, insurance rate change procedures have been revised with input from employee teams. For example, Milwaukee's compensation plan was crafted with input from employees to combine skill-based pay with the security of a base compensation plan that reflects prevailing local wages. All nonmanagement employees fall into eight pay grades. The broad pay bands allow employees to earn regular wage increases as they acquire skills and experience without the necessity of being promoted to a higher-level position. Movement into higher quartiles of a pay grade reflects a team member's career path and the attainment of more advanced skills. Thus the system allows employees within the same job grade to earn as much as two and a half times the starting hourly rate for that grade.

Team bonuses are based on each team's reported TCCP results and corporate financial results. Positive movement in one or all areas measured by TCCPs (productivity, customer service, and cost containment) results in team bonuses of as much as 8 percent of individual pay.

Individual merit increases are based on a *consensus review process,* which consists of criteria established by employees, other team members, and their managers. The areas covered include team interaction skills, job effectiveness, and customer responsiveness. The combination of individual, peer, and manager input provides an effective methodology to assess results and fashion development plans.

The move to teams has changed the role of leadership at Milwaukee. In insurance operations and other areas, teams started out with leaders—usually knowledgeable and experienced employees suggested by managers. But as teams evolved, the assigned leader gave way to shared leadership. Now small teams with eight or fewer members operate without formal leaders. Larger teams of twelve to fourteen or more pose greater coordination and communication challenges and often choose a leader by consensus on a rotating basis. Although leaders receive no extra compensation for their added duties, teams devise various ways to offset the leader's workload.

Other roles are assigned by consensus—including timekeeping (a legal requirement) and tracking TCCP measures. Team members express their interest for one of these rotating assignments during the self-assessment component of their performance evaluations. The team then discusses the need and makes the assignment during a regular team meeting.

Managers and Leaders

The senior management staff continues to guide overall strategic planning at Milwaukee and has had little trouble delegating tactical decisions to teams. Senior managers gave up exclusive rights to evaluate employees, set compensation, and oversee daily work flow, but they felt more than compensated by the positive results. For mid-level managers, who still have supervisory and management duties, the new environment continues to evolve. The management span of control at Milwaukee was increased from roughly 1:6 to 1:20. The company's goal remains the same: to transform managers into facilitators who coach and advise teams, communicate the company's philosophy and business plan to employees, and provide training in quality principles and techniques.

If there was a missing element in the company's carefully planned team implementation, it was the lack of a system to help managers understand and adjust to their new roles. Extensive employee involvement in developing and implementing new programs helped cement their enthusiasm for the team system. But many managers needed more help making the transition to teams. Adjusting to the new consensus performance review process was especially difficult for some managers, who feared that employees would never learn enough about various responsibilities to evaluate others or worried that employees would inflate the reviews of their peers.

Milwaukee has only recently begun tackling the problem. One step has been the creation of an employee group on the challenge of "management empowerment." Moreover, a new management training program was devised to clarify the roles of managers in the company. Milwaukee is developing a series of modular training programs for managers, too, including feedback skills, communication skills, conflict resolution, and quality tools such as statistical process control.

Results

Milwaukee calls its team transformation a "complete package." It feels it has linked all the elements that create an organization responsive to meeting customer needs and expectations. The foundation of this responsiveness is the self-directed work team, which operates almost entirely on performance measures directly tied to continuous improvement in meeting customer needs.

The transformation has had important results for Milwaukee's bottom line. One of the key financial indicators for an insurance company is its loss ratio—the amount paid out in claims to policyholders versus the amount taken in premiums. Although the loss ratio is tied to factors largely beyond an insurance company's control, including natural disasters, it is also influenced by the types of policies and products a company sells in the regions it serves.

Before 1990, Milwaukee's loss ratio was higher than the industry average. Now Milwaukee has a much improved loss ratio—indeed, in recent years it has outperformed the insurance industry. The difference, the company feels, is that while senior executives establish broad strategic goals for product lines, teams now set their own goals for the product line mixes in their territories. The idea is that teams, closely attuned to the unique needs and characteristics of their customers, will be less likely to pursue unprofitable lines of business. The result has been a drop in the company's loss ratio. This represents not only substantial cash savings but also income for investment purposes, which is where the real profits lie in the insurance industry.

Initial improvements in the company's loss ratio, lower operating costs, overall profitability—all have contributed to an increase in shareholder value of more than 160 percent since 1991. Numerous small and large efficiencies contributed to the lower operating costs, including much faster

new-policy processing time (on-time delivery on new policies went from 70 percent to more than 90 percent during
the period, a tribute to increased communication of the
cross-functional teams in insurance operations) and sharply
reduced personnel costs. Lower personnel costs were due in
large part to a lower annual employee turnover rate, which
dropped from 36 percent in 1987 (versus an industry average of 25 percent) to 5.2 percent in 1992. This improvement
dramatically reduced recruiting and training costs. And as its
workforce became more stable and experienced, Milwaukee
also realized significant gains in productivity.

Today's employees have more reasons for wanting to
stick around—including the compensation and benefit programs they designed. But the biggest reason employees stay
at Milwaukee is the new corporate culture, which is contributing to the company's growing reputation as an attractive,
exciting place to work. In fact, Milwaukee employees report
fewer work-related stress and complaints than employees at
other companies. Use of the company's employee assistance
program is now 40 percent below the industry average.

Of course Milwaukee's transformation was not all smooth
sailing. Some people felt that too many changes were set into
motion simultaneously. At times the pace overwhelmed employees. The team transformation hit employees with a new
job grading scheme, a new benefits plan, and a variable compensation plan all at once—on top of introducing them to an
entirely new way of working as part of self-directed work
teams. Fortunately, the employees' role in planning and implementing the changes, communicating the reasons for
changes to their peers, and providing cross-training to other
team members helped ensure that the new system would
take root and eventually blossom. But mistakes were made
along the way that a more measured rollout might have
avoided. Some teams tied their own performance to measures that had not yet been tested, for example, while other

teams tried to rate their performance on financial indicators that proved to be beyond their control, making it difficult to participate in the variable compensation plan. Exception had to be made to ensure fairness.

Ultimately, the true test of Milwaukee's team system might not come for years, as the effects of a five-year strategic plan for growth are realized. The plan is the first in the company's history. Before, one-year operational plans were all senior executives could contemplate—the insurance business was too risky to look much beyond. Now, with employee teams contributing to product strategies and a stable, highly motivated, and flexible workforce, Milwaukee has been emboldened to develop a five-year vision of where it wants to go. Most important, it now understands how to get there.

16

How Empowered Teams Helped Win The Malcolm Baldrige Award

Eastman Chemical Company—Tennessee Eastman Division, Kingsport, Tennessee

Industry	Chemicals, fibers, and plastics
Union	None
Type of team implementation	Problem-solving teams, natural unit teams, and empowered self-directed work teams
First teams started	1983
Employees	8,370 at Tennessee Eastman (18,470 Eastman employees worldwide)
Percentage in teams	100 percent in natural unit teams, continuous improvement teams, and special project teams; 30 percent in self-directed work teams
Team size	4 to 30 (usually 10)
Team responsibilities	Mature self-directed work teams are responsible for meeting production requirements within agreed standards and expectations; assuring safety; operating, maintaining, and controlling equipment; improving processes; making work assignments; training team members; and improving individual and team effectiveness by providing peer feedback.

Organization-wide team responsibilities	Teams are used at various levels to guide the development of effective teams and support systems. Such teams include the Manufacturing Team, the Quality Council, the Compensation Steering Team, and the Apprenticeship Steering Team. Within each division and department, comparable steering teams are established as needed.
Team leadership and governance	Leadership is shared by team members serving as team coordinators. Coordinators ensure that teams meet requirements and objectives in safety, quality, production, maintenance, labor, housekeeping. Coordinators work within their own teams and as part of standing teams.
Leadership outside teams	Team managers (formerly supervisors) coach teams to build capability and set performance goals. Team managers guide team development and assist members in developing team and technical skills. They also help manage boundary issues and obtain resources for the teams. At some facilities, only one team manager per shift is needed, mainly for emergency management.
Team compensation	Work teams receive recognition for meeting minimum requirements for maturity. They also earn the right to participate in the six-level pay-for-applied-skills-and-knowledge system (PASK). Transition to this pay system may include a team-earned pay increase.
First-year team member training	About eighty hours of nontechnical training: understanding empowering work sys-

tems, the role of technicians in the system, and skills for coping with change; team interaction and communication skills; problem-solving skills; safety techniques.

Subsequent team member training

Members spend 8 to 10 percent of their time in team and technical-skills training—the amount is established in the annual operating plan. Technical training is provided largely by team members certified as trainers.

First-year leadership training

More than 100 hours of training: change management, interaction skills, questioning and counseling techniques, reinforcement techniques, receiving and giving feedback, developing and improving performance measures, and coaching. Some divisions offer managers a six-month, full-time training program to prepare for their new roles.

Subsequent leadership training

Team coaches spend 5 to 10 percent of their time in continuing development.

How team members are selected

At a recent plant start-up, candidates went through extensive screening and selection. This process was based on criteria determined by a job analysis to contribute success in empowered workteam environments. Tests, job simulations, and targeted behavioral interviews guided the hiring process. The process was so successful it is being considered for future use throughout the company.

How team performance is evaluated

Teams develop key result indicators (KRIs) that are tied to business unit objectives. KRIs are the primary means of monitoring team performance. Team maturity expectations ("rites of passage criteria") help teams develop plans to achieve fully functional, self-regulating status. Once teams have met the minimum expectations, they regularly review their progress to ensure they are continuing to meet those expectations and are improving effectiveness.

Team impact on organization

Eastman Chemical has become one of the country's most profitable chemical companies, thanks in part to productivity improvements at Tennessee Eastman. Many improvements are attributable to various team initiatives. Productivity has improved by 70 percent since the mid-1980s. In 1991, Eastman had the best earnings/sales ratios of the top fifteen U.S. chemical companies. Company surveys show that 75 percent of Tennessee Eastman's customers rate it the leader in customer satisfaction. In 1991, Tennessee Eastman was selected as one of the ten best plants in America by *IndustryWeek* magazine. In 1993, Eastman Chemical received the Malcolm Baldrige National Quality Award for the large manufacturing category.

Key lessons

- Commitment to change must be made throughout the organization. People must understand the need for change in order to become committed to it.

- Coaching effectiveness is critical in the transition to an empowered, self-directed team environment, making the development of coaches one of the keys to the process.

- High performance is possible when the work system is designed and managed using empowerment and quality management principles.

- Multiskill training and mastery of skills by technicians provide the specialization and flexibility needed to satisfy customers and other stakeholders.

Background

Tennessee Eastman Division, located in Kingsport, Tennessee, is the largest unit of the Eastman Chemical Company. Tennessee Eastman was established in 1920 to make raw materials for Kodak film. Today Tennessee Eastman occupies more than 3,700 acres and includes more than 470 buildings. Eastman Chemical's products include more than four hundred industrial chemicals, one basic fiber, and three basic types of plastics. Together Tennessee Eastman and Eastman Chemical employ more than thirteen thousand at Kingsport—making Eastman the largest employer in Tennessee.

Eastman's "quality management journey," as the company calls it, began in the late 1970s when worldwide competition began to increase. In previous decades Eastman had seen strong growth and a greatly expanded market share. But European and North American competitors began challenging its position. The competitors' main weapon was quality. The performance characteristics of Eastman's products weren't slipping, but the competition was getting better. When one of Eastman's largest industrial customers threatened to take its business elsewhere, it served as what Eastman termed a "wake-up call." With a core product line under pressure and major customers threatening to bolt, senior management decided to take action. In the past, cost reduction was used to justify capital improvements. Now Eastman would begin to spend on capital improvements designed to improve quality.

In 1980, Eastman established a broad goal: to be "first in quality." During the next several years, various changes were made—a sharper marketing focus on customer needs, the establishment of statistical process control systems to improve manufacturing processes, and the introduction of a companywide "customer emphasis" campaign to direct employee attention to the importance of internal and external customers. Results followed fairly quickly: customer complaints declined by 92 percent without large capital expenditures, manufacturing costs were reduced substantially, and market share grew. Subsequent steps included the creation of a quality management staff support group consisting of statisticians and industrial engineers and, in 1983, the formulation of an official Eastman Chemical quality policy. Training was beefed up in statistical process control, problem solving, and performance management. Quality improvement and problem-solving teams, some cross-functional, then were formed in all parts of the company to look at specific improvement opportunities.

A turning point for the company came in 1985. An in-depth study of Eastman's overall quality culture resulted in the "Eastman Way"—a document detailing how the company wanted to conduct its business and stressing the importance of integrity, trust, creativity, innovation, and teamwork. The document helped the company remove the barriers to teamwork. Around the same time, Eastman began moving its continuous quality improvement focus beyond manufacturing into all areas of the company. And it took the first steps toward establishing a quality management process that would be used by all employees—from operators to senior managers in all functions. Training was based on a "cascade" approach, starting with senior managers, who then trained division and department heads. Senior managers were among the first to use team principles in reaching decisions, setting an example they hoped would influence the rest of the organization.

The implementation of team management, or the quality management process, resulted in "natural unit" teams being formed within the existing organizational structure. The supervisor or manager became the team leader and the direct reports became the team members. These teams met once a week to share business information and work on continuous improvement activities for their work areas. When needed, cross-functional teams were formed to address issues beyond the natural unit team's boundary. The natural unit team system was eventually adopted companywide, and by the end of the decade nearly all Eastman employees were spending time every week in team activities.

The Move to Self-Directed Teams

The early success with natural and cross-functional teams, along with an interest in expanding the team concept, led to the formation of a steering team of senior managers from most functions to explore high-performance team concepts. The steering team made benchmarking visits to many plants with high-involvement work systems in place. And they learned a lot:

- Mature work teams could manage day-to-day tasks and meet requirements and commitments with very little direct supervision other than coaching.

- Team boundaries that are based on sound design principles result in teams with better business focus and a greater ability to prevent variances (and reduce their impact when they do occur). Using natural unit teams based on existing organizational boundaries was not the best team design for Eastman.
- Selection, training, development, and reward systems must be changed to support the new expectations of a team-based system.
- Extensive training is needed in technical, business and team skills.

The steering team also attended a four-day, on-site seminar conducted by quality guru W. Edwards Deming. He taught Eastman management that if performance is to improve, management must work on the system, not on the people.

The steering team then appointed several focus teams to study how the company's HR systems could be more aligned with a team culture. (Ultimately the company's HR systems were modified.) The steering team also sanctioned three "beachheads" in manufacturing to gain experience with high-performance work systems. Their initial work system designs resulted in much higher levels of multiskilling in technical and administrative tasks. New team boundaries were established that were far broader in scope and responsibility than previous natural unit team boundaries. Given the great expectations of work teams, however, the transition was time consuming and difficult.

By 1991 the steering team had achieved its goals. At that time the Tennessee Eastman Manufacturing Team, composed of Tennessee Eastman's president, vice presidents, and division-level managers, assumed responsibility for steering the implementation of the empowered work systems. To aid the implementation, the team developed key documents—an empowerment definition, a vision, and central features and implementation principles. Through Eastman's policy deployment and functional planning system, empowerment became a major area of management focus and in fact was incorporated into the improvement management process. Each division was responsible for developing plans to support this initiative using the key documents for guidance. During the regularly scheduled functional planning reviews at the Manufacturing Team meetings, divisions learned from one another's experiences. Although terminology and job titles differed slightly among divisions, all work systems were based on common principles and central features developed by the Manufacturing Team.

Today about 30 percent of Tennessee Eastman's employees have made the transition to self-directed, empowered work teams. A good example of the fundamental changes is illustrated by the filter tow manufacturing teams, which are responsible for spinning, processing, and packaging, as well as shift maintenance and various laboratory functions. In the old days, operators typically performed one or two functions within these areas and received all their direction from shift supervisors or foremen. Now teams of twelve to eighteen operators are responsible for the entire filter tow manufacturing process—and each team has the expertise needed to operate processes, prevent and correct variances at the source, and check for compliance with standard operating procedures. Team managers (formerly supervisors) assist teams as needed, but the teams make most of the decisions regarding their work output.

The filter tow team and teams like it use a system of coordinators to share leadership roles. These team coordinators typically are involved with administration, data keeping, and continuous improvement in about ten areas, including safety, quality, environment, production, maintenance, housekeeping, and training. As team leadership must be demonstrated in order to advance through Eastman's pay-for-skills system, team members are especially eager to volunteer for leadership roles.

All Tennessee Eastman teams meet regularly. For self-directed work teams, handoff meetings are held at the beginning of every shift. Some incoming coordinators arrive thirty minutes before a shift begins to meet with the coordinators from the outgoing shift to discuss the status and needs of the operation. The entire team arrives about ten minutes later, and coordinators summarize any quality problems or production changes that occurred during the preceding shift, explain the staffing needs for the current shift, and make work assignments. Apart from these daily shift handoff meetings, teams meet periodically to work on improvement projects and team development issues. Meanwhile, team production coordinators may meet with production planners to discuss schedules and special customer orders. Finally, coordinators from all shift teams in a unit meet regularly to resolve issues affecting their functional part of the business. The Standing Training Team, for example, made up of all team training coordinators, meets to improve standardization and training processes.

Tennessee Eastman's team success is due, in part, to its commitment to team development. Team members go through extensive training not only in technical skills but in business and team interaction skills as well. Training includes team meeting skills, communication skills, problem-solving processes, and creating high-performance work systems. These skills are required for advancement in the pay-for-applied-skills system.

Team Maturity and Compensation

Nearly all Tennessee Eastman teams must demonstrate their maturation as a "fully functioning empowered work team" by meeting a set of team maturity expectations. Once a team is certified as reaching this stage, its members are eligible to participate in a new compensation system that pays them for acquiring and applying skills and knowledge. Some areas of the company call this process, which can take many months, a team's "rites of passage."

For teams, certification requires building up the mix of technical skills called for in the team skill profile, which fixes the minimum and maximum number of skills each team needs. Teams must also acquire a basic understanding of the business, establish and use performance indicators linked to business success, and use peer feedback for improving individual and team effectiveness. Specific skills needed by coordinators are outlined in the team maturity expectations as well. For team members, certification means demonstrating basic knowledge in such areas as customer expectations, business conditions, safety, and housekeeping.

When a team feels it's ready for team maturity certification, it makes a presentation before a panel composed of team managers and coordinators from other teams. This panel uses a series of assessment forms to determine the team's readiness. If certification is achieved, the team must review its own maturity status at least once a year by comparing itself against a "fully functioning team" checklist. This list is divided into six broad areas that cover business objectives, quality standards, and performance goals.

Team certification qualifies team members to participate in Eastman's pay-for-applied-skills-and-knowledge (PASK) systems. The first two or three levels of the six-level system represent the core set of competencies expected of all team members—becoming skilled in two or three technical areas (such as mixing, refining, and finishing), for example, and demonstrating increasing competency in managing and business skills (such as quality, safety, computer, teamwork, business). To qualify for advancement in PASK, people must demonstrate they can apply the required skill and knowledge. Certified team trainers provide the majority of technical training.

By level three, team members also are expected to have served in at least two team leadership roles. By levels four and five, team members have gained additional technical skills and have begun specializing in a career path. In most business units, three or four career paths are open to team members—specialization in operations, maintenance, laboratory work, or training, for example. Whatever the choice, it must fit into the "skill profile" established for the team during the team design process. Thus the team has to authorize the training choices of team members. In addition, the employee must use the newly acquired skills at least 10 percent of the time. Most individual compensation is based on the employee's level in the PASK system.

Individual development plans are mandatory. Twice a year employees receive formal feedback on their performance from the team in sessions designed to help them increase their effectiveness. In addition to formal feedback sessions, team members may provide informal comments when a colleague is failing to meet the team's standards (for example, not wearing appropriate safety attire or not following standard procedures). If attempts to correct the behavior are unsuccessful, a team can ask for help from its team manager.

Supervisors and Managers

In areas of Tennessee Eastman where teams are starting to mature, the traditional role of supervisor has been eliminated—today many areas operate with 50 to 75 percent fewer first-level managers. Managers who remain in these areas have been renamed team managers or coaches and have assumed a dramatically different set of responsibilities—including helping new teams with the decision-making process, training coordinators to manage their roles, helping teams set performance goals, assisting teams in resolving personnel problems, and managing upsets and emergencies. Because the coordinator role rotates every twelve to eighteen months, training the coordinators is an ongoing process. If a team decides it is not maintaining its maturity status, the team manager will work with it to take corrective action. All teams have a team manager who helps them continually improve their capability and performance. Even the best teams benefit from coaching.

Results

Eastman's productivity has been rising steadily for years. Only the fifteenth largest chemical company in the United States at the end of 1991, Eastman was fifth in earnings and the leader in earnings as a percentage of sales. And Tennessee Eastman, which has increased productivity by nearly 70 percent since it first started major internal changes in the early 1980s, certainly can take some credit for Eastman's performance. Significantly, the quality concerns that shook the company out of its complacency are a distant memory. First-pass yields have continually improved each year and now stand at a record high.

In 1988, Tennessee Eastman applied for the first Malcolm Baldrige National Quality Award and received a site visit as part of the final selection process. Since then the company has used Baldrige criteria as a self-assessment tool. In 1993, Eastman Chemical Company again applied for the award and it was recognized as the winner of the large manufacturing category. Most important, surveys show that more than 70 percent of Eastman's 4,500 customers rate it number one among all chemical companies with which they do business.

While self-directed work teams have yet to be implemented in all areas of Tennessee Eastman, years of experimentation with special process improvement teams, natural unit teams, and various quality management approaches have built a strong foundation. Perhaps Tennessee Eastman's biggest lesson from the experience is that empowered work teams have organizational and team boundaries that are simply better suited for variance prevention, cost reduction, and other continuous improvements.

Teams also have taught the company some important lessons about change. First among them is that change begins with management. Managers must make a compelling case for change and articulate an exciting vision for the future. They must communicate the message that change is tough and takes time, patience, and persistence. The importance of this behavior extends to all levels of management, especially first-line management. Accepting responsibility can be difficult for operators who are accustomed to following orders, and employees invariably learn and develop at different rates. Without the right coach, equipped with the right skills, these barriers to team development might never be overcome. From the beginning Tennessee Eastman recognized the importance of guiding shift supervisors away from their traditional directing and controlling roles and toward guiding and coaching roles.

A second important change lesson is that team implementations must include a process for continual improvement—like all Eastman processes—which they call *organizational renewal*. As part of the renewal process, team members meet to talk about what's going well and to identify areas for improvement. One finding was the need to better balance mastery of a particular skill area with the need for flexibility through cross-training. Through Eastman's renewal process, empowered work systems continue to improve adaptability, capability, and performance.

17

The Baldrige and Beyond: Sustaining Systemwide Reengineering and Empowerment

Texas Instruments—Defense System and Electronics Group Dallas, Texas

Industry	Defense electronics
Union	None
Type of team implementation	Self-directed natural and redesigned teams phased in at six facilities over several years; extensive use of cross-functional teams to work on process improvements
First teams started	Early 1980s
Employees	13,000
Percentage in teams	Approaching 100 percent
Team size	10
Team responsibilities	Depending on the type and maturity of teams, responsibilities include determining workplace design, planning work schedules, reducing costs, determining and deploying training needs, scheduling vacations and overtime, interfacing with other teams to eliminate production bottlenecks and implement new processes, selecting

new team members, and evaluating team members. Teams also are responsible for meeting quality and production goals and, in some cases, working with suppliers on quality issues.

Organization-wide team responsibilities

New product planning and design through multifunctional project teams.

Team leadership and governance

Ranges from shared leadership to distributed leadership. Most teams periodically rotate leadership in such areas as tracking safety and quality data and attendance and coordinating training and communication with other teams. Many teams do not officially have leaders, but most rotate responsibilities for overall team coordination.

Leadership outside teams

The number of frontline supervisors has been greatly reduced and their role has become one of facilitation. Often production, manufacturing, and quality engineers assume facilitation responsibilities. Facilitators might work with as many as six teams.

Team compensation

Pilot programs at three facilities include a pay-for-performance system that rewards teams for meeting business goals and a pay-for-knowledge system that encourages employees to develop skills related to team needs.

First-year team member training

About forty hours: team meeting skills, quality tools, problem-solving techniques.

Subsequent team member training	An additional forty hours: team interaction skills, general business knowledge, team and workplace design.
First-year leadership training	About forty hours: team meeting skills, quality tools and problem-solving techniques, team and workplace design, facilitation and coaching skills.
Subsequent leadership training	An additional forty hours in the same areas plus training skills.
How team members are selected	As few outside workers have been hired in recent years, most new team members come from within the company. Most teams interview proposed members. Candidates from outside the company typically are screened by DSEG's human resources department and then interviewed by team members.
How team performance is evaluated	Teams set goals in conjunction with facilitators, managers, and other teams because many team goals have to be closely coordinated with other teams in a business unit. Improving quality, reducing costs, and meeting schedules have become the key team goals—along with a "stretch" goal tied to a business unit need such as reducing cycle time. Most teams also have special project goals.
Team impact on organization	DSEG has reduced its workforce by approximately 40 percent since the beginning of the decade, but revenues per employee have increased and output has

remained stable. The unit believes the results can be attributed largely to the impact of teams. As teams vary widely by stages of development, few data are available for many. Mature teams, however, have reduced costs by as much as 50 percent and improved on-time deliveries to customers tenfold. In 1992, DSEG received the Malcolm Baldrige National Quality Award.

Key lessons

- Some early teams were rushed into existence without adequate process redesign. A lack of clear objectives, as well as old-style job boundaries and support systems, limited team effectiveness. More effort was needed to make sure all employees understood the meaning of empowerment.

- The huge implications of adopting an organizationwide, empowered team design were difficult for some parts of the organization to grasp. Success came after everyone understood that all systems and processes had to be reengineered and all parts of the organization needed to make a genuine commitment to change.

Background

Texas Instruments' Defense System and Electronics Group (DSEG) has frequently pioneered quality management techniques. Its experiences were similar to other companies on the cutting edge of change: some innovations worked well enough to become permanent; others were abandoned as just another idea that sounds good in theory but proves difficult in practice.

Teams are nothing new at DSEG. Almost all its employees (13,000 out of Texas Instruments' 60,000) participate in some type of problem-solving or project team. Some engineers serve on as many as six teams. The team focus took root in the mid-1980s as DSEG started applying quality management techniques that would eventually fall under the rubric of total quality management. By the end of the decade DSEG had specified three elements—customer focus, employee involvement, and continuous improvement—as the cornerstones of its business strategy.

Until the end of the decade, most teams at DSEG were set up to handle a project or problem and then disband once the goal was accomplished. This approach served the company well during the 1980s and helped propel it to the top of the defense electronics business. In the late 1980s several simultaneous processes began to pull the company in the direction of self-directed process teams. Top management began championing the use of criteria from the Malcolm Baldrige National Quality Award as self-assessment tools and internal benchmarks. Empowerment and employee responsibility were increased so that everyone could have a role in meeting the company's objectives. At the same time, the move to convert as many processes as possible to just-in-time manufacturing accelerated.

Meanwhile, the defense industry's boom years were coming to an end. Downsizing, paring non-value-added process steps, improving productivity, and speeding up cycle time for new products became important priorities. Most significantly, pilot programs in process teams, or work cells, suggested some clear options for making breakthroughs in productivity and quality. The development of process teams was largely a grass-roots effort undertaken by site and business unit managers to meet the demands of just-in-time manufacturing processes that were sweeping through the company.

Some of DSEG's earliest successes in self-directed teams occurred at its Denison plant near Dallas. In one pilot program, twenty-five of Denison's three hundred employees were organized in teams and gradually given increasing responsibility for their work schedules, production costs, and relations with internal Texas Instruments customers. Support functions and supervision were reduced as teams matured and assumed these responsibilities. The results, in terms of on-time delivery and cost reduction, far surpassed anything traditionally managed work groups had achieved, including a 53 percent drop in costs for expensive components for a tank thermal siting system.

Top management noticed the results. The Denison experience contributed to the decision in 1991 to form a support group called the High-Performing Organizations Development unit. The idea was to promote the development of empowered teams in other parts of the organization and create a unified team and empowerment strategy that would guide the company through the turbulent 1990s. Steve Leven, DSEG's human resource manager, lobbied hard to create the unit. From his research and visits to other organizations using self-directed teams he became convinced of their benefits. Hank Hayes, DSEG's president, also recognized that self-directed process teams could be a powerful tool.

A DSEG road map was developed to guide the teaming and empowerment. Some facilities already were thriving with teams; others were still traditionally managed. Therefore, each business set its own pace. Leadership came from management teams within business units composed of a cross section of managers from functional areas including quality, engineering, manufacturing, tooling, human resources, finance, and others. Their charter was to create the boundaries, define the objectives, and articulate a vision to move business units toward empowered team-based organizations.

The objective of all such efforts, says Fred Eintracht, a former site manager at Denison and now head of the High-Performing Organizations Development unit, was to implement a shift in philosophy that had in fact been developing for years. The shift involved moving away from directing business performance through conventional management techniques to achieving business performance through employee "ownership" of complete products or processes. Part of that shift included replacing DSEG's management structure with a decentralized form of decision making that pushes responsibility down to those who are performing the work. "We started to notice that when people took ownership of results good things started to happen," says Eintracht. More important, Eintracht says, DSEG realized that just creating teams is not nearly enough. The entire organization has to be designed around what Eintracht calls "the empowerment teaming philosophy"—which means that leadership, organizational design, work design, and support systems must all be aligned.

Design teams were appointed to redesign DSEG's work processes. Design team members include quality managers and engineers, facilitators (formerly called line managers or supervisors), assemblers, and other employees involved in manufacturing. Early teams at Texas Instruments had been limited mostly to employees performing similar duties within single functions. Later design teams focused on broad, multiskilled teams responsible for a product from start to finish.

At DSEG's McKinney plant north of Dallas, for example, the printed wiring board shop used to be organized by functions, with groups of single-function employees partitioned by steps in the production process. After benchmarking similar operations in other companies and analyzing the work flow at McKinney, a design team determined that multifunctional teams could achieve breakthrough performance. The training plan created for the new teams carefully considered individual cross-training needs and the transfer of supervisory and support groups tasks to teams. Within six months of team start-up in the printed wiring board shop, dramatic results were realized—including a 50 percent reduction in cycle time, a 60 percent reduction in scrap, and a 30 percent improvement in productivity. Success at McKinney helped set the stage for similar efforts in other parts of the company.

Teams Today

While the pace of change has varied, in several DSEG production areas separate assembly, testing, and quality control jobs have been consolidated into one and several management layers have been eliminated. Cross-functional integrated product development teams also have taken deep root. In these teams, specialists in planning, engineering, quality control, manufacturing, and other areas share responsibility for developing and producing new products. This represents a dramatic change from the traditional functional approach.

One factor in particular has influenced the pace of empowered team development: the level of trust established within certain business units. Where relations between managers and employees are open and cooperative, empowerment has developed rapidly. Where relations lack trust, empowerment has stalled. Unfortunately, such divisive issues typically develop over long periods of time and are not easily resolved.

The team system in many areas of DSEG has had several years to mature. Typically a production team meets at the beginning of each shift to determine resource availability, study the day's production schedule, and assign responsibilities. Decisions are made about needed resources or overtime. Because many teams depend on other teams, an engineer or a member of another team often is present, and interteam issues, such as production bottlenecks or new processes, might be high on the agenda. Engineers might serve as a resource to six or more teams—sometimes clustered in what DSEG calls "responsibility centers." Depending on their needs, teams share personnel with other teams. Teams are largely responsible for resolving quality issues, which can involve visits to suppliers experiencing quality problems to track down root causes.

DSEG's most successful teams use an informal shared-management system in which members rotate responsibilities for tracking data in such areas as production, training, safety, quality, and communications. Few teams have a team leader, but some have a team coordinator who handles administration and logistics, including setting up meetings.

Training

As teams spread throughout the organization, training has become a priority at DSEG. The organization's goal is to increase the minimum training for team members each year. Much of the early training focuses on team-building skills and cross-training to support team flexibility and develop core team skills. Much of the later training is the team's responsibility. Support personnel and team facilitators are responsible for transferring their technical or process knowledge to teams. Because teams are assuming increasing responsibility for meeting customer expectations, controlling costs, scheduling, and handling other general business issues, a new priority is business knowledge training. Managers and facilitators play a key role in this training.

Compensation and Performance

To support team development, DSEG is considering changes in its compensation system. Pilot programs at three sites use a dual system that includes a pay-for-performance component to reward teams for meeting business goals and a pay-for-knowledge component that encourages continual learning among individual team members.

The pay-for-performance component includes goals related to quality, costs, and on-time performance as well as more ambitious stretch goals worked out between teams and management. The pay-for-knowledge component includes basic "knowledge blocks" related to effective team interaction and understanding the business process as well as advanced skills in such areas as leadership, administration, and problem solving. The team decides what skills people need to meet its objectives. Team members are certified for achieving new skill levels, usually after demonstrating proficiency on the job. The system was designed to ensure that team goals and individual skill development are linked. Otherwise, a pay-for-knowledge system alone might encourage learning unrelated to actual team needs—an expensive but common mistake that does little to improve team productivity.

Evaluating employees' performance is a team-driven process and is not linked to the compensation system in order to encourage objective input from team members during peer evaluations. Until 1993, team members were evaluated by their supervisors (now called facilitators). With the new peer review system, team members evaluate their coworkers, other teams they work closely with, and internal customers and suppliers. Evaluations focus on each employee's contributions to the team and any training and development that may be lacking. Numerical performance ratings (one equals "outstanding," two equals "above average," and so forth) were eliminated. Team members now focus on such issues as how well employees are expanding and upgrading their skill levels to support the team, how well they handle team administrative duties, and how well they communicate and listen during team meetings.

In the pilot program, individual evaluations were not tied to pay increases because linking the two might make it difficult for those involved in the peer appraisal to be objective. Ultimately, however, the system is intended to reinforce the idea that individual contributions affect team performance, which in turn affects pay. Thus individual performance is rewarded, but only within the context of the team environment.

Managers and Leaders

While many DSEG employees have had experience with teams of one kind or another, managers and leaders find themselves moving into areas where there are few precedents. Many of the old job classifications and functional units nominally remain, but they offer few guides to behavior because most managers find themselves working much differently than they did a few years ago. Duties are much broader and boundaries more permeable. Previous career paths have disappeared to be replaced by what DSEG calls "criteria for success" in a new, flatter organization. Titles are discouraged. Above all, managers are asked to transfer both their expertise and authority to teams—a task they must be willing to do and understand how to do.

The shift from controlling to "partnering," a process that still contains many unknowns, is proving to be a big challenge. First-line supervisors have been among the most affected. Total employment is down by more than 40 percent since the beginning of the decade because of defense budget cutbacks and productivity gains. Management layers also have shrunk—from eight a few years ago to four or five now depending on the business unit. The span of management control has roughly doubled. Remaining supervisors, or facilitators, have rapidly assumed roles of coaches and change agents in the transfer of knowledge and skills to teams. Many former supervisory tasks have been transferred to production, quality, and other engineers who serve as resources to many teams. As the transition continues and DSEG pushes responsibility down through the organization, even fewer supervisors and managers will be needed to operate in their traditional roles.

Use of the Baldrige Award criteria has focused management on removing obstacles to further team development rather than on day-to-day financial indicators. This shift demands much closer attention to the relationships between work processes and long-term strategy—primarily through middle and upper-level management reengineering teams in six key areas, with about a dozen other teams working on lower-level processes. DSEG might need fewer managers, but its need for problem solvers has never been greater.

Results

DSEG is leaner and more productive than it was at the beginning of the 1990s. Revenues per employee have increased substantially. New capital investments and automation have contributed to much of the productivity gains, but some of the most spectacular improvements have been noted in areas where the team transformation has advanced the farthest. In DSEG's microwave board unit, for example, 120 employees accomplish the same amount of work it took 190 employees during the unit's employment peak—and they do it in 40 percent less time. Meanwhile, unit managers have been reduced from fourteen to two. The Denison plant has reduced costs by more than 50 percent in some product areas. A few miles away at DSEG's McKinney operation, an internal customer return rate of 3 percent was reduced to 0.03 percent.

DSEG is not ready to judge the team transformation a complete success. Too much work remains. "This is the way we're going to run our business—as a team-based organization that stresses empowerment," Fred Eintracht says. "Unlike organizations that think teaming is only applicable to certain levels, we're looking at every aspect of the business, from production to engineering to new product development to leadership." This is a more difficult and in some ways more painful process, Eintracht adds, and it will take time.

DSEG's approach is based on lessons it learned through the latter half of the 1980s and early 1990s—and continues to learn as the team process unfolds. Early on, management, enamored with the promises of total quality management, pushed hard for the creation of teams. As a result, teams were created with little understanding of how job boundaries and support systems would have to change to increase the new teams' chances of success. Cast free from traditional supervision, lacking adequate training, clear objectives, and understanding of customer needs, and typically doing the same narrowly focused work as before, early teams were often ineffectual. As these teams struggled for a purpose, some managers who resisted the transition to teams could point to problems to justify their skepticism. From that experience emerged a key lesson: all employees, from assemblers to senior executives, must understand the concepts and realities of empowerment before teams can succeed. And no team effort should be undertaken without a strong plan that aligns leadership, work design, and the support system.

DSEG also had to work with existing facilities—which meant that the employees in place when the team transformation began were not hired for their flexibility and learning ability. Eintracht admits, "We just wanted them to sit at a station and perform a task." Experience showed that to transform such a workforce required substantial organizationwide training—and the budgets to match it at a time when financial pressures were fierce.

Maybe the biggest eye-opener for DSEG was the fact that empowered teams required major changes in nearly all the company's systems, policies, and practices. It is nearly impossible to impose a team structure on a traditional hierarchical organization. After early stumbles, DSEG learned that most systems and practices in the organization would have to be refashioned. It took time for some parts of the organization to realize the implications.

18

The Language of Teams
Can Be Spoken Anywhere

Texas Instruments Malaysia
Kuala Lumpur, Malaysia

Industry	Electronics
Union	None
Type of team implementation	Self-managed natural work teams introduced over a period of years through programs that gave operators increasing control over equipment and processes
First teams started	1989
Employees	3,000
Percentage in teams	100 percent
Team size	6 to 18
Team responsibilities	Team responsibilities fall into two main categories: maintenance (equipment maintenance and daily administrative activities such as managing cost, delivery, safety, housekeeping, equipment setup, tracking attendance, and assigning daily duties and responsibilities) and customer satisfaction. For the second category, teams carry out special problem-solving or ongoing process improvement activities.

Organization-wide team responsibilities	Except for a plantwide environmental safety and industrial hygiene team, no formal systems have been set up to include operator teams in plantwide activities.
Team leadership and governance	Teams may have up to four coordinator positions that are rotated among members, typically every six months. Coordinators handle many responsibilities: tracking attendance, making team assignments, reassigning members to other teams, maintaining inventory levels, housekeeping, and monitoring downtime, cycle time, and production quality.
Leadership outside teams	Supervisors have been retrained as facilitators and are responsible for overseeing up to twelve teams. TIM has one facilitator to every two hundred employees.
Team compensation	No special team compensation. Problem-solving and process improvement teams are rewarded with gift certificates. A continuous improvement reward program was recently introduced.
First-year team member training	More than forty hours: team meeting skills, quality tools, problem-solving techniques, cross-training skills, peer appraisal skills.
Subsequent team member training	More than forty hours: team interaction skills, team and workplace design, facilitation and coaching, cross-training skills.
First-year leadership training	More than a hundred hours: team meeting skills, quality tools, problem-solving techniques, decision-making techniques, cross-training skills.

Subsequent leadership training	More than a hundred hours: team interaction skills, team and workplace design, facilitation and coaching, cross-training skills.
How team members are selected	By the HR department. Applicants are tested in basic math and English.
How team performance is evaluated	Teams keep statistics on their productivity, cycle time, costs, and quality.
Team impact on organization	Cycle time has been reduced by 50 percent for most products during the past several years. Output has more than doubled even though the workforce has remained stable. Mean time between failures on essential equipment has increased by a factor of four. Savings for problem-solving team averages $10,000 annually. Quality has become outstanding. Shipments to Japan have increased from zero in 1985 to 35 percent of output today.
Key lessons	• TIM credits standardization of documentation and methodologies for smoothing the transfer of skills and knowledge to team members. • Some companies in Asia feel that technology and automation reduce the need for "people skills" training. TIM says the opposite is true. Meeting, communication, and other interpersonal skills training has proved vital. • Training team members in problem-solving and decision-making skills, ac-

complished over a period of years, was
another cornerstone of team development. It was also instrumental in reducing the amount of supervision
needed.

- Communication from management on
business issues and conditions, unusual for an Asian company, helped employees understand the rationale for
teams. TIM's general manager speaks
to all employees in small groups
monthly.

Background

Texas Instruments Malaysia (TIM) was formed more than
twenty years ago in Kuala Lumpur, Malaysia's sprawling capital, to serve growing regional and global demand for integrated circuits for computers and related products. Today
TIM has more than three thousand employees. Its growth has
paralleled Malaysia's emergence as a powerhouse in the
semiconductor business. Indeed, Malaysia itself is one of the
most remarkable success stories of the past decade among
emerging industrialized nations. Islam is the country's main
religion. Nearly 90 percent of TIM's production employees
are Muslim women; they observe the Muslim stricture to
cover their heads, and they dress in bright, intricately
stitched local fashion, making TIM's production areas in-
congruously colorful.

Though TIM is thousands of miles from Texas Instruments' Dallas home base, local managers are determined to
keep pace with the parent company's tradition of workplace
innovation. TIM has played largely by its own rules, however.

Working without formal steering and design committees, TIM has crafted work systems that can match any facility in the world for flexible, high-volume integrated circuit production. Moreover, TIM's success has defied the belief (held by Asian and Western managers alike) that hierarchical, traditional Asian cultures, with their automatic deference to authority figures, are opposed to empowered team environments.

In the early 1980s, when new ideas for organizing and managing work were rippling through Texas Instruments' entire worldwide organization, TIM installed quality circles and problem-solving teams, with modest successes in cost savings and productivity improvements. Jerry W. Lee, the American who served as TIM's country managing director until 1993, Mohd. Azmi Abdullah, Texas Instruments' Asian training and education manager, and other senior managers were especially influenced by the emerging literature on total quality management. Like managers everywhere, they became convinced that productivity and quality could be improved by giving employees control of their jobs and the information needed to make intelligent decisions. The goal, says Azmi Abdullah, was "empowering our employees on a broad scale." While that goal was not unusual by Texas Instruments' standards, it represented uncharted territory for operations in Southeast Asia.

For TIM, the "operator self-control" principles of quality guru Joseph Juran provided a framework for the process of employee empowerment. Juran advocated giving employees a combination of technical job knowledge plus training in statistical process control, problem solving, and other quality tools. Under Juran's system, operators would regulate their own quality and be empowered to shut down their machines when quality specifications were out of variance—something only quality control inspectors were allowed to do in the past. Juran's ideas helped TIM reduce special quality control personnel while improving process yields and quality. Eventually TIM began operating largely by "management by exception." This meant that with processes controlled by operators, the managers and supervisors intervened in daily production only for exceptional events that fell outside operators' decision-making guidelines. The operator self-control concept focused on a narrow range of decision-making opportunities, however, and ultimately fell short of TIM's empowerment goals.

In 1989 and 1990, TIM took another step forward—a pilot program in team self-management. By this time operators had been trained to perform many equipment maintenance routines as part of a "total productive maintenance" program borrowed from Japan. In addition, all levels of the organization had been trained to analyze the causes of problems in terms of internal and external "customer satisfaction drivers," such as quality, cost, delivery, and service. TIM's new self-managed work teams were a home-brewed version of the redesigns that many U.S. companies were undertaking. There were no formal steering or design committees. Team guidelines were drafted by Azmi Abdullah, regional training and education manager Subramaniam Applanaidu, and other managers. The guidelines called for two types of self-managed work team activities. The first, maintenance activities, included equipment maintenance, daily administrative activities (managing cost, delivery, safety, housekeeping, equipment setup, attendance, and other areas), and managing customer satisfaction drivers related to team activity. The second category, improvement activities, encompassed special project and process improvement teams. These teams within teams met regularly on projects they chose themselves or projects assigned by managers.

As teams developed, TIM's training staff added eight new trainers (former supervisors) in anticipation of expanded training needs, especially in coaching and team facilitation skills. Finally, to recognize the magnitude of the change and the support of top management, the self-managed work team concept became part of the plant's official objectives.

TIM Teams

Today all TIM's production employees are organized in self-managed work teams, although teams vary widely in their stages of maturity. About half of TIM's teams are responsible for most factors related to their work inputs and outputs—dealing with internal suppliers, monitoring productivity and quality, assigning work within teams, and scheduling vacations. A typical twelve-person team might have as many as four coordinators, each with multiple responsibilities (unlike many shared leadership systems in which coordinators have one responsibility at a time). TIM's coordinators are responsible for tracking attendance, making team assignments, reassigning team members to other teams (if machines are down or another team is short staffed), maintaining inventory levels, housekeeping, and monitoring downtime, cycle time, and production quality. Coordinator spots are rotated among team members according to the team's own schedule, typically once a year. Usually team coordinators meet once a day midway through a shift, review team charts on attendance and productivity, and determine if team members need help in various areas. They also note how the equipment is performing and determine what information to leave for the next shift.

Job assignments are rotated within teams, as well, but because the automated semiconductor fabricating equipment is so complex, most team members hold specific jobs for at least one year. Usually the team member responsible for a specific job trains the next member slated to hold that job.

TIM's appraisal system includes self-assessment and peer

evaluations. The process is coordinated by a facilitator who collects evaluations and discusses them with the employee. If performance standards are met, team members receive an automatic merit increase. TIM also uses informal incentives, such as gift certificates and lunches, to recognize team achievement. The ultimate achievement for a TIM team is to win a "best team" competition, a popular pursuit in Southeast Asia in recent years.

Managers and Leaders

The number of supervisors at TIM has dwindled from eighty in 1984 to eight "facilitators" in 1993. Each facilitator coaches six to twelve teams, about two hundred employees.

The transformation to teams was accomplished with little confusion or anxiety among TIM's frontline managers. No one lost their jobs during the process. Instead, many supervisors were redeployed into other functions, primarily training. When they were removed from active supervision roles, for example, facilitators helped teams develop matrices of the tasks and assignments for which teams would be responsible—in effect systematizing their experiences and transferring this knowledge to teams. Also helpful in the transition was the fact that top managers had long been effective communicators, especially former country managing director Jerry Lee, who was respected by the Malaysian workforce.

By most standards TIM's management structure is highly unusual. Facilitators report to process management teams of four mid-level managers who oversee specific processes within the plant, ranging from assembly to testing. Process management teams report to the quality steering team, which includes the fifteen senior managers at the plant and Lee. The structure is based on a high degree of consensus; there are few skirmishes over departmental turf or managerial rights and responsibilities. The structure serves TIM well because manufacturing is based on very high production volumes but short production runs. Because specifications change so rapidly in the semiconductor business, staying competitive means being able to turn on a dime—an art that TIM seems to have mastered.

Results

Texas Instruments Malaysia has become one of the most productive Texas Instruments facilities—and perhaps a model for the rapidly developing high-tech industries of Southeast Asia. Thanks both to automation and to TIM's team system, cycle time has steadily declined in recent years and now stands at about half 1980-1990 levels. Quality has improved, as well, with defects plunging to an extremely low level. Other measures are equally impressive. Indeed, quality is high enough at TIM to make it a prime exporter to Japan, where component standards are among the most stringent in the world.

TIM credits several things for its smooth transition to teams. Standardization of documentation and methodologies was essential to the transfer of skills and knowledge to team members. This process took time, however, because much of this information was locked in the heads of supervisors and engineers, who were accustomed to telling operators what to do instead of teaching them. TIM also believes training and orientation for supervisors helped with the transition. This way supervisors clearly understood and were committed to their new roles in a team-based environment—an essential first step on the path to teams.

Training team members in problem-solving skills and quality tools was another cornerstone of team development. It also helped gradually reduce the amount of supervision needed. TIM made sure that operators had the training and confidence to solve problems on their own before placing them in teams. As the next step in operator training, TIM plans to introduce more business management education to team members as they become more involved in product planning and marketing.

The world is beginning to notice TIM. Visitors have included delegations from other companies in the semiconductor industry as well as professors and students from business schools ranging from the University of Maryland to the University of Iceland. TIM is spreading its message on its own, too. Current country managing director James Lamm has extensively toured Asia. His message: Empowerment and self-managed teams can work as effectively in Asia as anywhere—perhaps even more so when coupled with the unique cultural strengths of Southeast Asian countries.

19

Aligning Systems to Keep Teams on the High-Performance Track

Westinghouse Electronic Assembly Plant
College Station, Texas

Industry	Defense and commercial electronics
Union	None
Type of team implementation	Natural and redesigned multifunctional, self-directed work teams; cross-functional teams
First teams started	1983
Employees	185
Percentage in teams	100 percent
Team size	8 to 20 (most have 14)
Team responsibilities	Budgeting materials and expenses; monitoring safety; handling quality assurance; making daily work assignments; meeting production goals; scheduling shifts, vacations, and some overtime; coaching and cross-training.
Organization-wide team responsibilities	Teams typically play a role in decisions affecting major human resources and process systems. Employee-led teams have

analyzed and recommended changes in performance evaluation and compensation systems.

Team leadership and governance

Teams have officers who monitor production, budgets, quality, safety, and other areas and provide information to team members. Officers are volunteers and rotate every six months to a year. Decisions about work and vacation scheduling are usually made by consensus.

Leadership outside teams

Team advisers have replaced the traditional supervisory positions. Usually technical specialists, they facilitate team interaction, help teams with resources and training needs, and evaluate members' performance. Advisers work with up to three teams.

Team compensation

Team members are salaried and fall within the same broad pay category except for employees with highly technical skills. There are no individual or team bonuses, but a reward system awards bonuses to all employees when certain plantwide goals are met.

First-year team member training

180 hours: technical skills, team meeting skills and interaction skills, interviewing, cross-training, product and process skills.

Subsequent team member training

60 hours: overall business knowledge, meeting skills, quality tools and problem-solving techniques, team interaction skills, interviewing, facilitation and coaching, cross-training.

First-year leadership training	180 hours: team meeting and team inter-action skills, workplace design, interview-ing skills, facilitation and coaching skills, cross-training, product and process skills.
Subsequent leadership training	Sixty hours: overall business knowledge, meeting skills, quality tools and problem-solving techniques, team interaction skills, workplace design, interviewing skills, facil-itation and coaching, cross-training.
How team members are selected	Initially a comprehensive selection system included interviews of applicants by team members. Now a targeted selection system involves only team advisers, managers, and HR personnel. Applicants are assessed on desired behavioral dimensions.
How team performance is evaluated	Team advisers help teams set and meet production and quality goals. Team mem-bers are evaluated by peers and team advis-ers, but the adviser's evaluations have the greatest weight.
Team impact on organization	Although there has been tremendous tur-moil in the defense industry, costs at EAP have fallen by about 60 percent since the mid-1980s and cycle time for some prod-ucts has been reduced from twelve weeks to less than two. During the same period, work in process has been sharply reduced and rework requirements have been cut in half.
Key lessons	• Members' involvement in interviewing and selection and peer evaluations had to be scaled back because of unex-

pectedly high production demands
and an unanticipated turnover rate.
Employees with little job experience
have had an especially difficult time
with peer evaluations.

- A pay-for-knowledge-and-skills system
  hampered the development of stable,
  long-term teams because it encouraged employees to outgrow their
  teams.

- Designing systems that encourage
  long-term team stability and providing
  teams with vast information about
  business costs and requirements has
  created flexible teams able to respond
  quickly to fast-changing production
  requirements.

Background

When Westinghouse's Electronic Assembly Plant (EAP)
opened in College Station, Texas, in 1983, it represented the
best efforts of one of America's leading research-driven organizations to merge advanced technology with the latest
workplace design. Everything about EAP was leading edge—
from its self-managing teams to its automated robotics. Ten
years later, much has changed, including the original team
design. EAP learned several valuable lessons about teams and
empowerment in a volatile and constantly changing business.
Thanks to that experience, EAP may be uniquely positioned
to thrive in what promises to be even more unpredictable
times ahead.

Planning for EAP began in the early 1980s, when Westinghouse's Electronic Systems Group (ESG) was growing rapidly. As the division had won contracts to build the radar systems for the F-16 fighter and B-1 bomber programs, a new and more flexible manufacturing capacity became a priority. A strategy was developed that focused on what Westinghouse called "Centers of Excellence." Each center would embody the latest principles of organizational efficiency. The Materials Acquisition Center, located near the business unit's main manufacturing facility in Baltimore, would consolidate all ESG's purchasing and procurement. The Manufacturing Systems and Technology Center, also in Baltimore, would bring together several hundred scientists and engineers to develop advanced manufacturing processes.

Both centers would support a third center: the new EAP. The new EAP would take a fresh approach to fabricating printed wiring assemblies—the core of the division's products—and overcome many of the problems that bedeviled existing manufacturing processes. Those problems were daunting. In 1980 at ESG's Baltimore facility, for example, more than 80 percent of first-time-through printed wiring assemblies required some type of rework or repair. That record was typical of other U.S. companies that supplied Department of Defense contractors. While some of this rework could be attributed to stringent military design specifications and testing and retesting requirements, Westinghouse knew that yields could be improved. Indeed, benchmarking comparisons with Japanese and European companies that built similar printed wiring assemblies, although mostly for commercial companies, showed that much higher first-time yields were possible. Some Japanese companies were achieving first-time yields as high as 90 percent. To Westinghouse, the disparity suggested a huge opportunity—a U.S. operation that could reduce cycle time for printed wiring assemblies while substantially improving quality would give the ESG a commanding competitive edge in winning military contracts.

The success of Japanese manufacturers was especially interesting to Tom Murrin, president of Westinghouse's Energy and Advanced Technology Group at that time. Murrin, who had closely followed Japanese production techniques for decades, oversaw the steering group assembled to plan the College Station facility and its integration into the new Centers of Excellence framework. When the group, which consisted of ESG managers and engineers, came back with a traditional plant design for the new EAP, Murrin told them to start over.

Because Westinghouse was making a major financial commitment to the new facility, it expected EAP not only to provide much needed manufacturing capacity but also to radically improve yields. Murrin reasoned that a traditional design would result in traditional problems. His advice: Visit companies around the world and select the best ideas in human resource management. Come back with a plan that truly represents the next generation in workplace design.

Early Teams

The steering group, which later formed the core management and engineering team for the new facility, worked together for a year before EAP at College Station opened. Most of the steering group members also worked as a design team for the new facility's team structure, which for the early 1980s was quite advanced. Hiring began in early 1983. Applicants spent nearly forty hours in a process consisting of paper-and-pencil tests, simulated job assessments, and interviews with managers, human resource personnel, and team leaders. After the first few teams were formed, team members also would interview applicants.

While EAP's products were quite complex, the selection process focused on attitudes and behavior rather than prior experience or technical skills. Few jobs provided the kind of background skills that might prove useful at EAP, where there would be little design standardization and production would consist of a high mix of products and very low volumes, sometimes as low as one. The newness of the technical and team skills made the training requirements at EAP extraordinarily intense—to bring new employees up to speed technically, and to provide ongoing training in team and interpersonal skills, would be vital.

The new workforce was structured unlike any other within Westinghouse at the time. All employees were salaried. Although there were four job classifications, 95 percent of nonexempt employees fell into one classification—technicians, a name employees chose themselves. Technicians included everyone involved in building, inspecting, and supporting the product, even office and clerical employees. Several pay grades within the technician classification covered employees with key electronic or maintenance skills.

EAP's first teams were formed around steps in the assembly process. Some teams focused on component insertion, for example, other teams on soldering. To improve communication among team members, workstations were grouped in clusters facing one another. Because products were complex and product demands were constantly changing, the clusters would make it easy for team members to answer one another's questions, facilitate cross-training, and ensure that all team members were alerted to quality or production problems. The cluster design also reduced the need for separate team meetings away from the production floor; teams could meet informally at virtually any time. Looming over all team clusters were "visibility" boards that tracked the vital statistics of specific teams—production and quality levels, team attendance, and several areas related to customer acceptance of products.

Each team also included "officers" who served on a voluntary and rotating basis (typically six months). They were responsible for team and organizationwide data collection in such areas as attendance, safety, production, and quality. Each team also had an adviser, usually a Westinghouse engineer, who was responsible for training and coaching new team members in technical skills. As teams matured, members who developed technical skills quickly and were especially adept at training others took over many of the training and coaching roles.

Westinghouse knew the success of the team design depended on training. During EAP's first year or two of operation, employees received nearly 180 hours of ongoing training in addition to a six-week orientation. While training for technical skills certainly was not ignored, EAP focused especially on communication, team development, facilitating and coaching, interviewing, and interpersonal skills training—all the areas the core design team thought would be needed to achieve the facility's ambitious goals.

Midcourse Correction

EAP's first two years were hectic and challenging. Luckily for the new facility, production consisted of fairly tested and stable products, and the production pace grew in a measured fashion. Throughout the first year, team members shared a sense of challenge and adventure. By the end of the first year, only a hundred local people had been hired as team technicians. The operation was small enough that the entire plant, from managers to technicians, could meet once a week at a College Station pizza parlor to socialize.

Cracks in the team system started to develop in 1984 and 1985, however, as EAP really began to grow. The pay-for-skills-and-knowledge system seemed to discourage the development of stable, long-term teams. The system, designed to

reward employees who developed new skills with pay increases and new job responsibilities every six months, resulted in constant movement within and among teams. Most
jobs on teams, however, took time to master, and teams often
didn't have the time to mature into cohesive working units.
EAP encountered problems with its coaching system as well.
It relied on team members to develop skills and then coach
others, who in turn went on to coach still others. With few
standardized training modules developed for many of the
jobs, training became diluted—as knowledge was passed
from one employee to another, a little bit was lost in every
transfer. This ultimately led to a decline in skills.

The peer evaluation system did not work as planned,
either, partly because developing a stable workforce was un-
expectedly difficult. Turnover rates were higher than anticipated. Many EAP employees were spouses of students or
teachers at nearby Texas A&M University who moved in and
out of the area. The problem was compounded by College
Station's location amid Texas oil country—the industry's
boom-and-bust cycle made it even more difficult to maintain
a stable workforce. The result, despite EAP's careful selection
process and focus on training, was an employee attrition rate
of more than 20 percent—a rate never envisioned by the
original steering and design committee.

The biggest challenge to the team system came from
Westinghouse itself. As new military contracts were won in
1984 and 1985, EAP had to deal with an increasingly heavy
flow of new products. Many of the products required complex, new processes and were based on new designs that
weren't yet stable. As EAP was required to build more and
more new products, hiring grew rapidly. During much of
1984 and 1985, EAP hired as many as forty new team technicians a month. Because the original team design called for
team members to interview job candidates, some employees

spent as much as two hours a day, for months at a time, conducting interviews.

Time spent in team meetings, peer evaluations, and selecting new employees added up to what many employees felt was too little time spent mastering the challenging production process—and too little time actually building products. Dissatisfaction led to a midcourse correction in 1985 after an ad hoc committee of team technicians, team advisers, and managers was formed to reevaluate the team design and recommend changes. Those changes included reduced team members' involvement in interviewing and selecting employees, a revamped evaluation process that relied more on input from team advisers, and replacement of the pay-for-knowledge-and-skills system with a new scheme that rewarded individual performance based on quantifiable quality, attendance, and productivity objectives. Later EAP created the Performance Achievement Reward (PAR) system, which provided lump-sum payments to everyone for plantwide quality, cost, and productivity improvements.

One thing that didn't change was the decision not to award team bonuses. The EAP's original design team visited several facilities that used bonus systems and didn't like what they saw. At some facilities it appeared much easier for teams working on simpler products to qualify for productivity bonuses—not because of differences in motivation and performance but rather because of the degree of challenge posed by the products. Because EAP would be working on hundreds of products, some easy, others untested, the design team concluded that a team bonus system might not be fair.

Teams Today

"We were given the chance to stumble," says Larry Teverbaugh, EAP's plant manager since 1988, "and we ended up profiting from our mistakes." Since 1985, EAP has experienced the same ups and downs as the defense industry, including layoffs when weapons contracts were canceled. And, like similar operations, EAP is trying to wean itself from a near-total dependence on the weapons business. To Teverbaugh and other EAP managers, EAP's biggest advantage is the flexibility of its workforce—no matter what sector EAP supplies, the business always will be dominated by demands for unique, highly specialized products and increasingly short delivery schedules. Thanks to the lessons EAP has learned in its ten-year team journey, the facility has what Teverbaugh calls a "depth of resources" that few other operations can match.

The development of mature, flexible teams since 1991 has been particularly fast. During this period, EAP has been rocked by a series of outside events, including the cancellation of two major contracts, which put more stress than usual on production and increased demands of team flexibility. As a result, team member training has become focused on understanding what it costs to run a manufacturing facility like EAP, the financial measurements that must be monitored under fixed contracts—and, above all, how teams contribute to profit and loss. In the past, for example, a team adviser or manager would keep track of personnel and material costs associated with specific contracts. Today that function is performed by rotating budgeting officers within EAP teams, which have advanced beyond such areas as safety, work assignments, and cross-training.

"Teams have evolved from thinking about the best ways to manage themselves," says Teverbaugh, "to thinking about the most effective ways to run the business." Monthly business meetings with all team members include a discussion of EAP's monthly costing rate (the cost of running the facility divided by the number of productive hours, expressed as a rate per hour) and the effects of salary, benefits, health care costs, and other expenses on profitability. As part of ongoing training, the plant's financial and training managers help employees understand this information, which once would have been carefully guarded, and relate it to team performance. Now, when presented with new production demands or unique product requirements, teams seldom need to be told what to do, says Teverbaugh. Instead managers focus on making sure team members know the basic business parameters. The production details are left to the teams.

EAP's cycle time reduction program required rethinking the manufacturing process. Under the old system, teams could be highly functional. On one production line, for example, robots partially assembled printed wiring assemblies, which then were passed on to a series of teams that handled assembly, soldering, mechanical insertion, and inspection. But these teams depended on the output of the teams that maintained the robots. To reduce cycle time, a just-in-time manufacturing operation was introduced that required creating cross-functional teams—each team member was trained to operate the robots as well as perform the assembly, soldering, and testing required to complete the boards. The change reduced work in process by a factor of four and cut in half the number of people needed to produce the same output.

Results

Like dozens of electronics operations that once served military contractors almost exclusively, EAP is undergoing a period of dramatic change. Currently only about 7 percent of its products go into nonmilitary products, but by 1995 Westinghouse hopes EAP will conduct 60 percent of its business with commercial builders of avionics, radar, and air traffic management equipment. In the meantime, defense industry cutbacks have taken a toll, including a major layoff in 1992 that idled almost 25 percent of EAP employees.

EAP's experience with self-managed teams may give it a clear advantage as the defense electronics industry emerges from its shakeout. In terms of cost and quality, few facilities can match EAP's record. Its per-product costs have fallen by more than 60 percent since the mid-1980s. An impressive list of reductions contributed to the improvement—including cycle time (from an average of twelve weeks to less than two), work in process inventories (reduced by 65 percent), and rework (down by 50 percent). Today EAP can produce as many as 950 different types of printed wiring assemblies and electronic assemblies in batch sizes as small as one. All have high reliability requirements and little design standardization.

Teverbaugh attributes EAP's early missteps to a "lack of clear and quantifiable objectives and the ability to measure progress toward those objectives." The objectives for the pay-for-knowledge-and-skills system were poorly defined, for example, which led to learning unrelated to team needs as well as frequent job rotations. As a greenfield site, EAP also had more than its share of teething problems, which made it necessary to recast the original team design. For example, EAP had to take a more rigorous approach to technical training after the informality of the team coaching system diluted training quality. Team coaches still provide most of the training, but now EAP has more than three hundred training modules and testing procedures in place to ensure competency. Rapid production increases tested the team system, too, especially peer evaluations and team participation in the hiring process. Events also suggested that EAP focused too much on changing behavior. Teverbaugh says, "We spent so much time focusing on the behavioral aspects of things that we forgot we had customers paying the bills. We weren't focusing on the value-added steps of the business that would keep us in business."

Team members seemed to do the most to redirect EAP's focus on the value-added steps of the business. Their efforts contributed to what Teverbaugh calls "superior performance over time." At EAP this means the ability to handle unexpected events in a business increasingly dominated by them. Even when the odds are the greatest, "people just do not give up," says Teverbaugh. That attitude may be even more essential in the years ahead.

20

Leading Teams:
Transforming Managers into Coaches

Wilson Sporting Goods Company
Humboldt, Tennessee

Industry	Sporting goods (golf balls)
Union	None
Type of team implementation	Permanent, cross-functional, or work-area continuous improvement teams; some natural self-directed work teams are emerging.
First teams started	1987
Employees	650
Percentage in teams	75 percent
Team size	15
Team responsibilities	Teams meet weekly or biweekly to plan process improvements or solve quality and productivity problems. They establish their own goals aligned with the plant's mission. Team participation is voluntary.
Organization-wide team responsibilities	None

Team leadership and governance	"Coaches" (formerly supervisors) usually facilitate and provide backup and direction to teams; hourly associates colead with coaches.
Leadership outside teams	Coaches still perform fairly traditional supervisory functions.
Team compensation	Humboldt's compensation system has not been changed by teams. Cash incentives are never used to reward team activities; team rewards generally are honorary and consist of plaques, awards, and other gestures, such as lunches and dinners. Teams also are rewarded with gift certificates at a company store that carries Wilson golf equipment and other sporting goods.
First-year team member training	Twenty-six hours: meeting skills, quality and problem-solving techniques, team interaction skills.
Subsequent team member training	Sixteen hours: all the same areas plus team and workplace design and cross-training others.
First-year leadership training	Twenty-six hours: meeting skills, quality and problem-solving techniques, team interaction skills.
Subsequent leadership training	Sixteen hours: all the same areas plus team and workplace design, facilitation and coaching skills, cross-training others.
How team members are selected	Employees volunteer.

How team performance is evaluated	Teams evaluate themselves on their ability to work as a team and their accomplishments.
Team impact on organization	Since a team approach to continuous improvement was initiated, scrap rates have fallen by 64 percent, rework by 91 percent, and cycle time by 30 percent. Annual inventory turnover has risen from 6.5 times to 90 times. Numerous team projects have resulted in one-time and ongoing savings.
Key lessons	• Coaches and team leaders need extensive and ongoing training. • Senior managers should maintain a high profile throughout the team-building process, lending support and credibility to team activities. • Quick responses to ideas and projects and team needs are important to maintaining momentum.

Background

Wilson Sporting Goods, one of the world's strongest brand names in athletic equipment, started its Humboldt, Tennessee, plant in 1977 to make rubber and leather basketballs and softballs. At the time, Wilson was a unit of PepsiCo. But neither PepsiCo's marketing clout nor Wilson's name recognition could save the Humboldt venture from getting off on the wrong foot. For one thing, Humboldt's opening coincided with growing Asian competition in athletic equipment. With higher labor and raw material costs than its competitors in Taiwan, Hong Kong, Malaysia, and other Asian countries, Humboldt had trouble making money from the start.

This didn't sit well with PepsiCo. As a result, the general manager's office at Humboldt became a revolving door. With seven general managers during a five-year period, employees found little reason to put their faith in each new manager's program to turn the operation around. Similarly, middle managers grew distrustful and uncertain. The situation deteriorated even further during an organizing campaign by the United Rubber Workers in 1980. After a hard-fought battle, the union achieved a narrow victory that set the stage for years of divisive labor relations. Ultimately the union was decertified, but the mistrust among managers and employees did not easily subside.

The cloud started to lift at Humboldt only after it abandoned its original product line and Wilson was acquired by a new set of owners. In 1983, while still under PepsiCo, Humboldt started shifting production to golf balls, a more promising area, and by 1985 the plant was in the golf ball business exclusively. That same year, PepsiCo concluded that Wilson no longer fit its corporate strategy and sold the company to Wesray, the holding company set up by former Treasury Secretary William Simon and a group of investors. Wesray was determined to turn Wilson into a lucrative business—and perhaps sell it for a profit. Although Humboldt still was losing money, Wilson's new owners felt that with a little patience, some needed capital investments, and more stable management, the Humboldt operation could be salvaged. But when Al Scott arrived as plant manager in 1985, Wesray's optimism looked a little misplaced: standards had dropped in quality, in safety, in productivity, and in morale. "The atmosphere was very confused, very political," recalls one manager. "People were thinking about survival, not how to build the business."

Scott's arrival marked a turning point for Humboldt. He

brought with him a belief that employee involvement, empowerment, and pushing decision making down to the front line could make a difference. He knew from experience that change would have to be introduced prudently—without careful preparation, such changes could be not only expensive but ineffectual. Scott believed that changing management's attitudes and behavior had to be the first priority. He had seen what happened when employees received team training, had their expectations raised, and then were confronted by an unmovable wall of old-line supervisory and management techniques. Therefore, Scott launched an ambitious training program for Humboldt's managers, who would then train employees, using a "cascading" approach.

For the next two years, Humboldt's supervisors and managers went through a series of programs in coaching and reinforcing effective performance, delegating responsibility, and other aspects of an empowering management style. Then the issue of getting the right quality and quantity of coaches in key positions had to be addressed. Once the staff management was reorganized, managers began studying quality tools, problem-solving techniques, and other total quality management concepts. Determined to replace the anxious, fear-ridden mindsets of the past, Scott drew upon a variety of sources. Managers received rigorous training in behavioral and quality skills and attended courses on setting goals and managing time. They also attended a variety of image-boosting "peak performance" workshops from such figures as Zig Ziglar.

Team Wilson

In 1987, after two years of intensive training for managers, Scott and his management team felt the time was ripe to roll out a comprehensive employee involvement initiative. Using sports metaphors, Scott called the initiative "Team Wilson" and renamed managers and supervisors "coaches." A new mission statement, consisting of five key "operating philosophies," was drafted. The five tenets committed Humboldt to continuous improvement, associate involvement, employing just-in-time manufacturing, total quality management (TQM), and becoming the "lowest total cost manufacturer" in the golf ball business. While the statements were not extraordinary, they signaled a sharp break with the past.

That same year, team guidelines were drafted by the management team. (Since then the guidelines have undergone minor revisions but remain largely unchanged.) Their goal was to implement "applied management" at the production employee level. Team participation was voluntary and would not affect salary. Teams were defined in the guidelines as "a group of associates performing similar or multifunctional work who meet weekly for not more than one hour to learn about and apply basic quality team techniques." Teams were to use these techniques to analyze problems within their areas and recommend solutions to management. When possible, teams could take action themselves to implement the solution.

Thirteen team objectives were outlined—ranging from looking for ways to reduce costs and improve quality to such general targets as building a "can-do attitude on continuous improvement" and developing "harmonious management/worker relationships." Management pledged to allow an hour a week for formal team meetings, to provide meeting space and materials, to avoid taking on projects teams claimed as their own, and to furnish training and support for team activities. Although management reserved the right to suggest problems for teams to tackle, the teams had the right of refusal. In turn, teams were obligated to focus on work-related problems within their control, to coordinate their meeting schedules with company workloads, and to review their progress periodically with management. Certain areas, however, were off limits to teams: benefits and salaries, employment policies and handbook changes, and employee performance or disciplinary procedures.

As envisioned by the management team, team leaders would be coaches or supervisors chosen by company managers; later, teams would choose hourly associates to colead. The management team took an active role in the team system by acting as a review board for team recommendations, rejecting team projects if they didn't fit team guidelines, and coordinating team recognition events (which became very important to teams). Managers also met at least monthly with every team.

The team system got off to a slow start. The first formal teams, considered pilots, were put together with considerable assistance from managers, who hoped the pilot teams would expose any flaws in the team development plan. One such flaw did emerge: without early training in quality tools and problem-solving techniques, teams tended to pick fairly trivial process improvement projects. Compounding the problem, in most cases coaches served as team leaders—as a result, despite their previous training, they needed more "train the trainer" training.

By the end of 1987, Humboldt had implemented four teams representing only about 5 percent of the workforce. But during the next several years the team concept gained widespread acceptance—thanks to continued training for managers and coaches as well as management's high-profile efforts to nurture the team system. In 1991, for example, as part of the philosophy of "cascading" training to associates, department managers received fifty-three hours of formal training in TQM techniques while coaches received up to seventy hours. During that time, team members received only eight hours of formal TQM training but benefited from a great deal of informal training during weekly team meetings. During these meetings, coaches provided most of the training, covering a different topic (such as goal setting or some aspect of team interaction skills) every two or three months.

By the end of 1993, Humboldt had thirty-eight active teams; 88 percent of all employees were participating; more than a thousand projects had been completed. Most of these projects fell into four broad areas: quality improvements, reductions in scrap and rework, inventory reductions, and safety and housekeeping improvements. Teams were permitted to spend up to $500 on improvement projects that met team guidelines. Otherwise, the management team had to approve team projects (which it did 90 percent of the time). Many team projects resulted in substantial savings or process changes.

Today, while the main team activity is brainstorming solutions to problems or improving processes, teams vary widely in their approaches—which is just what the management team had hoped for from the beginning. For example, some teams work directly with suppliers providing nearly instant feedback on supplier quality or delivery programs (It's not unusual to see a supplier representative attending a 6:30 A.M. team meeting.) One such partnership resulted in an annual savings of $30,000 when the team and a supplier devised a cardboard box recycling arrangement. Moreover, cross-functional teams are becoming more widespread. Usually formed into task forces, cross-functional teams have made improvements to internal systems ranging from accounting to materials management.

Team Wilson teams now are led jointly by hourly associates and management coaches. Typically, associates rotate coleadership based on a schedule the team establishes. While a self-directed work team framework was not part of the original concept, several teams are moving in that direction with informal assistance from the management team. The first self-directed team was organized in the plant's special order unit, where production demands are especially volatile. The team schedules production orders, monitors and controls its own work in progress, schedules overtime, audits its own safety and housekeeping, and troubleshoots equipment.

Team Activity As Its Own Reward

There is no formal team performance tracking system at Humboldt. In an effort to keep team participation stress-free and rewarding, Wilson intentionally keeps the team evaluation process informal. Teams don't set performance targets. Instead they set organizationwide objectives, which may be initiated by team members or suggested by coaches or management. Teams keep track of their own performance, and once or twice a year they report their progress to the steering committee during formal presentations.

The sports team concept influences Humboldt's team reward system, as well, which deliberately eschews big team bonuses or other cash incentives. (About the only tangible rewards for team achievement are gift certificates for Wilson sporting goods from the plant's on-site store.) The plant's fifteen job classifications and pay grades have not been affected by the team system. The management team hoped that enthusiasm for the team system would be spurred by the rewards of improving processes and operations, being given the chance to help the plant's competitive position—and, above all, playing a part in assuring the plant's future.

Team achievements, however, are extensively recognized with plaques, T-shirts, pictures, and posters displayed throughout the plant. At the annual team recognition and rewards dinner, which is attended by Wilson corporate executives, gold, silver, and bronze achievement medals are awarded. The event is hugely popular and more than a thousand associates and guests attend.

Individual evaluations are fairly traditional. Associates meet with their coach or manager every six months to discuss job responsibilities and duties as well as brainstorming, troubleshooting, use of quality tools, and team cooperation and communication. Coaches, in turn, are evaluated by the associates they work with in such matters as team facilitation and coaching skills.

Results

Wesray and later Amer—a Finnish corporation that purchased Wilson from Wesray in 1989—have plenty of reasons to be pleased with Humboldt's performance since the dismal mid-1980s. The decision to abandon basketballs in favor of golf balls has paid off spectacularly, and Wilson's share of the $1 billion U.S. market has climbed steadily since 1990. Since Al Scott and the current management group climbed on board—and stayed there—Humboldt has seen its workforce rise from less than 200 to more than 650. Managers believe the plant is the best-run facility in the Wilson Corporation— possibly the best-run in the whole sporting goods industry— and they've got plenty of data to back up that belief.

While Humboldt's turnaround is undoubtedly due to smart marketing moves (including the introduction of new golf balls such as the wildly popular Ultra®) and stable management, its team system has certainly played a key role. While the team system has never been a numbers game, plant managers estimate that team projects have resulted in a savings of more than $25 million—attributed to less scrap, less rework, and above all fewer carrying costs for inventory. Meanwhile, first-time yields in crucial operations, such as injection molding, have increased substantially.

The goals of Team Wilson were modest but far-reaching. One goal was to increase empowerment without spending months on an elaborate design. The success at Wilson did depend, however, on a profound change in Humboldt's culture—a change that had to start at the top with extensive management training. The management team was determined, too, to avoid the problem of organizational inertia. It knew that interest in teams might founder if managers didn't maintain a high profile throughout the team-building process, lending support and credibility to team activities. Today managers meet with three or four teams a month, regardless of the shift, and the entire management team attends formal team presentations once or twice a month. Humboldt's managers know that quick response to team proposals and team needs is essential to success.

The team approach has helped Humboldt manage the internal stress of rapid growth. In 1989, Humboldt's peak expansion year, production increased dramatically as market share grew. Employees worked most Saturdays and many Sundays to keep up with the demand—yet there were few complaints and no loss in quality. Management's confidence in high morale and team spirit was confirmed by an employee survey conducted by an independent consulting firm in 1991. The survey was designed to measure, among other things, employees' perceptions of management support for a new, more empowering workplace and the degree of their commitment to the team system. While the survey results showed room for improvement, managers were glad to see associates' strong acceptance of the team system. If Humboldt has proved anything, it's that a team system can be simple, fun, and highly productive.

PART THREE

Lessons Learned

21

Taking a Deeper Look
Inside Teams:
A Summary of Best Practices

In this chapter, we take a closer look inside our twenty teams. We will point out some differences among the implementations and spotlight unique case studies. More important, we will highlight the "best practices" that thread throughout all twenty implementations, allowing you to benchmark your own team initiatives and progress.

Teams, Teams Everywhere

In our visits to organizations, we frequently are asked, "Are teams for every type of organization?" More often than not, this question is asked by line managers who hope the answer is "Of course not." They hope to continue along the present course, avoiding change at all costs. While there are undoubtedly a few jobs or departments that might not be conducive to a team approach, we often find that where there's a need, there's a means. As Table 1.1 shows, teams can work in just about any type of organization. Let's take a quick look:

- Teams were implemented in enterprises as small as sixty employees to as large as thirteen thousand.
- We used to hear that teams worked fine for manufacturing firms but not for white-collar service organizations. While most early implementations seemed to be in manufacturing, team applications in service industries are coming on strong. Kodak Customer Service Center, Mil-

299

waukee Insurance Company, and Cape Coral Hospital cases are just a few of hundreds of service organizations that are now implementing teams. Teams span a wide range of industries, too, including food warehousing and distribution, pharmaceuticals, electronics, consumer products, chemicals—and, yes, even peat farming.

- Not only do teams work in a wide range of industries, they work with many different types of jobs. Operators, managers, trainers, engineers, customer service representatives, senior executives, quality control specialists, maintenance technicians, nurses, press operators, and research scientists are all serving as team members.

- Teams work in both plant start-ups and established operations. Four of the twenty organizations (Miller, Westinghouse, Colgate, and Hannaford Brothers) were greenfield sites that implemented the team concept along with the opening of a new facility. The remainder converted their traditional organizations into team-based cultures.

- We are often asked if teams can be implemented in unionized organizations. This book indicates that teams are alive and well in companies with organized workforces (Miller, Hannaford Brothers, K Shoes, Bord na Mona, Sterling, and UCAR). In fact, two of these companies, UCAR and Hannaford Brothers, have teams at both union and nonunion facilities.

- Finally, teams are not just a North American phenomenon. Self-directed work teams are sprouting up all over the globe. *Inside Teams* tells the story of four international applications (Bord na Mona, Ireland; Texas Instruments, Malaysia; K Shoes, United Kingdom; and Sterling Winthrop, Australia). However, we are aware of and have worked directly with organizations throughout the world, including companies in Eastern Europe, which are attempting to match a newfound personal freedom with workplace democracy.

So here's an important lesson learned: Don't be too quick to write off the applicability of teams to your own company, department, or job. Teams have been implemented successfully in a wide range of organizations and situations. In fact, the type of organization has far less to do with team success than the nature of the implementation itself.

Getting Started

Moving to teams must be dictated by business needs. Simply reading an article, visiting a team-based facility, or hearing a presentation are hardly reasons for going through the trials and tribulations of a team rollout.

All twenty teams had clear and strong business reasons for establishing teams. By far the overwhelming reason was increasing competitive pressure. Both K Shoes and Ampex were losing business to overseas competitors. Milwaukee Insurance was facing increasing pressure from the national giants. Cape Coral, like many hospitals, found itself in an increasingly competitive market. Mine Safety Appliances, once the industry leader, began losing market share to competitors who were turning out products quicker, at lower cost, and of equal quality. With a more difficult business environment, faced with losing significant market share, the leaders in most of these organizations realized they needed to work on containing costs, improving quality, and doing things faster. They saw teams and teamwork as a powerful strategy for changing "business as usual."

We're not implying that you must be in a "do or die" mode to start teams. Several of the organizations used teams to enhance their current business position. The changes at

Kodak's Customer Assistance Center came about as a way of creating a superior service image. When Westinghouse built its new facility, it was faced with a strong demand for its products—what the company wanted was a new high-performance organization to ensure its long-term success. DDI's team implementation was driven not by a crisis but by a vision of a more productive work environment and a different culture.

Here's another important lesson: Whether you are initiating teams as a response to current conditions, as a way of building a more secure future, or both, the message is clear: Simply because teams are in vogue is not a good reason for starting them in your own company. Business conditions, business needs, and business goals must serve as the catalyst for change.

Change Starts at the Top

A strong message was revealed as these companies told us how their campaign got off the ground: Senior management must drive and support the change effort. People at the top of the organization (CEOs, COOs, division leaders) were almost universally involved in sending out a strong, consistent signal: We must change. Here are some examples of such change:

- Paddy Hughes, CEO of Bord na Mona's Peat Energy Division, reflecting on his role in the move to teams, said, "We were looking for radical change, so we had to make radical proposals to get people thinking sufficiently about the change that was required."
- Similarly, Robert Perkins, K Shoes' manufacturing manager, really got his organization behind the move to teams after visiting a competitor, US Shoes. He came

back with a message: "They [US Shoes] are talking about teams while we are still talking about individuals; they are talking about flexibility and productivity while we are talking about narrowly defined tasks."

- At Wilson Sporting Goods, the plant's general manager, Al Scott, made it clear that he needed to shift people's focus from "thinking about survival to thinking about building the business."

More than communicating the need to change, senior management also took an active role in supporting the team process. They not only became involved, it became their passion. They stood by their belief in teams during good and bad times. Six organizations (Ampex, DDI, Sterling Winthrop, Tennessee Eastman, Kodak Customer Assistance Center, and Wilson Sporting Goods) specifically mentioned that a high degree of senior management support was essential to their success.

How Change Occurred

"There is more than one way to skin a cat," the adage goes. It certainly applies to the process these twenty organizations employed in getting their teams up and running. Each implementation had a unique plan. Basically, though, the organizations approached their team implementations in one of two ways.

A handful of organizations seemed to hit upon work teams as a result of previous initiatives. In other words, it was not their original intent to establish self-directed work teams. For example, Milwaukee Mutual Insurance Company started its change process with a program that focused on four improvement areas: team efficiency, customer service, operational proficiency, and unit-loss ratios. More than thirty individual departments were asked to improve on the areas most relevant to their operations. As they began to work, problem-solving teams realized they could make more dramatic improvements if they redesigned cumbersome processes and broke down some of the functional silos that required numerous handoffs. This led to the formation of both redesigned and natural work teams. A similar change process was followed at Wilson Sporting Goods. Intact work groups and cross-functional problem-solving teams were asked to work on thirteen designated improvement objectives, which set the foundation for the later formation of "pilot" self-directed work teams.

But the majority of the organizations did start out with a vision of a team-based organization. In these cases, a decision was made, usually by senior management, that teams were the way to do business in the future. Then, usually, an implementation plan was developed. Teams were formed around existing work processes (natural work teams) or around redesigned processes (redesigned work teams)—all with varying degrees of shared leadership. Examples of implementations involving natural work teams included our own CSI, Bord na Mona, and Texas Instruments Malaysia. Implementations involving redesign of key processes, structures, and systems include, among others, Colgate, Ampex, and Hannaford Brothers.

Regardless of their approach to change, the twenty organizations used a number of common strategies:

• The move to teams often involved some sort of steering team. This team, composed of senior executives (but sometimes involving leaders from other levels, team representatives, functional specialists, and union representatives), guided and supported the team rollout. For example, the steering team at Cape Coral, which consisted of the hospital's top officers, helped establish a set of organizational values, a clear mission, and broad goals and parameters for the redesign effort. Similarly, at Sterling Winthrop, senior managers got together for a two-day meeting at a remote site to hammer out their approach to teams. The steering team not only guides the team implementation but is a valuable way to build management's commitment and consensus as well. It often becomes a permanent group.

- While the steering team supports the team implementation, the real work of designing and implementing often is left to a design team. The design team takes on the often arduous task of redesigning key processes, establishing team boundaries, defining responsibilities for team members and their leaders, aligning support systems, and developing an organizationwide communication plan. The design team usually is composed of a representative sample of associates across several organizational levels and functions. The design team approach not only capitalizes on the perspectives and expertise each person brings to the party but, as many of the organizations pointed out, ensures widespread commitment. Not all organizations used a two-tiered steering team/design team approach. In some cases these teams were combined into one implementation team that filled the roles of both.

- Large organizations, or those geographically dispersed, pose a special implementation dilemma. For organizations such as UCAR, with nearly one thousand employees around the Southeast; Texas Instruments, with thirteen thousand employees mostly in Dallas; and Tennessee Eastman, with over eight thousand employees in Kingsport, Tennessee, a single design team would have had an insurmountable task. Thus in these organizations the guiding philosophy seemed to be "think strategically, but act locally." A senior management steering team provided overall direction of team efforts, but each plant or division charted local design teams (and, in some cases, local steering teams) to plan and implement their own team rollouts. Note that in these organizations teams are evolving over long periods of time (up to two or three years). With thousands of employees, you don't simply wake up one morning and find hundreds of work teams up and running.

- It's important to learn about the team concept. In many of the organizations, both steering and design team members often made site visits to learn from other organizations. The lesson learned is that there are hundreds of organizations implementing work teams. Taking the time to learn from them will help you form your own vision for teams, may save you from reinventing the wheel, and will help you avoid some of the typical pitfalls.

- Gain the commitment of all the stakeholders in the team initiative. Steering and design teams serve as "representatives" of the entire workforce. Resistance usually comes from those outside these teams—because they have not been involved. Two-way communication, widespread involvement, and initial training are critical elements in ensuring a smooth start. At Ampex, senior management met regularly with employees early in the implementation to listen and address their concerns. At Kodak Customer Assistance Center, all associates were asked to attend a paid Saturday session in which the company introduced the vision and implementation plan for its new team-based approach to service. Perhaps even more important, that very afternoon the reorganized teams held their first team meetings, which included electing team members to serve on various facilitywide process and business councils.

Union Partnerships

Five of the twenty organizations (UCAR, Sterling Winthrop, Bord na Mona, K Shoes, Miller, and Hannaford Brothers) are represented by unions in at least some of their facilities. In most cases, the relationship between union and management was, and still is, positive—mainly because unions were viewed as partners in implementing teams and union representatives were actively involved in the change process. But the partnership does not stop at implementation—it must be ongoing. At Miller Brewing, the union president and team representatives serve on a plantwide policy review team to work on broad issues affecting team performance. At Bord na Mona, a similar joint policy team is in place to develop and realign the company's approach to teams.

Redesigning Team Roles and Responsibilities

One major difference between the team implementations was the degree to which they redesigned their processes and roles. In fact, sixteen of the twenty organizations made major changes in the way work was accomplished, products were manufactured, and services were delivered. All twenty redefined the roles of their team members—in general, expanding the breadth and depth of their jobs.

Conducting "business as usual" presented the biggest barrier to their competitive position. Work tended to be organized around a mass production model. Employees were taught to do one or two jobs. Dozens of specialists, from engineers to quality control experts, told them how to do their work. Armies of supervisors and managers controlled, checked, and rechecked everything they did. The workforce felt bored and brainless. No one felt much accountability for anything meaningful. And manufacturing companies were not alone. Insurance, banking, even health care became bureaucratic and cumbersome.

This traditional approach may have worked well in the past. But as organizations face the pressures cited earlier, the need for radical change becomes paramount. Customers want things quickly, at value prices, of exceptionally high quality, and tailored to *their* unique needs. As we survey the twenty organizations, we note six recurring principles that guided the redesign of processes and responsibilities:

Traditional Structure	*Team Design*
Work designed around functions.	Work designed around processes.
No sense of ownership.	Team owns a product, service, or process.
Single-skilled jobs.	Multiskilled/cross-trained.
Leaders govern teams.	Teams govern teams.
Support staff/skills outside team.	Support staff/skills incorporated into team.
Managers make all organizational decisions.	Teams involved in organizationwide decisions.

Process Redesign

Most of the twenty organizations made the transition—sometimes slowly—from work organized around multiple functions to work organized around meaningful processes. Processes take some type of input and change it to some type of output in a way that provides value to a customer. Here are some examples:

- Rather than requiring up to 150 separate operations, K Shoes is reorganizing into "modular" teams responsible for taking shoes from "cut to box." When they are done, a pair of shoes will take four hours instead of twelve days to produce.

- At Sterling Winthrop, manufacturing liquid analgesics once involved more than twenty-one different department interfaces. Then Sterling Winthrop redesigned its entire production operation. Vendor scheduling, material receipt, production scheduling, blending, and so forth are now handled by multifunctional teams responsible for the entire production process. The impact: virtually all backorder problems have been eliminated.

- Texas Instruments redesigned its new product development process. Instead of functional experts throwing their work "over the wall," specialists in planning, engineering, manufacturing, and quality control work together to design and launch new products.

Ownership

A basic principle of the team concept is to create a sense of job ownership. It's hard to feel you're part of something meaningful if you are doing the same job over and over and you don't see how your work ties into the bigger picture. Creating ownership usually involves giving teams responsibility for whole products, services, or groups of customers. Our twenty organizations present some excellent examples of creating a greater sense of individual and team ownership by redesigning their processes:

- Cape Coral Hospital's forty-plus departments are being redesigned into four primary patient care centers (surgical, general, specialty medical, and outpatient) that will function much like mini-hospitals within the Cape Coral system. In addition to increasing efficiency, Cape Coral's new system is meant to encourage hospital professionals to feel a greater sense of ownership and responsibility for their patients.

- Bord na Mona has found a particularly unique way of creating a sense of ownership. Although the company did not use extensive work redesign, the massive peat farming system was divided into mini-enterprise units with teams running each unit. Teams became responsible for budgeting, hiring seasonal workers, maintaining equipment, and more. In essence, each team owns its own turf.

- At the Colgate plant in Cambridge, Ohio, teams are responsible for accomplishing all the tasks necessary to produce liquid detergent—including blowing, labeling, and filling bottles and then delivering them to the loading dock.

Multiskilling/Cross-Training

As the twenty organizations moved to teams, single jobs virtually disappeared. A premium was placed on cross-training team members to handle many different jobs—thus increasing the organization's flexibility and employees' job satisfaction. Organizations that functioned with dozens of job categories (which inevitably led to a "that's not my job, you do it" attitude) were reduced, in many cases, to just a few major job classifications. Examples abound:

- At UCAR, up to nine different jobs are now combined into one.

- At Milwaukee Insurance, a typical policy went from a policy rater to an underwriter to a processor. Thanks to cross-training, team members now perform all three tasks—and they do them well.

- At Westinghouse's Electronics Assembly Plant, work was

performed by several different specialty teams. Westinghouse redesigned its operations into highly cross-functional product teams that learned robotic tasks, assembly, soldering, and testing. Through extensive cross-training, these teams were able to reduce work in process by a factor of four.

Expanded Team Responsibilities

In addition to extensive cross-training in technical tasks, employees in these organizations were required to assume a broad array of other responsibilities, many of them typically reserved for supervisors and managers. As Table 21.1 illustrates, it's quite common for teams to pick up those responsibilities that are directly job related. For example, most of the teams are responsible for quality improvement, work, vacation, and production scheduling, for safety and environmental concerns, for continuous process improvement, and for cross-training in various technical skills. Teams also are asked to assume leadership responsibilities. Indeed, many of these teams routinely handle leadership tasks—selecting new team members, evaluating team performance, handling customer and supplier interfaces, and controlling budgets and expenses.

Integration of Support Jobs and Responsibilities

Before the move to teams, many of these organizations had large "staff" departments—maintenance, engineering, human resources—that provided expertise and services to the line organization. But many also realized that maintaining separate support departments hindered the progress of their team implementations. One problem was that these support departments often caused delays. At one plant, an equipment breakdown caused a whole chain of events: the equipment

Table 21.1. Team Responsibilities.

Organization	Quality Improvement/Control	Work/Vacation Scheduling	Production Scheduling	Team Budget/Expenses Control	Selection	Discipline	Maintenance/Equipment Repair
Ampex	X	X	X		X		
Bord na Mora	X	X	X	X	X	X	X
Cape Coral Hospital	X	X		X			
Colgate	X	X		X	X		X
Development Dimensions International	X	X	X	X	X		X
Hannaford Brothers	X	X	X	X	X	X	X
Harris	X						
K Shoes	X		X	X			
Kodak	X	X	X		X		
Miller Brewing	X	X			X	X	X
Milwaukee Mutual	X	X	X		X		
Mine Safety Appliances	X		X	X			X
Pfizer	X						
Sterling Winthrop	X	X	X				X
Tennessee Eastman	X	X			X	X	X
Texas Instruments	X	X	X	X	X	X	X
Texas Instruments Malaysia	X	X	X	X		X	X
Westinghouse	X	X	X	X			X
Wilson Sporting Goods	X	X	X		X		X
UCAR	X	X	X				X

operator had go to a supervisor, who in turn had to call the support department, which, depending on its own scheduling demands, would fix the problem. Moreover, these support departments frequently were not customer-oriented—in fact, they often viewed themselves as the "customer." And they often did little to impart their skills and responsibilities to teams.

Team Measurement/ Goal Setting	Team Appraisal	Safety/ Environmental	Housekeeping	Business Direction "Input"	Process Improvement (Problem Solving/ Quality/ Customer) Teams	Plant/ Facility-wide Coordination/ Input	Shift/ Coordination	Technical Cross-Training	Training Other Team Members	Customer/ Supplier Interactions
					X				X	X
X		X				X				
		X	X					X		X
X	X	X	X			X		X	X	X
X		X	X		X	X	X	X	X	X
X	X	X	X	X	X	X	X	X	X	X
					X			X	X	X
X		X						X		
X	X			X	X	X		X	X	X
X	X	X	X		X	X	X	X	X	X
X	X			X	X	X		X	X	X
X		X	X		X			X	X	X
			X	X			X			
X			X					X	X	X
X	X	X		X	X	X	X	X		
X	X	X	X	X	X			X	X	X
		X	X	X		X	X	X		
		X	X		X	X	X	X	X	
X	X	X	X		X	X	X	X	X	
X	X	X	X		X	X	X	X		

Our twenty organizations have integrated support services into the teams in one of two ways. One approach is to keep functional specialists together as a team—but rather than serving the entire organization, they serve certain internal customers. Often they are cross-trained in support skills so they can address a variety of team needs. At Milwaukee Insurance, the HR department has assigned specialists to each line team. These specialists are cross-trained in all aspects of human resources: hiring, benefits, employee relations. When team members have benefits questions, they now go directly to their HR specialist rather than a benefits specialist. At Texas Instruments, engineers are clustered into "responsibility centers." Each responsibility center serves five or six production teams so that engineers feel they have a defined set of internal customers.

Assigning support specialists to teams resolves some of the conflict and built-in inefficiencies. The support staff tends to be more responsive to the needs of their internal customers, and team members, in turn, form closer alliances with their assigned support staff. However, problems still exist. Team members may be reluctant to expand their skills and knowledge in any of the technical support areas and continue to rely on their assigned support resources.

A second, more dramatic, approach is to incorporate functional specialists into the teams. These support specialists may even transfer their skills to the team. At Ampex, teams have assumed many responsibilities that specialists once handled, including material support, quality assurance, and production control. Teams do not handle highly technical engineering responsibilities, however. Instead, engineers are assigned to serve on specific teams. At K Shoes, the quality inspector's job has been virtually eliminated. The teams themselves are now trained to handle inspection and quality control.

There is no right or wrong way to integrate support functions into line teams. How an organization goes about it is determined by many factors—the team's maturity, the team members' skill level, the depth of technical expertise required, and the ratio of support professionals to team members. Many organizations are far too cautious in asking teams to assume certain support responsibilities. Ultimately, we feel, additional responsibilities will provide greater job satisfaction to team members and greater efficiencies to the organization.

Assuming Broader Organizational Responsibilities

Most of the changes we've discussed here pertain to shifts in responsibilities and roles within the team. But many of these organizations are going even further by giving team members even greater responsibility. The idea is that those who are closest to the job should have a say in decisions affecting the entire organization. It also sends a strong message: We value your opinions and we're partners in this organization. Here are some examples:

- At Hannaford Brothers, team members serve on intradistribution center teams that advise management on human resource policies or changes in operations. A task force of team members and HR people were involved in developing Hannaford's new pay-for-knowledge-and-skills system.

- At Westinghouse, a team of plant leaders and team members was formed to reevaluate the team process in order to continually improve the various systems that support the team concept (such as appraisal and selection).

- At Tennessee Eastman, teams participate in quality councils, a cross-functional manufacturing council, and various team steering committees that work on facilitywide policies and procedures. One cross-functional team, for example, is working on the apprentice system.

- At Kodak Customer Assistance Center, team members and managers serve on business councils and process councils. Business councils are responsible for understanding the marketing and product support requirements of the businesses they serve. They educate cus-

tomer service representatives about the products and set
up performance measurements to ensure that customer
service representatives meet the needs of internal and
external customers. Process councils are internally focused. Composed of managers and team members, these
councils help determine internal staffing needs, interview and select new employees, and help establish policies on team recognition systems.

The Changing Role of Leadership

No group felt the impact of the move to teams more than the
leaders in these organizations. As teams mature, they assume
greater responsibilities—many of which used to be the exclusive domain of first- and second-level leaders. This means
the role of leadership must change, as well, or the team
implementation will stagnate. As Robert Perkins, head of K
Shoes manufacturing operations, put it: "It's like Pandora's
Box. You build these teams and, at some point, they are going
to knock on your door and tell you things you don't want to
hear, like, 'We don't think you're being empowering enough.'
We realized that unless we were prepared to face that challenge, the teams would outgrow us as managers." The
change is not easy. In the words of Jeff Priano, a supervisor
who became a team leader in DDI's new system: "It felt like
the rug was being pulled out from under me."

In fact, five of the twenty organizations said that taking
the time to build management and line commitment to the
team process was imperative to their eventual success. What
happens to leaders in a team environment? How is the leadership role handled (inside and outside the team)? What
new responsibilities do supervisors and managers acquire?
All the organizations grappled with these questions as they

shifted to teams, and here they provide us with some of the answers.

Fewer Leadership Positions

Thirteen of the organizations report they now function with fewer managers than before their team implementation: UCAR reduced the number of managers by 40 percent; Milwaukee Insurance eliminated management positions by two-thirds; Tennessee Eastman operates with one-half the managers it once did; at Texas Instruments Malaysia, eighty supervisors were replaced by eight facilitators. Only two organizations, however, reported involuntary termination. While we suspect this number might be a bit larger, it's important to note that most of the organizations thinned their leadership ranks through early retirement programs, attrition, and reassignment, rather than layoffs and terminations.

Fewer Management Layers

Closely correlated with the need for fewer leaders is a significant reduction in the number of management layers. With empowered teams, there is just no need for checks and balances up and down an extensive chain of command. One-half of the organizations reported functioning with fewer layers. Cape Coral, for example, will go from seven management layers to three as it establishes patient-focused care centers. At Texas Instruments, layers have shrunk from eight to four or five.

Greater Span of Control

As the number of layers and managers is reduced, there is a corresponding increase in the span of control. (Actually, we prefer to call it "span of responsibility.") In some cases, this increase is quite dramatic. K Shoes is currently operating with a 1 to 60 span of responsibility (one leader per sixty team members). At Milwaukee, the span has increased from 1 to 6 to 1 to 20. At Miller, a leader may have fifty to sixty team members; at Texas Instruments Malaysia, a facilitator may be responsible for two hundred team members. Clearly the expanded span of responsibility requires a more empowering leadership style. You can't have the same degree of checks and controls with two hundred employees that you did with twenty.

What Happens to Former Managers?

Many leaders will move out of formal leadership positions into other jobs. At K Shoes, former supervisors were offered technical or retail jobs. At Milwaukee Insurance, managers were redeployed into technical or marketing positions. Texas Instruments Malaysia asked former supervisors to assist in the massive training initiative. At UCAR and Bord na Mona, some supervisors were recast into line team member roles, assuming production responsibilities.

Leaders who are not reassigned remain supervisors or managers—but with far different roles and different titles. Because spans of responsibility have increased and teams have assumed many traditional governance responsibilities, the remaining supervisors truly must become leaders. Their responsibilities to the team, as defined by nearly all twenty organizations, include coaching, facilitating, handling disciplinary problems, reviewing team/individual performance, training, and communication. Their new job is to help teams perform and grow. This change is often reflected in their new titles: Wilson and others use the word "coach," Sterling Winthrop likes "facilitator," Colgate calls its single management layer "area leaders," while Hannaford Brothers relabeled the role "operations coordinator." Apart from facilitating team performance, leaders often assume strategic responsibilities. At UCAR and Texas Instruments, leaders play a key role on process reengineering teams, which cross business functions. Kodak's Customer Assistance Center involves its leaders extensively in its process and business councils. At DDI, team leaders play active roles on numerous cross-functional quality improvement teams.

Not all leaders are successful in their new roles. Some mistake empowerment for abdication. As one team member said of his leader: "He used to come down and talk to us and let us know what was going on, and he really acted concerned. Since this empowerment thing started, we don't see him anymore." Knowing when to "hang on" and when to "let go" is a skill that leaders must master. Some leaders, however, simply can't make the transition. As one Sterling Winthrop manager explained, some "were washing their hands of the whole thing." The company ended up creating a new facilitator position for which the supervisors had to apply—along with anyone else in the organization who was interested. After an extensive assessment process, only a handful of the former supervisors were selected to be facilitators.

Leaders on Leadership Teams

Some of the organizations are trying to support their team implementations by practicing what they preach—modeling teamwork at managerial levels. Leaders are asked to serve on various teams, composed of other leaders, to work on special organizational issues or provide overall guidance to the organization. The basic concept is that—rather than having a hierarchy at the top and teams at the bottom—leaders must become more team oriented. At Texas Instruments Malaysia, team facilitators report to process management teams of four mid-level managers who function as a team. Facilitators obtain coaching, support, and advice from anyone on the mid-level management team. Kodak's Customer Assistance Center has an overall leadership council composed primarily of managers who help set overall policy and direction for the organization. At UCAR, middle and senior managers are involved on various management teams that deal with business development, process improvement, and site coordination. Jim McKnight, manager of UCAR operations, says it's critical that "we do the same thing at the business team level that we're asking production work teams to do."

Leadership Within the Team

So far we've been talking about the role of formal leaders outside the team. But as teams assume many governance responsibilities, we are often asked whether they need an internal leadership function. In most cases, there is indeed a formal process for leadership within the team, but it varies considerably. Seven of the twenty organizations had a person on the team who was the designated leader. At Texas Instruments, many teams have an inside team leader called a coordinator. Colgate teams appoint a "point of contact" who serves as a coordinator between teams and various plantwide groups. At Wilson, outside leaders help a team coleader to develop greater leadership skills and responsibilities. In general, the team leader coordinates internal team activities and serves as a point of communication—bringing outside information to the team and sharing key information about team activities with other teams and managers. Problems can arise, however, when those who are designated for these roles are not particularly models of empowerment. Rather than serving as internal coaches and coordinators, they end up serving as internal bosses, causing resentment and conflict.

Team leadership can also be handled on a rotating basis. At UCAR, Westinghouse, Mine Safety Appliances, Harris, and

Hannaford Brothers, internal leaders are chosen to serve for a certain period of time. In the case of Hannaford Brothers, teams elect a coordinator who serves—for no longer than two consecutive six-month terms—as an interface with other teams in the distribution facility. Teams at Mine Safety Appliances choose a new "team captain" every two weeks to three months to handle the team's paperwork, production, and coordination. Westinghouse has rotating team leader volunteers, called officers, who, for a period of about six months, monitor and provide information to team members on production, budgets, quality, safety, and the like.

Half the organizations have no formal person responsible for team leadership. In these organizations, various governance responsibilities are shared among team members. Many use a formal system of assigning and rotating various leadership responsibilities to their team members, some using the star point concept explained earlier. At Texas Instruments Malaysia, each team has four coordinator positions, with each coordinator handling three or four different responsibilities that range from tracking attendance to maintaining inventory levels. At Tennessee Eastman, each team has up to ten coordinators who handle such things as safety, maintenance, housekeeping, and training. Mastering these coordinator roles is tied directly to a pay-for-applied-skills-and-knowledge system.

Those organizations that use a more formal star point system usually rotate the star points every four to twelve months. Thus, a person may be a star point for safety during half the year and move over to the training star point for the other half. However, not every team member has a star point assignment. A team may have only six to eight star points, but twenty team members.

An important point to keep in mind: systems that do not have internal team leaders are not necessarily more empowered—perhaps the organization simply wants outside leaders to play a stronger role in guiding team performance.

Aligning Organizational Systems

Fred Eintract at Texas Instruments thinks that one of the biggest eye-openers was the realization that shifting to empowered teams demands major changes in almost all systems, policies, and practices. It's nearly impossible to impose a team structure on a traditional organizational structure. "It took a while for some parts of the organization to realize the implications," says Eintract, "but once they did, you see it's eventually going to affect the whole culture of the organization." Most of the twenty organizations overhauled four key systems in their move to teams: selection, training, rewards/compensation, and monitoring performance.

Selecting Team Members

Working in a team environment calls for a different set of skills and motivations than those required in traditional workplaces. A premium is placed on the ability to learn, teamwork and collaboration, a continuous improvement ethic, high initiative, a focus on the customer, and problem-solving skills. And leaders need additional skills, as well, in coaching, facilitation, encouraging continuous improvement, and running meetings. Making sure you have the best people on board will dramatically increase your chances for a successful team implementation. Most of these organizations made a transition to teams with their current workforce. Thus the need for revamping the selection process was not high on their list of priorities. But some of the organizations (especially new plant start-ups) wisely realized that a new and high-powered approach to selection would pay off in

years to come. Several of the organizations used a selection
process with these basic features:

- A job analysis is conducted to identify the skills and motivations called for in the new team environment—not
  only the "can do" (the skills) but the "will do" (the desire to do it).

- Multiple assessment techniques are used to evaluate the
  complex skills required for team performance—a combination of paper-and-pencil tests, job motivation instruments, realistic job previews, interviews, technical skill
  tests, and simulations. These measures, requiring up to
  twenty hours of applicant time in all, are administered
  and observed by several assessors so that more than one
  perspective goes into these critical selection decisions.

- The assessment techniques are organized into a selection system that begins with easy-to-use and cost-
  effective screens for large numbers of applicants and
  progresses to in-depth evaluation tools as applicants advance past successive hurdles. Colgate, for example, was
  faced with ten thousand applicants for a mere two
  hundred jobs—fifty applicants for every position. Thus a
  phased approach to selection is imperative.

- Those involved in the selection process are trained in
  their roles. They are taught to observe and evaluate behavior, conduct targeted interviews, and integrate all the
  data to reach sound decisions.

Organizations using these high-powered selection systems at
start-up tend to continue using them in hiring for open positions. In fact, hiring for a new plant start-up is only one
reason for using a comprehensive selection process. Pfizer,
DDI, Sterling Winthrop, Kodak Customer Assistance Center,
and Ampex use a systematic approach to selecting team

members and leaders. Kodak and Ampex, for example, maintain ongoing selection committees responsible for new hiring or promotion decisions. Sterling Winthrop designed a selection process to screen volunteers from its workforce to serve on pilot teams as well as to select team coaches (team leaders) from its managerial ranks.

One last point regarding selection: teams would hardly be empowered if all the selection decisions were made by management. Thus in organizations like Miller, Pfizer, and Ampex make sure that team members get involved in selecting new team members.

Developing Team Skills

One of the primary lessons here is that organizations must ensure sufficient time, commitment, and resources to implement team training. Cape Coral, Kodak's Customer Assistance Center, Miller, Texas Instruments Malaysia, Sterling Winthrop—all said that training could make or break the success of a team implementation. Yet they admit that training time was often the first thing sacrificed to the many demands on a team's time—with detrimental effects.

Although when it comes to team training enough might never be enough, these twenty organizations outpace traditional companies by far: average first-year training time runs from a low of 8 hours to a high of 180. Training does not end after the first year, however. Teams receive another 20 to 40 hours of training as they enter their second year, and thereafter the commitment to training continues at an equal or greater rate. Here are the common types of training provided to teams:

- Orientation and training in the team concept and the principles of team design

- Training in problem solving and quality improvement to help teams carry out their responsibilities to continuously improve process and quality
- Training in a whole range of team social skills: meeting skills, resolving conflict, coaching/facilitation, and more
- Training in business knowledge and understanding basic financial concepts—critical if teams are to play a role in budgeting or must interact directly with other teams as well as outside customers and suppliers
- Technical cross-training to acquire the breadth and depth of multiple skills that are often part of a team redesign effort

There are a number of important lessons about training that are worth considering as you continue with your own team training plans:

- Lesson 1: Training must be spread over a period of time and should be given when the teams will be able to use the skills (just-in-time training). It makes little sense to train team members in interviewing skills six months before they will be involved in a hiring decision. One training manager said, "We were thinking that if a little training is good, a lot of training is even better." The company later found out that some of the skills taught early had diminished by the time teams were ready to use them.
- Lesson 2: Don't neglect the need for management/leadership development in the zeal to get team members trained. Harris admits to shortcutting middle leadership levels in training and involvement in the team approach. Most of the company's initial culture training was confined to senior managers and team members, leaving middle managers out of the loop. This only heightened

their confusion about their new roles—a problem Harris was quick to correct.

- Lesson 3: Involve team members in the training plan. At Colgate, team members did an excellent job of developing and standardizing the technical curriculum for the newly designed liquid detergent plant. In some organizations, union members teach team and technical skills to their work teams.

- Lesson 4: Management must show active support. Frank Gambino, Mine Safety Appliances' plant manager, took a major role in teaching teams more about the financial aspects of running the business.

Rewards and Compensation

Traditional compensation and reward systems simply don't cut it in a team environment. In the organizations surveyed here, a great premium is being placed on multiskilling, flexibility, teamwork, continuous quality improvement, self-management, and customer focus. But the traditional method of compensation and rewards—automatic cost-of-living increases, merit increases, emphasis on individual recognition—does not support such changes. Moreover, it seldom relates pay increases to the organization's financial performance. (Increases are given at the same rate regardless of how well or how poorly the company is doing.) Finally, it fails to answer a key question asked by new team members: "What's in it for us if we help change things around here?" Perhaps that's why fourteen out of the twenty organizations decided to change their compensation and reward systems to support their team cultures. There are three general approaches to compensation being used by these organizations: skill-based pay, gain-sharing systems, and team bonus schemes.

Skill-Based Pay.   Skill-based pay (or pay-for-skill systems) are used by Milwaukee Insurance, Hannaford Brothers, Tennessee Eastman, Colgate, and Sterling Winthrop (whose systems were in place prior to the team implementation). Miller Brewing, Texas Instruments, Pfizer, and Kodak Customer Assistance Center are designing and piloting pay-for-skill systems. Tennessee Eastman's system is one of the most innovative we've come across. Teams are first required to demonstrate their "team maturity" by meeting a set of expectations—technical, social, and business knowledge skills—defined by a cross-functional compensation policy team. No team member may participate in the pay-for-applied-skills-and-knowledge (PASK) plan until all team members meet the initial set of expectations. The PASK system has six levels and spans a whole range of "skill areas." At first team members are expected to master additional technical skills, business skills (safety, computers, broad business knowledge), and team interaction skills. They also are expected to serve in at least two team leadership roles. As team members advance through the system, there is a shift from learning a wide range of skills to specialization. Team members are then asked to pick a career path in, say, operations, maintenance, laboratory work, or training.

In addition to the ingenuity of the system, Tennessee Eastman has established unique administration guidelines. For example, each team must annually review its maturity status by comparing itself against a "fully functioning" team checklist. Team members also need to demonstrate that they use their newly acquired skills 10 percent of the time (a "use-or-lose" policy, so to speak). Finally, team members must chose skills or career paths that fit in with an overall team skills profile to ensure that the team has the range of skills it needs to accomplish its goals. A team couldn't function effectively if, for example, every team member picked laboratory work as its career path.

How much do these companies add to base compensation in a pay-for-skill plan? At Hannaford, team members can increase their base pay by up to 20 percent. Colgate was allowing an additional $0.30 cents an hour per skill up to a maximum of $1.50 (five skills). Regardless of the design of the system, skill-based pay plans offer several advantages—including a big increase in team and organizational flexibility to meet shifting production/customer demands, more cohesive and smoother-running teams (especially if team social skills are part of the plan), and greater opportunities for growth and challenge in ever-flattening organizations.

Gain-Sharing Plans.   Several of the organizations (Hannaford, Bord na Mona, Westinghouse, Texas Instruments Malaysia, Kodak Customer Assistance Center) have some sort of companywide gain-sharing plan. These plans usually reward *all* team members from *all* teams for reaching performance goals for the entire enterprise (usually at the company or plant level). Often these bonuses are based on a gain over some previous baseline of performance (hence the name "gain sharing"). Westinghouse, for example, gives an equal lump-sum payment to everyone in the plant based on plant-wide improvements in quality, cost, and productivity.

There are several advantages to this type of plan. It encourages teamwork throughout a business unit; it answers the question "What's in it for us?"; and it allows a variable approach to compensation based on the organization's performance. The plan has its shortcomings, though: the workforce will be disappointed if business conditions outside their direct control preclude a payout, and some teams or employees inevitably claim that they performed better than everyone else and thus deserve a greater piece of the pie.

Team Bonuses.   Team bonuses are similar to companywide gain-sharing bonuses except they are based on the performance of individual teams rather than the enterprise as a whole. Organizations that use this approach include Milwaukee Insurance, DDI, Colgate, and Harris. The team bonus approach rewards only those teams that perform and it promotes collaboration on a team. But there is a major drawback: if only some of the teams cash in while others lose out, resentment may make it difficult for the entire facility to work well together. This was a major reason why Westinghouse opted for a plantwide bonus system instead of a team bonus scheme.

Choosing the Right Option.   While no compensation system is perfect, these three options represent a fundamental shift from compensation based on individual performance to compensation based on the underlying goals of team-based organizations. As you go about designing or modifying your current reward system, keep a few things in mind:

- Changes in compensation plans are often emotional issues and hard to implement—attention can immediately shift from the wide range of teamwork benefits to "What's going to happen to my earnings?" This is why several of these organizations are just now designing new compensation systems. Sometimes it's better to tackle this problem later rather than sooner.

- The options reviewed here are not mutually exclusive. Many of the organizations couple individual-based compensation with a pay-for-skills plan or a bonus plan. Each plan accomplishes different objectives and together they can have a synergistic impact.

- Place as much emphasis on informal rewards and recognition as you do on changing compensation plans. Wilson Sporting Goods, for example, thinks internal motivation is far more important than special pay sys-

tems. Thus they have an ongoing program of award certificates for team achievements and, like the Harris Corporation, host an annual recognition awards dinner
attended by associates, spouses, and friends.

Managing Performance

We just visited an organization that is deciding how to redesign its organization, including the use of highly empowered
teams. Here's how the company currently conducts its performance appraisals:

Step 1: The manager sits down with each employee and
communicates key goals and measures. They are not
negotiable.

Step 2: One year later, the manager sits down and rates
each employee on achieving goals during the year. The
ratings are largely nonnegotiable and are based solely
on the manager's occasional interaction with the employee. They are supposedly tied to compensation, but
no one really sees the connection.

This system is in direct conflict with a team-based work culture—and is why many of the organizations in this book have
changed their approach to monitoring performance.

Above all, goal setting and monitoring are no longer top-
down and one-way. Without exception, all twenty of the
organizations get team members involved in establishing
team goals and monitoring performance against these goals.
At Westinghouse, teams (within the parameters of companywide goals and standards) set their own team goals. Similarly,
at Sterling Winthrop, teams track their own performance in
six areas: material and labor variances, quality measurements,
customer complaints, back order performance, and line fill

rates. They also are learning how to set team goals that tie directly to corporate and strategic planning goals. These organizations are finding that participative goal setting increases everyone's commitment to achieving the goals while team monitoring allows the team to improve itself—usually far quicker than management's feedback and less likely to elicit excuses and resistance.

In the appraisal process we are seeing two major changes. First, at six of our organizations (Milwaukee Insurance, DDI, the current Miller Brewing system, Westinghouse, Texas Instruments, Colgate) team members solicit feedback from other team members and from internal and even external customers. At Colgate, for example, team members gather performance feedback from other team members as well as complete a self-appraisal. Each team member then will meet with his or her area leader (the only layer of management between the plant manager and the team) and discuss performance and agree on a developmental plan. The process is highly participative. Input primarily comes from the team member being evaluated and his or her peers. The area leader is more a facilitator than a judge, and the focus is on development rather than evaluation.

A second group of organizations (UCAR, Kodak Customer Assistance Center, Miller Brewing, Texas Instruments, and Tennessee Eastman) are carrying things even further and developing a more elaborate team appraisal process. For example, our colleagues are working with one organization to develop a new team appraisal process and accompanying training system. The process starts with an annual discussion with each team on plantwide key result areas (major critical areas of accountability) and corresponding objectives. Each team then sets its own goals around four or five key areas (for example, one team is focusing on product waste). In addition, each team member targets two "dimensional," or behavioral, areas to work on (such as teamwork, initiative, or problem-solving skills). One dimensional area is selected by the team member, the other is assigned to the team member by the team. Twice a year, the team appraises its performance against the quantitative goals and objectives it set for itself. Once a year, the team provides constructive feedback to each individual team member on the two dimensional areas. A similar approach to team appraisal is being used by Kodak Customer Assistance Center (see Chapter Fourteen).

Here are a few guidelines for making your team appraisal successful:

- Appraisal should not be the first activity assigned to a team. Teams need time to mature, get used to working together, and build trust before they can evaluate one another, especially face to face.

- A team approach to appraisal requires training. Team members must learn how to establish goals, measure performance, assess individual strengths and weaknesses, and give constructive, balanced feedback—all difficult skills to learn.

- Don't assume that teams will be too easy on themselves. In reality, the opposite is often true—a team's expectations might well be higher than management's. At the Kodak Customer Assistance Center, teams were setting goals for themselves that were often more ambitious than those set by the leadership council.

The Payoff

Table 21.2 summarizes the results our organizations achieved by implementing teams. As we looked at the twenty organizations, we couldn't help but be impressed by three things:

Table 21.2. Team Results.

Organization	Impact of Teams
Ampex	• Inventory costs declined from $80 million to $20 million. • Scrap and rework costs were cut nearly tenfold. • On-time customer delivery figures rose to 98 percent. • On-time supplier delivery rose from 70 percent to 99 percent.
Bord na Mona	• Annual output per employee rose from 1,700 tons to 3,400 tons. • Absenteeism was reduced from 10–15 percent to 1–2 percent.
Cape Coral Hospital	(Early implementation; quantitative data not yet available.)
Colgate	• 30 percent increase in line efficiency.
Development Dimensions International	• 43 percent reduction in client-reported errors. • Revenue per employee rose nearly 65 percent.
Hannaford Brothers	• Top 15 percent of cost-efficient distribution centers nationwide. • Fewer on-the-job injuries—resulting in savings of more than $500,000 in worker compensation costs.
Harris	• $4.5 million in team improvement savings. • 18 percent reduction in costs.
K Shoes	• From 5,000 rejects per million to 250. • Output per employee up 19 percent. • On-time delivery up from 80 percent to 97 percent.
Kodak	• Turnover half the industry average. • Calls handled per hour up 100 percent. • First-time accuracy levels up 100 percent.
Miller Brewing	• 30 percent reduction in labor costs and requirements and a corresponding increase in productivity.
Milwaukee Mutual	• Shareholder value increased by more than 160 percent. • On-time policy delivery up from 70 percent to 90 percent. • Employee turnover dropped dramatically. • 20 percent cut in policy processing time. • Employee assistance program usage 40 percent below the industry average.
Mine Safety Appliances	• Output for several products increased by 25 to 65 percent. • Scrap and rework reduced by about 50 percent.
Pfizer	(Early implementation; quantitative data not yet available.)
Sterling Winthrop	• Lead time for shipping orders cut from 15 days to 5. • 40 percent increase in productivity. • 75 percent reduction in line changeover time.
Tennessee Eastman	• Awarded the 1993 Baldrige Award. • Productivity up 70 percent.

Table 21.2. Team Results, Cont'd.

Organization	Impact of Teams
	• Number one in customer satisfaction in its industry. • Best earnings/sales ratio of top 15 U.S. chemical companies.
Texas Instruments	• Awarded the 1992 Baldrige Award. • Revenue per employee up 50 percent. • Costs reduced by more than 50 percent. • Customer return rates reduced from 3 percent to 0.03 percent.
Texas Instruments Malaysia	• Defects dropped to extremely low level. • Cycle time reduced by approximately 50 percent. • Output per employee up 100 percent.
Westinghouse	• Cost for products down 60 percent. • Cycle time reduced from 12 weeks to 2. • Work in progress inventories reduced by 65 percent. • Rework down by 50 percent.
Wilson Sporting Goods	• Cost savings of more than $25 million (average of $5 million a year). • Inventory turnover has risen from 6.5 times to 90 times a year. • Scrap rates have dropped by 64 percent, rework by 91 percent, and cycle time by 30 percent.
UCAR	• Cycle time reduced by 40 percent. • Inventory reduced by 50 percent. • $10 million productivity improvement savings annually.

- The payoffs from teams are consistent across all the organizations. With the exception of Cape Coral Hospital (which is just in the early phases of implementation) and Pfizer (which is working on quantifying the impact of its teams), every organization has cashed in on its investment.

- The impact is significant. In many cases improvements are in the range of 50 to 100 percent.

- Teams improve many facets of the organization's business—from quality to turnover.

Let's highlight some of the major areas affected by teams:

- *Cost Savings:* Many of these organizations empower teams to work on continuous improvement. The payoff is enormous. UCAR teams save $10 million annually. Wilson Sporting Goods has achieved savings of $5 million a year for the past five years—an average of about $10,000 per associate. Harris reports cost savings of $4.5 million in a single year.

- *Labor Productivity:* Teams enabled these organizations to do much more with less. K Shoes reports a 19 percent increase in productivity; Sterling Winthrop, 40 percent; Miller, about 30 percent; Tennessee Eastman, 70 percent; Kodak Customer Assistance Center, topping 100 percent. By capitalizing on the collective brainpower of those closest to the work, teams are able to eliminate those things that simply don't add value.

- *Quality and Service Improvement:* Every organization today must focus not only on doing things at lower cost, but doing things better—continuously working to improve product and service. At Texas Instruments' McKinney facility, customer return rates have dropped from 3 percent to .03 percent. At Westinghouse, rework is down by 50 percent. At Texas Instruments Malaysia, defect rates shrank significantly. And, thanks to teams, Tennessee Eastman is first in customer satisfaction among its competitors.

- *Speed:* Doing things faster is yet another competitive edge in today's business environment. And again teams deliver. At UCAR, cycle time has been reduced by 40 percent. K Shoes has reduced the time to make a pair of shoes from twelve days to one.

- *Human Resource Benefits:* Teamwork affects the bottom line in other ways as well. Increased company loyalty spurred by teamwork results in less absenteeism, less turnover, and fewer worker's compensation claims.

Colgate's technician turnover, for example, is extremely low; 90 percent of those hired in 1988 are still on board. There are other people benefits as well. Hannaford Brothers' savings in worker's compensation costs translates into a labor savings of 79 cents an hour for every associate, which Hannaford feels gives the company a critical competitive advantage in a low-margin industry.

Moreover, these organizations have reported performance improvements in inventory reduction, supplier performance, lower maintenance costs, and greater overall production line efficiencies. Two of the organizations were awarded the Malcolm Baldrige National Quality Award (Texas Instruments in 1992 and Tennessee Eastman in 1993).

Perhaps even more important than the hard numbers is the impact teams have on the morale and motivation of the workforce itself. We've said earlier that the decision to implement teams must be backed by hardheaded business reasons. Yet it should be comforting to know that implementing teams is usually the "right thing to do" for the workforce. More than ever, people want to feel they can make a difference—that they are valued for their ideas and decisions, not just getting the job done.

Our interviews consistently revealed the power of teams. As one Mine Safety Appliances team member said: "Everyone feels the change. Being listened to, respected, involved in what's going on, has made a huge difference to people who have been doing the same things for years." Phillip Lloyd, Sterling Winthrop's HR manager, believes that those involved with teams "feel they have a destiny in the business and a role in determining that destiny." And Don Edgar, Cape Coral's CEO, believes "it's rewarding to see people who in the past have seen their role as 'do as we're told' begin to take ownership in their jobs."

Perhaps the most powerful team testimony, however, was made by Larry Teverbaugh at Westinghouse: "When business organizations create the right kind of team environment, ordinary people can create extraordinary value to support customers and stockholders. It becomes a family environment where we all look after the interests of the business and each other."

22

The Future of Teams: Predictions About the Journey Toward Empowerment

When we wrote *Empowered Teams* in 1991, we made several predictions about the future of teams. As revealed in our *Inside Teams* journey, many of these predictions have become reality.

We predicted that the use of teams would increase dramatically. Research we conducted for *Empowered Teams* indicated that only about one-quarter of surveyed organizations were using teams, involving only a small portion of the workforce. Only two years later, a similar study by Lakewood Publications (Gordon, 1992) showed that 35 percent of U.S. organizations were using self-directed teams, and if the twenty companies featured in this book are any indication, teams are being implemented in increasingly greater numbers.

We also predicted greater use of teams in white-collar service organizations. We've seen three leading-edge examples—Milwaukee Insurance, Cape Coral Hospital, and Kodak Customer Service Center—that indicate the dramatic increase of teams in nonmanufacturing organizations as well as in white-collar departments of manufacturing companies. Team implementations are surfacing in banks, software companies, and even government agencies.

We expected to see more team implementations around the world. Again, organizations featured in this book (Texas Instruments Malaysia, K Shoes, Bord na Mona, and Sterling Winthrop) demonstrated the cross-cultural applicability of teams. But these are not isolated examples. Bausch and Lomb implemented teams in Ireland. Semco, a manufacturer of food service equipment in Brazil, has been using the team concept for nearly a decade. And from 1992 to 1994 we have helped implement teams in multinational start-ups for cloth-ing and paper companies in Poland.

Our final prediction called for greater national support of the team concept. Certainly, the Malcolm Baldrige National Quality Award has prompted an increase in American indus-tries' emphasis on quality as well as high-involvement lead-ership practices. It's no accident that award recipients from 1992 (Texas Instruments' Defense System and Electronic Group) and 1993 (Tennessee Eastman) are model high-performance workplaces with widespread team implementa-tions. Further support is on the way. "The Future of the American Workplace," conference, sponsored by the Clinton administration in 1994, focused on "case histories" of orga-nizations that successfully implemented high-involvement, team-centered workplaces.

What's in store for teams in the future? If we were to revisit these twenty organizations in five years, where would they be with their teams? Although the rapid pace of change makes looking into the future a risky business, here are some of the trends we'd expect to see.

Teams will expand exponentially.   Lawler, Mohrman, and Ledford (1992) recently completed a survey of high-involve-ment work practices in 313 U.S. organizations. When they asked the organizations how they planned to use self-managed teams in the future, 60 percent of the respondents said they would increase or greatly increase their use of teams, 37 percent said they would stay the same, and only 3 percent said they would reduce or discontinue the use of teams. As pres-sures to compete will only get tougher and our workforce will expect a more democratic workplace, organizations will continue to transform—based on proven strategies that will have an enduring impact on their businesses.

Service industries, still lagging behind manufacturing in workforce innovations, will expand the use of teams. For example, we estimate that a high percentage of U.S. health care organizations will move toward the "patient-focused care" concept explained in our Cape Coral Hospital case (Chapter One). Further, team applications will continue to expand in different cultures and countries. Five years from now, we'd most assuredly be able to present case studies from Eastern Europe and mainland China. Teams no longer will be a phenomenon. They will be the way work gets done.

Support systems will continue to evolve. In this book we have focused on three systems: compensation, performance management, and training. These three systems will continue to evolve in order to support the team concept. Here are just a few of the changes we expect:

- Team training will increase from an annual average of 40-60 hours to 160-200 hours. Changing technology, more tailoring of products and services, increasing leadership spans of control, and growing cross-training requirements will necessitate continuous learning.

- Learning will become largely team-directed or self-directed. A centralized approach to training, requiring HR specialists, will no longer be able to keep up with the demand. Everyone will need to become a trainer and a learner. Various technologies for delivering team training (computer-based training, interactive media, distance learning) will become far more commonplace.

- Team training will include broader business knowledge—understanding customer needs and markets, financial performance, the range of the company's products or services, the links between one's own team and other teams. This type of training will be essential if team members are to have increasing job flexibility and make sound decisions about their products and services and valuable contributions to their enterprise as a whole.

- Performance management will become largely team-directed and self-directed. Through computerized networks, team members will be able to seek performance feedback from peers, bosses, suppliers, and customers. They will have mastered the skills to give and receive feedback. Although individual appraisals will still be conducted by the team, far greater emphasis will be placed on the entire team's performance. As their span of control encompasses forty to eighty team members, leaders will need to coach at the team level rather than evaluating each team member's performance.

- Expect a radical increase in the use of skill-based pay and variable compensation tied to individual, team, and organizational performance at all levels. The link between compensation and individual worth (in terms of depth and breadth of skills and knowledge) will become much stronger. And as teams contribute more directly to the well-being of an entire organization by assuming greater responsibility, the question of "what's in it for us" will be addressed by more and more organizations.

Radical organizational changes will increase the need for teams.   Organizational structures, as we know them today, will gradually disappear. Through a highly strategic change known as reengineering, many organizations are breaking down functional silos (marketing, sales, human resources) and organizing their entire companies around the *processes* its customers consider essential to its success (order fulfillment, client acquisition, new product realization). The principles of reengineering closely parallel those of empowered work teams. Hammer and Champy (1993), two leaders in the field, propose that many reengineering projects are built around the following recurrent themes:

- Several jobs are combined into one.
- Workers make decisions.
- Process steps are followed in a logical order.
- Checks and controls are reduced.
- Work is performed where it makes sense.

These themes have been the principal tenets of team redesign for the past two decades. Hammer and Champy (p. 71) say that as organizations reengineer around core processes, "teams of one person or several, performing process-oriented work, are inevitably self-directing. Within the boundaries of their obligations to the organization . . . they decide how and when work is going to be done. If they have to wait for supervisory direction of their tasks, they aren't process teams." But reengineering, by definition, requires extensive process redesign. There is little room for "natural" work teams in a reengineering effort. Moreover, reengineering usually requires massive and radical change. It is revolutionary—not evolutionary like many of our team implementations.

We contend that empowered redesigned teams will be a logical outcome of reengineering. As the number of reengineering implementations grows, so too will the implementation of teams in those organizations. UCAR, for example, started a reengineering implementation that led to their corporatewide team rollout.

Permanent teams will be replaced by virtual teams. We anticipate that a new type of team structure—virtual teams—will become more prevalent. The major difference between most of the teams described in this book and virtual teams is their longevity. Virtual teams are temporary "work modules" made up of cross-functional team members who come together to work on a particular project or task. Once the project is completed, team members disband and are assigned to other new virtual teams. This highly flexible type of organizational structure can best be compared to modular furniture. People can be moved easily in accord with ever-changing business needs. The virtual team still can be largely self-directed, however, as it assumes most of its own leadership and work tasks. Consider, for example, the new product development teams at Development Dimensions International (DDI). We charter teams of marketing, program design, and production specialists to work on launching new products. Once a product is launched, the team disbands and is reassigned to other teams. Harris's cross-functional project teams are virtual teams, as well. Although these teams present challenges that are not inherent in permanent teams, the constantly changing and unique customer requirements of the future will require far more flexible organizations that can quickly deploy and redeploy their resources to accommodate the demands.

The role of the "boss" will disappear. In the twenty organizations surveyed in this book, you saw only a preview of the evolving leadership role. Downsizing, larger spans of control, leadership through coaching and influence—these are just a few of the hallmarks of the new team leader. And within the next five years, the leader's role will change even more profoundly:

- Organizations will continue to flatten their hierarchies while the number of teams that leaders must manage will increase. The increased span of responsibility will require a change in style and behavior.

- Checks and controls will need to be replaced by empowerment and trust.

- Leaders must get out of their own functional silos. As teams become more virtual, a leader's permanent job will be to coach different teams and champion process improvement. The use of formal authority to get work done will be replaced with the ability to inspire and facilitate.

- The team approach will be applied at the leadership level as well. Teams will have access to leadership councils, "boards," or support groups composed of leaders with different skills and expertise but all with excellent coaching skills. Forget any semblance of following the old "chain of command"—the chain won't even exist. These leadership teams also will begin to function as "real" teams: accomplishing organizational objectives, evaluating their own team performance, mastering cross-functional skills.

Moreover, leaders will need to master a whole new set of skills—beyond those we have called "coaching" and "facilitation." We propose that tomorrow's team leaders will have to be masters at improving process, leading through vision and values, building a culture based on trust, and developing strong business partnerships with other teams, customers, and suppliers. These skills will require far more training and practice than most organizations (including those surveyed here) currently provide.

Social changes will support organizational teamwork. Sharing responsibility, leadership, and recognition is not easy. Many of us were brought up in a time when getting ahead, even at the expense of others, was a driving social value. Even early childhood "team" sports activities can reinforce the value of stardom over teamwork.

In the near future, we expect our social and educational systems to begin to support and teach teamwork. Already there are encouraging signs. One of our children is in a second-grade class that regularly discusses a set of values. Teamwork and cooperation are high on the list. The second-grader's older sibling, a fifth-grader, is expected to complete two or three team projects during the year. Students must learn to plan and carry out the projects together. Finally, Harvard's MBA program is planning a new curriculum that will require that one-quarter of all course work must be completed by students working together in teams. Rather than grading students individually, the whole team will receive a grade.

It's time to end our benchmarking journey. We have toured through organizations that have made teams work. Given the tremendous impact these organizations have achieved with teams, it's tempting to think of teams as the most recent in a series of "get well" pills. But teams don't make things better with one easy swallow. Far from a panacea, they demand courage, persistence, and the ability to deal simultaneously with organizational and business ambiguity. As Roger Michaelsen, director of Kodak Customer Assistance Center, put it, "I couldn't have imagined how massive this undertaking would be."

Yet for those who stay the course, the rewards are many—not only in terms of the bottom line, but also in creating an organizational culture that demonstrates the value of people. Teams create a sense of job and business ownership we all have wanted for years. For those of you well into teams, take some pride in knowing you are ahead of the game. For those of you at an early stage of your implementation, we hope you've learned some valuable lessons for the upcoming years. For those of you who haven't yet started teams, we hope the experiences of these twenty organizations will inspire you to start your own journey.

References

Gordon, J. "Work Teams: How Far Have They Come?" *Training,* 1992, 29(10), 59-65.

Hammer, M., and Champy, J. *Reengineering the Corporation: A Manifesto for Business Revolution.* New York: HarperBusiness, 1993.

Lawler, E., III, Mohrman, S., Ledford, G., Jr. *Employee Involvement and Total Quality Management.* San Francisco: Jossey-Bass, 1992.

Index

A

A. E. Staley, 96, 99
Abdullah, A., 266, 267
Absenteeism reduction, 153, 161, 163, 181, 191, 336
Accountabilities, team, 108, 120. *See also* Responsibilities
Accounting system, 205-206
Accuracy improvement, 37
Advisors, team, 273, 274
Advisory teams, 130, 172-173, 180, 222, 315-316
Alignment, of organizational systems, 14-15, 322-332; in Bord na Mona, 158-159; in Development Dimensions International, 47-49; in Eastman Chemical Company, 241; in the future, 340-341; in Harris Corporation, 205-206; in Mine Safety Appliances Company, 81, 89; in Texas Instruments, 261; in Westinghouse Electronic Assembly Plant, 275. *See also* Compensation systems; Member selection; Performance management; Training
Amalgamated Engineering Union (AEU), 151
Amalgamated Transport and General Workers Union (ATGWU), 151
Amer, 295
Ampex Systems, 137-150; background information on, 140-141, 301; key lessons learned in, 140; results of team implementation in, 139, 149-150, 333; summary information on, 5, 137-140; team implementation in, 137, 143-146, 306; team responsibilities in, 137-138, 146, 312-313, 314
Analgesics industry, 109-110. *See also* Sterling Winthrop, Ltd.
Andres, P., 47
Applanaidu, S., 267

Appraisal process. *See* Compensation systems; Performance evaluation systems
Area forums, 91, 99, 105
Area leaders/managers, 165, 173, 175-176, 223, 318. *See also* Leaders, team
Asia, case-study organization in. *See* Texas Instruments Malaysia
Assessment techniques, for hiring, 323. *See also* Member selection
Association for Quality and Participation, 199
Auditing, of performance, 76. *See also* Performance evaluation systems; Performance management
Australia, case-study organization in. *See* Sterling Winthrop, Ltd.
Australian Workers Union, 106
Automation, 169, 171, 270, 275. *See also* Mechanization
Autonomous enterprise teams, 151; development of, 157-159; functioning of, 159-161

B

Backorder reduction, 88, 108, 109, 110, 119
Bausch and Lomb, 338
Beer brewing business, case study. *See* Miller Brewing Company
Benchmark information: case-study organizations, listed, 4-5; key points to watch, 2, 10-16; sources of, 16
Benchmarking trips, 14, 71, 96-97, 240-241, 306
Betchoski, A., 46, 47
Bonuses: organizationwide, 175, 208, 273, 329; team, 54, 62, 67, 75-76, 161, 165, 166, 172, 193, 203, 222, 229, 281, 328-329. *See also* Gain sharing plans
Bord na Mona, 151-163; background information on, 153-155; key les-

sons learned in, 153; management support in, 302; reorganization of, 153-159, 310, 318; results of team implementation in, 1, 153, 162-163, 333; summary information on, 5, 151-153; team implementation in, type of, 151; team responsibilities in, 151-152, 312-313; union relationships in, 151, 156, 158, 159-160

Boundaries: between councils and teams, 216-217; design principles for, 241, 247; between design teams, 114-115; management of, 235; between natural work teams, 99, 100-101; between steering and implementation teams, 21-22, 32-33

Boundary managers, 152, 153, 161-162

Bramson, E., 141

Breweries, 69-70. *See also* Miller Brewing Company

Budgeting, team involvement in, 282-283, 312

Bureaucracy, 3, 6-8, 9, 93; reengineering of, 126-127, 133, 143, 187-188, 307-308; team implementation in, 261. *See also* Reengineering

Business councils, 208, 216, 217, 218, 315-316

Business direction, team responsibility for, 313

Business needs, for implementing teams, 301-302

Business skills, of teams, 159, 160, 256, 271, 282-283

Business teams, 126, 133

Business types, of case-study organizations, 4-5

Business units, teams as. *See* Autonomous enterprise teams

C

C & J Clark, 56

Cape Coral Hospital, 19-33; background information on, 22-24, 301, 317; key lessons learned in, 21-22; results of reorganization of, 31-33, 309-310, 333, 334, 340;

summary information on, 4, 19-20; team responsibilities in, 19-20, 312-313; team implementation in, 19, 24-27

Care 2000, 23-24

Career advancement, expectations of, 176-177

Career paths, 245, 258

Case-study organizations, 15; listed, 4-5

Cavallo, M., 96, 97

Centers of excellence, 276

Central forum, 99, 101, 105

Certification: for skills training, 147, 174, 180, 188, 189-190, 217-218, 257; "team certified," 189-190; for team maturity, 243-244; "team qualified," 189; of team trainers, 245

Champy, J., 342

Change: approaches to initiating, 303-304; commitment to, organization-wide, 237, 247, 251, 260; commitment to, from senior management, 302-303; need for measured, 223, 232-233, 290; pace of, 92-93, 104, 124, 133-134, 141-143, 149-150; strategies for, 304-306

Charters: for Cape Coral Hospital Design Team, 25-26; need for clear, 194, 204; team, 21, 133

Chemicals business, case studies. *See* Pfizer, Inc.'s Vigo Food Science Group; Eastman Chemical Company

Clinton administration, 339

Cluster design, 278-279

Coaches, 318; in Eastman Chemical Company, 245-246, 247; in Milwaukee Mutual Insurance Company, 238; in Wilson Sporting Goods Company, 287, 288, 290, 291, 292, 295. *See also* Facilitators, team; Leaders, team

Colgate-Palmolive Company, 164-178; background information on, 168-170; key lessons learned in, 167-168; as manager training ground, 177-178; results of team implementation in, 166-167, 176-178, 333, 335-336; summary information on, 5, 164-168; team implementation in, 164, 170-176, 310, 320, 323, 328; team responsibilities in, 164-165, 171-172, 312-313

Colorado, case-study organization in. *See* Ampex Systems

Commitment, 98, 124, 237, 247, 251, 260, 306

Committees, plantwide, 165, 172-173

Commodity teams, 200

Communication: about changes, 109, 120; about customer demand, 61-62; with design team, 186; electronic mail, 74; in redesigned teams, 108; from senior managers, 140, 265, 269; for shift work, 38, 46, 51-52, 130; team leaders for, 165, 172

Compensation, fear of losing, 65

Compensation systems, 14-15; alignment of, 49, 326-330; in Ampex Systems, 138, 139, 148, 160-161; in Bord na Mona, 152, 156, 157; in Cape Coral Hospital, 20; changing of, 329; in Colgate-Palmolive Company, 165, 171, 174-175, 328; consensus review process in, 229; in Development Dimensions International, 36, 48-49; in Eastman Chemical Company, 235, 243-245, 327; for former supervisors, 103; in the future, 341; in Hannaford Brothers Company, 180, 189-190, 328; in Harris Corporation, 193, 203, 330; in K Shoes, Ltd., 54, 62; in Kodak Customer Assistance Center, 208, 217-218, 228-229; in Miller Brewing Company, 67, 73, 75-76; in Milwaukee Mutual Insurance Company, 222; in Mine Safety Appliances Company, 80, 87; pay-for-performance, 249, 257; pay-for-skills/knowledge, 91, 103, 148, 165, 174-175, 180, 188, 189-190, 208, 217, 222, 235, 243, 244-245, 249, 257, 275, 279-280, 281, 284, 327-328; in Pfizer, Inc., 91, 103; production-based, 152, 156, 157-158, 160-161; selection of, 329-330; in Sterling Winthrop, Ltd., 107, 118, 119; team-driven vs. individual, 49, 326, 329; and team per-

formance, 139; in Texas Instruments—Defense System and Electronics Group, 249, 257, 258; in Texas Instruments Malaysia, 263, 269; types of, 326-330; in UCAR Carbon, 122, 130; in Westinghouse Electronic Assembly Plant, 273, 275, 278; in Wilson Sporting Goods Company, 287, 294, 329-330

Competition, as motivation for team implementation, 301; in Ampex Systems, 141, 149; in Colgate-Palmolive Company, 168-169; in Eastman Chemical Company, 238-239; in Mine Safety Appliances Company, 81; in Sterling Winthrop, Ltd., 109, in Wilson Sporting Goods Company, 288-289

Computer networks, 341

Consensus: decision-making, 67, 74, 101, 107, 152, 189, 208; plantwide, 269-270; review process, 229, 230; role assignments by, 229

Consultants, for redesign, 14

Continuous improvement, 31-32, 139, 197, 198-200; in heavy work environment, 212, 220; of processes, 47; reward system for, 263; using TCCP process, 225-229, 231; of team implementation, 247, 315; work-area teams, 286, 288

Control: fear of losing, 40, 41-42, 60, 140, 150; increased span of, 317-318, 341. *See also* Leadership roles

Coordinators: shift, 130; team, 180, 188-189, 201-202, 235, 242-243, 256, 263, 268, 318, 320, 321. *See also* Leaders, team

Corporate management, and plant-level team implementation, 69, 78, 94. *See also* Executives; Management; Senior managers

Cost reduction: as evaluation criteria, 55; through sociotechnical systems approach, 190-191; through team implementation, 133, 153, 162-163, 167, 176, 181-182, 194, 205, 251, 274, 284, 334-335. *See also* Labor cost reduction

Councils, 207, 208, 214-215, 216-217, 315-316, 320

Cross-functional teams, 2, 9-10; coordination of, 188-189; in Eastman Chemical Company, 240; in Kodak Customer Assistance Center, 207, 217; in Milwaukee Mutual Insurance Company, 221, 226-229; in Pfizer, Inc., 90; for problem solving, 138, 164; for process improvement, 34, 53, 248; for product development, 255; for specific programs, 192-193, 196, 198, 200-201; in Sterling Winthrop, Ltd., 112, 114, 119; in Texas Instruments—Defense System and Electronics Group, 248, 254-255; in UCAR Carbon, 127-128; in Westinghouse Electronic Assembly Plant, 272, 280, 283; in Wilson Sporting Goods Company, 293. *See also* Permanent cross-functional teams; Temporary cross-functional teams

Cross-training, 310-311, 325; advantages of, 12; appropriate compensation for, 15, 103, 189-190; as benchmark key point, 2, 12; certification in, 147; and customer satisfaction, 238, 247; dilution in, 280; examples of, 8, 44-45; and job satisfaction, 38, 45; between maintenance and operator technician teams, 168, 177; in modular production system, 61; in natural work teams, 102-103; on-the-job, 146-147; for patient care teams, 19, 23, 30, 340; in permanent work teams, 144, 146-147; and productivity increase, 51; of specialists, 314; team responsibility for, 172, 173-174, 203, 215, 313; union attitudes towards, 159-160. *See also* Certification; Skills-based pay; Training, for team implementation; Training, for team leaders

CSI. *See* Development Dimensions International

Culture change: aligning systems with, 14-15, 47-49, 81, 322-332; training for, 21, 33. *See also* Training, for team implementation; Training, for team leaders

Customer complaint reduction, 110, 239

Customer demand, production based on, 61-62, 87, 129-130, 145

Customer order management, 126

Customer satisfaction, 141, 196, 237, 239, 246, 262, 267

Customer service, reengineering around, 126, 133, 224, 226

Customer Service Inc. (CSI), 35, 39. *See also* Development Dimensions International

Customer service support business, case study. *See* Kodak Customer Assistance Center

Customers: internal, 227-228, 312, 313-314; and mature teams, 15, 188; mission statement regarding, 100; team responsibility for, 313

Cycle time reduction, 123, 133, 194, 264, 270, 274, 276, 283, 284, 288, 335

D

Decentralization, 141, 149, 254

Defense electronics business, case studies. *See* Harris Corporation; Texas Instruments—Defense System and Electronics Group; Westinghouse

Delayering, 63, 132, 317. *See also* Managers, reduction of

Delivery times, 55, 64, 108, 109-110, 139, 150, 251

Deming, W. E., 241

Design teams, 305-306; in Ampex Systems, 143; in Cape Coral Hospital, 24-27; charters for, 25-26, 184; in Hannaford Brothers Company, 184, 185-186; in Kodak Customer Assistance Center, 210, 213; in Miller Brewing Company, 71, 72; multifunctional, 108; in Pfizer, Inc., 97-99, 101, 105; roles and membership of, 305; in Sterling Winthrop, Ltd., 108, 114-115; team process in, 213-214; in Texas Instruments—Defense System and Electronics Group, 254-255; in UCAR Carbon, 127, 128-129. *See also* Steering teams

Detergents business, case study. *See* Colgate-Palmolive Company

Development Dimensions International (DDI), 34-52; background information on, 38-39, 302; changing role of leaders in, 40-42, 319; a day in the life of, 46-47; key lessons learned in, 38; results of team implementation in, 37-38, 50-52, 333; summary information on, 4, 34-38; systems alignment in, 47-49; team implementation in, type of, 34; team responsibilities in, 34-35, 312-313; virtual teams in, 343

Disbanding, of teams, 54

Discipline, team responsibility for, 312

Dispute resolution procedure, 66-67, 75

Distributed leadership, 249

Distribution center, design of, 184-187

Downsizing, 56-57, 98, 103. *See also* Layoffs; Managers, reduction of

E

Eastern Europe, 300-301, 339, 340

Eastman Chemical Company (Tennessee Eastman Division), 234-247; background information on, 238-240, 317; key lessons learned in, 237-238; results of team implementation in, 237, 246-247, 333-334; summary information on, 5, 234-238; team implementation in, 234, 242-246, 321, 327; team responsibilities in, 234-235, 312-313, 315

Edgar, D., 28-29, 31-32, 336

Educational system, teaching teamwork in, 345

Efficiency improvement, 166, 176, 206, 231-232, 336

Eintracht, F., 254, 260-261, 322

Electronic mail, 74

Electronics business, case studies. *See* Ampex Systems; Harris Corporation; Texas Instruments—Defense System and Electronics Group; Texas Instruments Malaysia; Westinghouse

Employee involvement, 94-95; challenges of implementing, 95-99; curtailment of, due to time constraints, 274-275, 281, 284; in design/planning phases, 96-98, 104-105, 110, 186, 210, 213-214, 326; organizationwide, 124, 228-229, 260, 306; and team implementation, 103, 104-105, 290-295. *See also* Employees; Empowerment; Governance; Leadership roles

Employee involvement teams (EITs), 192, 194, 196, 198-206

Employees: loyalty of, 64-65, 335-337; morale of, 89, 133, 167, 176, 232, 296, 335-337; and manager relations, 255; motivated, 169-170, 183-184; reducing skepticism of, 81, 92, 97, 104, 119, 182; seasonal, 151, 156, 159. *See also* Absenteeism; Employee involvement; Empowerment, employee; Member selection; Resistance; Turnover

Employees, in case-study organizations: number of, 4-5; percentage of, in teams, 4-5

Empowered Teams, 338

Empowerment, employee: in Asia, 266-267, 271; and enhanced job responsibilities, 11; and governance responsibilities, 11-12; as management focus, 241-242; mission statement regarding, 100; and operator self-control, 266-267; as organizational value, 24; redesigning for, 253-255; and team leaders, 321-322. *See also* Teams, empowered

Empowerment, manager, 230

Engineers: continuous training for, 200-201; on product teams, 142, 143, 147, 256; resistance of, 140, 150

Equalization, of compensation, 49, 54, 62. *See also* Compensation systems

Executives: as facility leaders, 39; on implementation team, 28-29; on steering team, 24, 169, 184. *See also* Corporate management; Management; Senior managers

F

Facilitators, team, 54, 80, 88, 318; former foremen/supervisors as, 92,

99, 101, 103, 116-117, 122, 165, 249, 259, 263, 269; former managers as, 138, 222; as teams' support, 201-202. *See also* Leaders, team
Farley, D., 94
Farrington, H., 184
Farukhi, M. K., 212-213
Fibers business, case study. *See* Eastman Chemical Company
Flattened organization, 63, 72, 132, 258, 317
Florida, case-study organizations in. *See* Cape Coral Hospital; Harris Corporation
Florida Power and Light, 196
Food industry. *See* Hannaford Brothers Company; Pfizer, Inc.'s Vigo Food Science Group
Footwear, Knitwear, and Allied Trades, 53
Footwear manufacturing/retailing business, case study. *See* K Shoes, Ltd.
Foremen (former): as area leaders, 165; as boundary managers, 162; as facilitators, 92, 99, 101, 103, 104, 122; as process managers, 132. *See also* Supervisors
Forums, 91, 99, 101, 105
Functional organization, 3, 6-8, 9, 93; redesigning of, 221, 226-228, 255, 307-308; reengineering of, 126-127, 133, 143, 187-188; titles used in, 13
Future, of teams, 338-346
"Future of the American Workplace, The," 339

G

Gain sharing plans, 67, 75-76, 180, 181, 190, 208, 328
Gambino, F., 83, 85, 326
Geographic locations, of case-study organizations, 4-5
Goals: business, team alignment with, 194, 204; coordination of team, 250; setting challenging, 195, 204, 250; team involvement in setting, 313, 330-331, 332
Golembeski, W., 169
Golfball business. *See* Wilson Sporting Goods Company

Gordon, J., 338
Governance responsibilities, 3, 316-322; in Ampex Systems, 138; as benchmark key point, 11-12; in Bord na Mona, 152; in Cape Coral Hospital, 20, 30-31; in Colgate-Palmolive Company, 165; in Development Dimensions International, 35; in Eastman Chemical Company, 235; in Hannaford Brothers Company, 180; in Harris Corporation, 193; in K Shoes, Ltd., 54; in Kodak Customer Assistance Center, 208, 216-217; in Miller Brewing Company, 67; in Milwaukee Mutual Insurance Company, 222, 228-229; in Mine Safety Appliances Company, 80, 85-86; in Pfizer, Inc., 91, 99, 101-102; star allotment of, 9-10; in Sterling Winthrop, Ltd., 107; in Texas Instruments—Defense System and Electronics Group, 249; in Texas Instruments Malaysia, 263; in UCAR Carbon, 122, 128-129, 130; in Westinghouse Electronic Assembly Plant, 273; in Wilson Sporting Goods Company, 287. *See also* Leadership roles; Leaders, team
Graphite products business, case study. *See* UCAR Carbon
Grievance procedures, 66-67, 75, 160
Group leaders, 35, 39, 40-41
Growing points, 99, 100-101, 102

H

Hamilton, R., 47
Hammer, M., 342
Hannaford Brothers, 179-191; background information on, 182-184; key lessons learned in, 182; results of team implementation in, 181-182, 190-191, 333, 336; sociotechnical systems approach in, 184-187; star point system, 9-10, 188-189; summary information on, 5, 179-182; team implementation in, 179, 187-189, 321, 328; team responsibilities in, 179-180, 188, 312-313, 315; union relationships in, 179, 307
Harris Corporation, 192-206; back-

ground information on, 195-198; key lessons learned in, 194-195, 204-205; results of team implementation in, 194, 205-206, 333; summary information on, 5, 192-195; team implementation in, 192, 198-205, 320-321, 325-326; team responsibilities in, 192-193, 312-313; virtual teams in, 343

Hartman, M., 40-41

Harvard University, 345

Hayes, H., 253

Health care industry, reorganization in, 22-24, 32-33, 340. *See also* Cape Coral Hospital

Health care technology industry. *See* Pfizer, Inc.'s Vigo Food Science Group (FSG)

Hiring. *See* Member selection

Horton, S., 41, 45

Hospital industry, case study. *See* Cape Coral Hospital

Housekeeping, team responsibility for, 313

Hughes, K., 141-142

Hughes, P., 156, 158-159, 160, 302

Human resource benefits, to team implementation, 335-336

Human resource departments, 227-228, 241. *See also* Member selection

Humboldt. *See* Wilson Sporting Goods Company

I

Identification, organizational, 12. *See also* Employees, loyalty of

Imaging products, customer support for. *See* Kodak Customer Assistance Center

Impacts, of team implementation. *See* Results

Implementation methods, for shifting to teams, 2, 303-306. *See also* Team implementation

Implementation teams, 28-30, 187. *See also* Team implementation

Indiana, case-study organization in. *See* Pfizer's Vigo Food Science Group

Industry types: of case-study organizations, 4-5; suited for teams, 299-300

Industry Week, 237

Inspectors, elimination of, 63, 65. *See also* Managers; Supervisors

Insurance business, case study. *See* Milwaukee Mutual Insurance Company

Insurance company, redesign of, 6-8

International organizations, 300-301, 338-339. *See also* Bord na Mona; K Shoes, Ltd.; Sterling Winthrop, Ltd.; Texas Instruments Malaysia

Inventory reduction, 336; in Ampex Systems, 139, 145, 149; in UCAR Carbon, 123, 129, 133; in Westinghouse Electronic Assembly Plant, 284; in Wilson Sporting Goods Company, 288

Ireland, case-study organization in. *See* Bord na Mona

J

Jackson, S., 115

Japanese production techniques, 277

Job analysis, 323

Job fit, measurement of, 167, 170, 173, 323. *See also* Member selection

Job responsibilities, enhanced: as benchmark key point, 11, 311-315; decision making about, 3. *See also* Responsibilities, offered to teams

Job satisfaction: and cross-training, 38, 45; and empowerment, 11; and expanded responsibility, 314-315; and product design, 87; and team implementation, 50

Job types, suited for teams, 300

Johnson, J., 197, 201

Johnson & Johnson, 96, 97

Juran, J., 266

Just-in-time systems, 129-130, 253, 283

Just-in-time training, 325

K

K Shoes, Ltd., 53-65; background information on, 56-58, 301; key lessons learned in, 55-56; management support in, 302-303;

reorganization of, 58-60, 308-309, 318; results of team implementation in, 1, 55, 64-65, 333; summary information on, 4, 53-56; team implementation in, type of, 53; team responsibilities in, 53-54, 60-62, 312-313, 314, 318; union relationships in, 53, 307

Kelly, M., 57, 59, 60

Key result areas (KRAs), 37, 209, 218

Key result indicators (KRIs), 237

Key result measurements (KRMs), 209, 218

Kodak Customer Assistance Center (KCAC), 207-220; background information on, 210-214, 302; key lessons learned in, 210; results of team implementation in, 1, 209-210, 219-220, 333; summary information on, 5, 207-210; team implementation in, 207, 214-219, 306, 319, 320; team responsibilities in, 207-208, 215-216, 312-313, 315-316

Kolowski, D., 95

Kraft/General Foods, 71

Kuala Lumpur, case-study organization in. *See* Texas Instruments Malaysia

L

Labor cost reduction, 335; and autonomous enterprise teams, 155-159; and sociotechnical systems approach, 191; and team-based organization, 68-69, 72, 77, 232, 259-260; and training, 55

Labor unions. *See* Union status; Unions

Lakeland Regional Medical Center, 23

Lakewood publications, 338

Lamm, J., 271

Lasure, N., 131-132

Lawler, E., III, 339

Layoffs, 141, 148, 284; policy of no, 31, 98; of resistant employees, 65, 317. *See also* Downsizing

Lead operators, 91, 101

Lead times, 108, 110, 119

Leaders, team, 14, 318-319, 320-322; in Ampex Systems, 138, 143, 145, 161-162; in Cape Coral Hospital, 20, 28-29; in Colgate-Palmolive Company, 165, 170, 172, 175-176; in Development Dimensions International, 35, 40-42; focus on needs of, 38, 40-41, 51; in the future, 343-344; in Hannaford Brothers Company, 180, 188-189; in Harris Corporation, 193, 198-199; K Shoes, Ltd., 54, 61, 63-64; in Miller Brewing Company, 67, 72-73, 74; in Mine Safety Appliances Company, 80, 85-86; in Pfizer, Inc., 91, 101-102; "point of contact," 165, 172, 320; relationships of, with team members, 73; reporting to, 40; responsibilities of, 320-322; selection of, 72-73, 109, 120, 173, 198, 322; for shift subteams, 130; in Sterling Winthrop, Ltd., 107, 115, 116-118, 120; in Texas Instruments—Defense System and Electronics Group, 249, 256; in Texas Instruments Malaysia, 263, 268, 269-270; in UCAR Carbon, 122, 129, 130; in Westinghouse Electronic Assembly Plant, 273, 278-279; in Wilson Sporting Goods Company, 287, 292, 293-294; "working," 35, 41. *See also* Leadership roles; Rotating leadership; Shared leadership; Training, for team leaders

Leadership, outside teams: in Ampex Systems, 138; in Bord na Mona, 152; in Cape Coral Hospital, 20; in Colgate-Palmolive Company, 165, 172-173; in Development Dimensions International, 35; in Eastman Chemical Company, 235, 242-243; in Hannaford Brothers Company, 180; Harris Corporation, 193; in K Shoes, Ltd., 54; in Kodak Customer Assistance Center, 208; in Miller Brewing Company, 67; in Milwaukee Mutual Insurance Company, 222, 228; in Mine Safety Appliances Company, 80; in Pfizer, Inc., 91, 99, 101; in Sterling Winthrop, Ltd., 107; as team responsibility, 313; in Texas Instruments—Defense System and Electronics Group, 249; in Texas Instruments Malaysia, 263; in UCAR Carbon, 122; in Westing-

house Electronic Assembly Plant,
273
Leadership council, 216-217, 218-
219, 320. *See also* Councils
Leadership roles: ambiguous, 195,
205; in Ampex Systems, 138, 159,
161-162; as benchmark key point,
2, 14; in Bord na Mona, 152; in
Cape Coral Hospital, 20; changing
of, 39, 40-42, 55-56, 87-88, 92,
190, 316-322, 343-344; in
Colgate-Palmolive Company, 165,
172; in Development Dimensions
International, 35, 39; in Eastman
Chemical Company, 235, 242-243,
245; expanded, 311, 343-344; in
the future, 343-344; in Hannaford
Brothers Company, 180, 188-189;
in Harris Corporation, 193, 195,
201-202; in K Shoes, Ltd., 54, 55-
56; in Kodak Customer Assistance
Center, 208, 216-217; in Miller
Brewing Company, 67, 76-77; in
Milwaukee Mutual Insurance Company, 222, 229, 230; in Mine Safety
Appliances Company, 80, 85-86,
87-88; in Pfizer, Inc., 91, 101-102;
selecting right people for, 109; and
span of responsibility, increase in,
317-318, 341; star point system
for, 188-189; in Sterling Winthrop,
Ltd., 107, 115, 116-118, 119-120;
strategic, 319; in Texas Instruments—Defense System and Electronics Group, 249; in Texas
Instruments Malaysia, 263, 269-
270; in UCAR Carbon, 122, 127,
128-129; in Westinghouse Electronic Assembly Plant, 273; in Wilson Sporting Goods Company, 287.
See also Governance responsibilities; Leaders, team
Leadership teams, 344. *See also* Management teams
Ledford, G., Jr., 339
Lee, J. W., 266, 269
Leven, S., 253
Line managers, 67, 124. *See also*
Managers
Lloyd, P., 336
Loss ratio, 231

M

McKnight, J., 130, 133, 134
McLeod, P., 169
Magee, C., 158-159
Maine, case-study organization in. *See*
Hannaford Brothers Company
Maintenance cost reduction, 162-163
Maintenance program, total produc-
tive, 267
Maintenance teams/responsibility,
171, 177, 312
Malabar Production, 197. *See also* Har-
ris Corporation
Malaysia, case-study organization in.
See Texas Instruments Malaysia
Malcolm Baldrige National Quality
Award, 237, 246, 251, 252, 259,
336, 339
Management: as business partner to
teams, 152, 161; changing attitudes
of, 290; communication with, 109,
140, 150, 265, 269; delayering of,
63, 132, 317; relationship of, with
teams, 291-292; support from, 81,
140, 124, 247, 296, 326. *See also*
Corporate management; Executives; Managers; Senior managers
Management by exception, 267
Management teams, 193, 194, 201,
203, 204, 291-294, 320; council-
based, 207, 208, 214-215, 216-
217, 320; process, 269-270; team
guidelines drafted by, 291
Managers, 14; adjustment/training
needs of, 223, 230, 290, 296, 319,
325-326; boundary, 152, 153,
161-162; business, 208; changing
roles of, 54, 56, 316-319; effects of
team implementation on, 60, 63-
64, 65, 87-88, 104, 205, 223, 227,
230, 258-259, 316-319; as facilita-
tors/coaches, 138, 149, 222, 223,
230, 245-246, 291; former, new
roles of, 318-319; general, 119-
120; as group leaders, 35, 39, 40-
41; line, 67, 124; middle, 30-31,
63, 65, 201; as models for teamwork, 210, 213, 220, 319-320; process, 122; on product teams, 142-
143; production, as pipe leaders,
107, 115, 117-118; reduction of,

30-31, 63, 99, 132-133, 138, 143, 148-149, 161, 227, 258-259, 269, 317; relationships of, with team members, 73, 255; as steering team, 95, 126; as team leaders, 138, 143, 240; as team managers, 67, 72-73, 76-77, 235, 245-246; turnover of, 167, 175, 177-177. *See also* Corporate management; Leaders, team; Senior managers; Supervisors; Team managers
Manufacturing facility, redesign of, 6, 7
Manufacturing industries, case studies. *See* Ampex Systems; Colgate-Palmolive Company; Eastman Chemical Company; Harris Corporation; K Shoes, Ltd.; Mine Safety Appliances Company; Pfizer, Inc.; Sterling Winthrop, Ltd.; Texas Instruments; UCAR Carbon; Westinghouse; Wilson Sporting Goods Company
Martin, P., 110, 111-112
Mass production model, 57, 307-308. *See also* Functional organization
Matsushita, 141
Mature teams, 2, 15; case-study organizations listed, 5; supervision needs of, 240
Maturity level, 15; and compensation, 243-245, 327. *See also* Mature teams; New teams
Mechanization, 56-57, 65. *See also* Automation
Meetings, team, 61, 74-75; agenda-setting for, 128; of production teams, 145, 255-256; training in, 189, 292-293
Member selection: aligning systems of, 48, 322-324; in Ampex Systems, 139; in Bord na Mona, 153; in Cape Coral Hospital, 21; in Colgate-Palmolive Company, 166, 167, 173, 176, 177, 323; in Development Dimensions International, 36-37, 48; in Eastman Chemical Company, 236; in Hannaford Brothers Company, 181, 187, 188; in Harris Corporation, 194; importance of, 109, 120; in K Shoes, Ltd., 55; in Kodak Customer Assistance Center, 209;

in Miller Brewing Company, 68, 74; in Milwaukee Mutual Insurance Company, 223; in Mine Safety Appliances Company, 80; in Pfizer, Inc., 92; for pilot teams, 112; in Sterling Winthrop, Ltd., 107, 112, 120; team involvement in, 312, 324; techniques for, 323; in Texas Instruments—Defense System and Electronics Group, 250; in Texas Instruments Malaysia, 264; in UCAR Carbon, 123; in Westinghouse Electronic Assembly Plant, 274, 277-278, 280-281; in Wilson Sporting Goods Company, 287
Michaelsen, R., 211-212, 213, 216, 345
Miller Brewing Company, 66-78; background information on, 69-72; key lessons learned in, 69; summary information on, 4, 66-69; results of team implementation in, 68-69, 77-78, 333; team responsibilities in, 66-67, 73-75, 312-313; team implementation in, 66, 72-76; unions relationships in, 66, 71, 75, 78, 307
Milwaukee Mutual Insurance Company, 221-233; background information on, 224-225, 301, 317; key lessons learned in, 223-224; results of team implementation in, 1, 223, 231-233, 333; summary information on, 5, 221-224; team implementation in, 221, 225-229, 303-304, 310, 318; team responsibilities in, 221-222, 227-228, 312-313, 318
Mine Safety Appliances Company, 79-89; background information on, 81-83, 301; key lessons learned in, 81; results of team implementation in, 81, 88-89, 333; summary information on, 4, 79-81; team implementation in, 79, 83-87, 320-321; team responsibilities in, 79, 312-313
MineSpot team, 84-86
MIS department, 227, 228
Mission statements, 85, 98, 100-101, 112, 291
Mitchem, R., 133

Mitsubishi Trading Company, 124
Modular production system, 59, 61
Mohrman, S., 339
Moody, J., 184
Motivations, for shifting to teams, 2, 301-302
Motorola, 196
Multifunctional teams. *See* Cross-functional teams
Multiple skilling. *See* Cross-training
Murrin, T., 277

N

National Union of Workers, 106
Natural unit teams, 234, 240, 241
Natural work teams, 3, 8-9, 99, 304; in Development Dimensions International, 34, 39; establishing accountabilities in, 108, 120; in Miller Brewing Company, 67, 72-76; in Milwaukee Mutual Insurance Company, 221, 304; in Mine Safety Appliances Company, 79, 80; in Pfizer, Inc., 90, 95-103; star point system for, 9-10, 67, 74, 75; in Sterling Winthrop, Ltd., 115-116, 120; in Texas Instruments—Defense System and Electronics Group, 248; in Texas Instruments Malaysia, 262, 304; in UCAR Carbon, 121; in Westinghouse Electronic Assembly Plant, 272; in Wilson Sporting Goods Company, 286
New teams, 2, 15; case-study organizations listed, 4
New York State, case-study organizations in. *See* Hannaford Brothers Company; Kodak Customer Assistance Center
Noisefoe team, 86-87

O

O'Connor, E., 155
Objectives, need for clear, 284. *See also* Business needs; Goals
Obstetrics (OB) unit implementation team, 28-29
Officers, team, 273, 278-279
Ohio, case-study organizations in. *See*

Colgate-Palmolive Company; Miller Brewing Company
"On-error" training, 145
On-the-job coaching, 13. *See also* Cross-training; Training
On-time delivery rates, 55, 64, 139, 150, 251
Operating teams, 126, 214, 215-216
Operator Engineers, 121, 128
Operator self-control, 266-267
Organization types: case-study, listed, 4-5; large, implementation strategies for, 305-306; suited for team implementation, 299-301
Oversight council, 208
Overtime: compensation for, 103; scheduling of, 11, 74, 90, 106, 122, 128, 137, 164; stress of, 115; for team meetings, 74, 75; for training, 43
Ownership, sense of, 3, 12, 38, 254, 309-310

P

Partnering, 258; with unions, 307
Patient care teams, 19, 23, 32, 340
Pay-for-skill systems, 327-328; in Ampex Systems, 148; in Colgate-Palmolive Company, 165, 174-175; in Eastman Chemical Company, 235, 243, 244-245; in Hannaford Brothers, 180, 188, 189-190; in Kodak Customer Assistance Center, 208, 217; in Milwaukee Mutual Insurance Company, 222; in Pfizer, Inc., 91, 103; in Texas Instruments, 249, 257; in Westinghouse, 275, 279-280, 281, 284
Peat extraction business, case study. *See* Bord na Mona
Peer counseling, 76
Peer evaluation systems, 76, 130, 131, 176, 180, 181, 186, 190, 219, 222, 257-258, 268-269; curtailing of, 274-275, 280
Peer pressure, 160
Pennsylvania, case-study organizations in. *See* Development Dimensions International; Mine Safety Appliances
PEOPLE (Performance Excellence: Our People Lead the Effort), 197-

198, 201-202, 204. *See also* Harris Corporation

PepsiCo, 288-289

Performance baselines, need for realistic, 224, 233

Performance evaluation systems: alignment of, 330-332; in Ampex Systems, 139, 147-148, 160; in Bord na Mona, 153; in Cape Coral Hospital, 21; in Colgate-Palmolive Company, 166, 331; in Development Dimensions International, 36, 37, 48-49, 331; in Eastman Chemical Company, 237, 245, 331; guidelines for, 332; in Hannaford Brothers Company, 181; in Harris Corporation, 194, 203; for individuals, 130-131; in K Shoes, Ltd., 55; in Kodak Customer Assistance Center, 209, 218-219, 331, 332; management-team, 194; in Miller Brewing Company, 68, 74, 76, 331; in Milwaukee Mutual Insurance Company, 223, 225, 331; in Mine Safety Appliances Company, 81; peer-based, 76, 130, 131, 176, 180, 181, 186, 190, 222, 257-258, 268-269; in Pfizer, Inc., 92; production-based, 153; self assessment, 147, 148; in Sterling Winthrop, Ltd., 108, 118, 330-331; for teams, 130, 148, 175, 257-258; team involvement in, 14-15, 118, 123, 181, 209, 313, 331-332; in Texas Instruments—Defense System and Electronics Group, 250, 331; in Texas Instruments Malaysia, 264, 268-269; in UCAR Carbon, 123, 129, 130-131, 331; in Westinghouse Electronic Assembly Plant, 274, 330, 331; in Wilson Sporting Goods Company, 288, 294-295

Performance indicators: setting of, 124, 134, 209, 218; team involvement in setting, 330-331; tracking of, 129, 237

Performance management: aligning system of, 48, 330-332; as benchmark key point, 2, 14-15; in the future, 341; team-based, 76, 87, 331-332. *See also* Performance evaluation systems

Perkins, R., 57, 58, 59, 60, 62, 63, 64, 65, 302-303, 316

Permanent cross-functional teams, 9-10; in Ampex Systems, 143-144; in Wilson Sporting Goods Company, 286. *See also* Cross-functional teams

Permanent work teams, 2, 3, 6-9; in Ampex Systems, 143-144; in the future, 342-343; in Kodak Customer Assistance Center, 214. *See also* Natural work teams; Permanent cross-functional teams; Redesigned work teams

Pfizer, Inc.'s Vigo Food Science Group (FSG), 90-105; background information on, 93-95; key lessons learned in, 92-93; results of team implementation in, 92, 103-105, 333, 334; summary information on, 4, 90-93; team implementation in, initial stages, 95-99; team implementation in, loose framework for, 99-103; team implementation in, type of, 90; team responsibilities in, 90-91, 312-313

Pharmaceuticals business, case study. *See* Sterling Winthrop, Ltd.

Philip Morris Companies, 69

Physician involvement, in reorganization, 26-27

Pilot teams, 60, 80, 106, 115, 292; selecting members for, 112

Pipe leaders, 107, 115, 117-118

Pipe teams, 111-118

Plant managers, 61, 72, 91, 101, 169, 175

Plant start-up team, 169

Plastics business, case study. *See* Eastman Chemical Company

Policy setting, team involvement in, 130, 172-173, 180, 222, 315

Priano, J., 40, 41, 42, 45, 316

Pride, 12, 38

Printing/distribution business, case study. *See* Development Dimensions International

Problem-solving teams, 313; in Eastman Chemical Company, 234, 239; in Milwaukee Mutual Insurance Company, 221; in Pfizer, Inc., 94; in Texas Instruments, 252; in Texas

Instruments Malaysia, 263; in Wilson Sporting Goods Company, 293
Process councils, 208, 216, 217, 315, 316. *See also* Councils
Process improvement teams, 313; in Harris Corporation, 192, 194, 196, 198-200, 201-202; in Pfizer, Inc., 94; in Texas Instruments Malaysia, 263, 267; in Wilson Sporting Goods Company, 286, 293
Process managers, 122, 123, 132
Process redesign, 3, 308-309; and production realignment, 126; and redesigned teams, 108; seamless, 170-171; steering team vs. implementation teams roles in, 22; in Sterling Winthrop, Ltd., 108, 110-116, 309; and team implementation, 251; and team responsibilities, 73-74, 308-309; in Texas Instruments—Defense System and Electronics Group, 254-255, 309; by work teams, 47, 86-87. *See also* Redesign, organizational; Redesigned work teams
Process teams, 252-253
Process technology, computer-controlled, 169, 171
Processors, 143
Product teams, 6, 112-113, 115, 127
Production contracts, 152, 156, 157-158, 161
Production managers, 107, 115, 117-118
Production scheduling, 129, 312
Production teams, 121-122, 137, 138, 143-146, 255-256; operator technician, 171, 177
Productivity improvement: through autonomous employee teams, 162-163; continuous, 166, 176; and cross-training, 45; employee, 209-210, 219; as organizational value, 24; with redesigned teams, 108, 119; through sociotechnical systems approach, 190-191; through team implementation, 37, 51, 64, 77, 81, 88-89, 92, 104, 139, 149, 251, 259-260, 296, 335; through team initiatives, 237, 246
Program teams, 192-193, 196, 198,

200-201, 203. *See also* Project teams
Project '92, 125-132
Project Pipe, 111-114
Project teams: in Ampex Systems, 142-143; in Harris Corporation, 195; in Texas Instruments, 252; in Texas Instruments Malaysia, 267; in UCAR Carbon, 122, 126, 127, 130. *See also* Program teams

Q

Quality assurance: in-process testing for, 86; team-performed, 137-138, 146, 172
"Quality First" program, 196-197
Quality improvement/control: in case-study organizations, listed, 312; through team implementation, 50, 55, 64, 238-240, 246, 264, 270, 335. *See also* Total Quality Management
Quality management process/techniques, 239-240, 251-255

R

Recognition, team: alignment of system for, 49; honorary, 138, 193, 203, 263, 269, 287, 294-295, 329-330; for maturity, 235. *See also* Compensation systems; Reward systems
Redesign, organizational: for continuous improvement, 197-198; examples of, 6-8; principles guiding, 308; resources used for, 14; sociotechnical systems approach to, 184-189; TCCP process for, 225-229; and team implementation, 8-9, 253-255, 260-261, 307-316. *See also* Alignment, of organizational systems; Process redesign; Redesigned work teams
Redesigned work teams, 3, 6-8, 304; in Ampex Systems, 137, 304; in Colgate-Palmolive Company, 164, 304; in Eastman Chemical Company, 241; in the future, 342; in Hannaford Brothers Company, 179, 304; in Kodak Customer Assistance Center, 207; in Milwaukee Mutual

Insurance Company, 201, 304; in
Pfizer, Inc., 99; in Sterling Winthrop, Ltd., 106; in Texas Instruments—Defense System and
Electronics Group, 248; in UCAR
Carbon, 121, 127-128, 130
Reengineering: commitment to, 251;
through empowered teams, 121-
132; and need for teams, 341-342;
objectives of, 126
Reinforcement, 12, 13
Renewal, organizational, 247
Reorganization, 3, 6-9; of Bord na
Mona, 155-159; of Cape Coral Hospital, 22-33; culture-change training for, 21, 33; of K Shoes, 58-60,
308-309; and new language, 58-
60; steering team vs. implementation teams in, 21-22; of Sterling
Winthrop, 109-114, 309; using
TCCP process in, 225-229. *See
also* Alignment, of organizational
systems; Redesign, organizational;
Reengineering
Reporting: to managers, 161, 203; to
team leaders, 40
Resentment, employee, 22
Resistance: to organizational redesign,
8-9; and organizationwide involvement, 306; and pace of change, 92-
93, 104; to team implementation,
65, 81, 94-95, 103, 104, 140
Resources, in redesign, 14
Responsibilities, offered to teams, 2; in
Ampex Systems, 137-138, 146,
312-313; in Bord na Mona, 151-
152, 312-313; in Cape Coral Hospital, 19-20, 312-313; case-study
organizations, listed, 312-313; in
Colgate-Palmolive Company, 164-
165, 171-172, 312-313; in Development Dimensions International,
34-35, 312-313; in Eastman Chemical Company, 234-235, 312-313;
expanded, 311; in Hannaford
Brothers Company, 179-180, 188,
312-313; in Harris Corporation,
192-193, 199-200, 312-313; integration of, 311-315; and job satisfaction, 314-315; in K Shoes, Ltd.,
53, 312-313; in Kodak Customer
Assistance Center, 207-208, 215-

216, 312-313; listed, 312-313; in
mature vs. new teams, 15; in Miller
Brewing Company, 66-67, 73-76,
312-313; in Milwaukee Mutual Insurance Company, 221-222, 227-
228, 312-313; in Mine Safety Appliances Company, 79, 85, 312-
313; in natural work teams, 3; organizationwide, 20, 35, 54, 66-67,
91, 107, 122, 138, 152, 165, 180,
192-193, 208, 214-215, 222, 235,
249, 263, 272-273, 315-316; in
Pfizer, Inc., 90-91, 101-102; in
redesigned teams, 6, 106; rotating,
122, 128, 129, 133, 222, 229, 249,
256, 268, 321; in Sterling Winthrop, Ltd., 106-107, 116, 312-
313; in Texas Instruments—Defense System and Electronics
Group, 248-249, 312-313; in
Texas Instruments Malaysia, 262-
263, 268, 312-313; in UCAR Carbon, 121-122, 312-313; in Westinghouse Electronic Assembly
Plant, 272-273, 312-313; in Wilson Sporting Goods Company, 286,
291-292, 312-313. *See also* Governance responsibilities; Rotating
responsibilities
Responsibility: change in, 41-42, 60;
span of, 317-318, 341
Restructuring. *See* Redesign; Reengineering; Reorganization
Results, of team implementation: in
Ampex Systems, 139, 149-150,
333; as benchmark key point, 2; in
Bord na Mona, 153, 162-163, 333;
in Cape Coral Hospital 21, 333; of
case-study organizations, listed,
332-334; in Colgate-Palmolive
Company, 166-167, 176-178, 333;
in Development Dimensions International, 37-38, 50-52, 333; in
Eastman Chemical Company, 237,
246-247, 333-334; in Hannaford
Brothers Company, 181-182, 190-
191, 333; in Harris Corporation,
194, 205-206, 333; in K Shoes,
Ltd., 55, 64-65, 333; in Kodak Customer Assistance Center, 209-210,
219-220, 333; in Miller Brewing
Company, 68-69, 77-78, 333; in

Milwaukee Mutual Insurance Company, 223, 231-233, 333; in Mine Safety Appliances Company, 81, 88-89, 333; in Pfizer, Inc., 92, 103-105, 333; positive, 1, 332-337; in Sterling Winthrop, Ltd., 108, 118-120, 333; in Texas Instruments—Defense System and Electronics Group, 250-251, 259-261, 334; in Texas Instruments Malaysia, 264, 270-271, 334; in UCAR Carbon, 123, 133-134, 334; in Westinghouse Electronic Assembly Plant, 274, 283-285, 334; in Wilson Sporting Goods Company, 288, 295-296, 334

Retail food distribution business, case study. *See* Hannaford Brothers Company

Retirement, early, 138, 143, 148

Revenue improvement, 37, 50, 51. *See also* Results, of team implementation

Reward systems: alignment of, 49, 326-330; as benchmark key point, 2, 14-15; for patient care teams, 32; for problem-solving and process improvement teams, 263, 269. *See also* Bonuses; Compensation systems; Gain sharing plans; Recognition, team

Rework, 274, 276, 284, 288

Ritchie, G., 57, 59, 60, 61, 62, 64, 65

Rotating council-team membership, 216

Rotating leadership, 14, 320-321; in Ampex Systems, 138; in Cape Coral Hospital, 20, 28; in Colgate-Palmolive Company, 165; in Hannaford Brothers Company, 188; in Miller Brewing Company, 67, 74; in Mine Safety Appliances Company, 80, 85-86; in Milwaukee Mutual Insurance Company, 229; in Texas Instruments—Defense System and Electronics Group, 249; in Texas Instruments Malaysia, 263; in UCAR Carbon, 122, 127, 133; in Westinghouse Electronic Assembly Plant, 273, 278-279; in Wilson Sporting Goods Company, 293

Rutledge, R., 95-96, 97-98, 104

S

Safety, team responsibility for, 313

Safety equipment business, case study. *See* Mine Safety Appliances

Scheduling, team control over, 312. *See also* Overtime, scheduling of; Production scheduling; Vacation scheduling

Scott, A., 289-290, 295

Selection system. *See* Member selection

Selectors, 187

Self-directed teams, 3, 6; in Ampex Systems, 143, 160; in Cape Coral Hospital, 20, 29-30; in Colgate-Palmolive Company, 164; in Development Dimensions International, 34; in Eastman Chemical Company, 234, 240-243; in K Shoes, Ltd., 53, 59, 60-62; in Miller Brewing Company, 66, 71-72, 73-76; in Milwaukee Mutual Insurance Company, 224-225, 227-228; in Mine Safety Appliances Company, 79, 83-87; in Sterling Winthrop, Ltd., 106, 114-116; in Texas Instruments—Defense System and Electronics Group, 253-255; in UCAR Carbon, 127-128; in Wilson Sporting Goods Company, 293-294. *See also* Teams, empowered

Semco, 338-339

Semiconductor business. *See* Texas Instruments Malaysia

Senior managers, 126, 127; communication with, 140, 186; as steering team, 142, 169, 184, 240-241, 304-305; as strategic planners, 230; support from, 288, 296, 302-303, 326. *See also* Executives; Management

Service industries, teams in, 299-300, 338, 340. *See also* Cape Coral Hospital; Kodak Customer Service Center; Milwaukee Insurance Company

Services, Industrial, Professional Technical Union (SIPTU), 151, 156

Severance program, voluntary, 156, 161

Shared leadership, 14, 101, 229, 249,

304, 321-322. *See also* Leaders, team

Shift coordinators, 130

Shift work, 38, 46, 51-52; coordination of, 313; subteams based on, 130; teams based on, 99

Shoe industry, case study. *See* K Shoes, Ltd.

Shop Distributive and Allied Employees Association, 106

Simon, W., 289

Site visits, 14, 71, 96-97, 240-241, 306

Size, team. *See* Team size

Skill-based pay. *See* Pay-for-Skills systems

Social change, and organizational teamwork, 344-345

Sociotechnical systems approach, 184-187; implementation of, 187-189

Sony, 141

Space reduction, 37, 50, 61

Specialists, 307; incorporation of, in teams, 73, 314-315; replacement of, 57, 71, 85, 86, 87-88, 188, 227-228; as team advisors/support, 273, 314; teams of, 313-314; union support of, 159-160

Sporting goods business, case study. *See* Wilson Sporting Goods Company

Standardization, of documentation/methodologies, 264, 270

Star point system, 9-10, 321; in Hannaford Brothers, 188-189; in Miller Brewing Company, 74, 75; in UCAR Carbon, 122, 129. *See also* Responsibilities

Start-up organizations: among case studies, 4-5; team implementation in, 300. *See also* Colgate-Palmolive Company; Hannaford Brothers; Miller Brewing Company; Westinghouse Electronic Assembly Plant

Statistical process control, 170, 197, 239

Status, changing of perceived, 40-41, 60, 65, 140, 150

Steel industry, 124-126. *See also* UCAR Carbon

Steering teams/committees, 20, 305-306; in Ampex Systems, 142, 143; boundaries between, and implementation teams, 21-22, 32-33; in Cape Coral Hospital, 24-27, 304-305; in Colgate-Palmolive Company, 169; in Eastman Chemical Company, 235, 240-241; in Hannaford Brothers Company, 184, 185-186; in Harris Corporation, 197-198; in K Shoes, Ltd., 59; in large organizations, 306; in Mine Safety Appliances Company, 83-84; in Pfizer, Inc., 95, 99; roles and membership of, 304-305; in Sterling Winthrop, Ltd., 107, 112, 114, 115, 120; in Texas Instruments Malaysia, 269; training for, 24; in UCAR Carbon, 126, 128; unions on, 128; in Westinghouse Electronic Assembly Plant, 277. *See also* Senior management

Sterling Winthrop, Ltd., 106-120; background information on, 109-114; key lessons learned in, 108-109; restructuring of, 109-114, 309; results of team implementation in, 108, 118-120, 333; summary information on, 4, 106-109; team implementation in, 106, 114-116, 319, 330-331; team responsibilities in, 106, 116, 312-313; union relationships in, 106, 307

Stetar, K., 46

Stich, R., 41-42

Stix, B., 58

Subteams, for shift work, 130

Suburu-Isuzu, 96

Supermarket business, case study. *See* Hannaford Brothers Company

Supervisors (former), 14; as area leaders, 165; as boundary managers, 153, 161-162; changing roles of, 318-319; as coaches/facilitators, 54, 80, 88, 92, 99, 101, 103, 116-117, 122, 222, 238, 245-246, 247, 249, 263, 269, 287, 291; as coordinators, 180; effects of team implementation on, 55, 60, 63-64, 65, 87-88, 104, 116-117, 140, 150, 205, 316-322; reduction of, 132-133, 143, 148-149, 258, 317; as team leaders, 35, 39, 40, 41, 138,

148; as team managers, 67, 235. *See also* Managers

Suppliers: and mature teams, 15, 200; mission statement regarding, 100; on-time delivery rates of, 139, 149-150; reduction and selection of, 149, 200; team involvement with, 138, 139, 145-146, 200, 249, 293, 313

Support systems, integration of, 311-315. *See also* Systems, alignment of

System employee involvement team (SEIT), 199-200

System improvement project (SIP) team, 199

Systems, alignment of, 14-15, 322-332; in Bord na Mona, 158-159; in Development Dimensions International, 47-49; in Eastman Chemical Company, 241; in the future, 340-341; in Harris Corporation, 205-206; in Mine Safety Appliances Company, 81, 89; in Texas Instruments, 261; in Westinghouse, 275. *See also* Compensation systems; Member selection; Performance management; Training

T

Task force, for policy recommendations, 180

TCCP process, 225-229

Team-based organizations, titles used in, 13

Team implementation: aligning organizational systems to, 322-332; approaches to, 303-304; as evolutionary process, 182; getting started in, 301-307; in large organizations, 305-306; loose framework for, 98, 99-103; management support for, 302-303, 326; national support for, 339; organization types suited for, 299-301; reasons for, 2, 301-302; and redesigning team roles and responsibilities, 307-316; strategies for, 304-306. *See also* Results, of team implementation

Team managers, 67, 72-73, 76-77, 235, 245-246. *See also* Leaders, team; Managers

Team positions. *See* Titles

Team responsibilities. *See* Responsibilities, offered to teams

Team share system, 67, 75-76, 180, 181, 190, 208, 328

Team size: as benchmark key point, 2, 13; of case-study organizations, 4-5; and implementation strategies, 305-306

Teams, empowered: best practices for, 299-337; extent of, 338-339; extent of, in the future, 339-340; future, predictions about, 339-346; and social change, 344-345; types of, 2-3, 6-10. *See also* Cross-functional teams; Design teams; Implementation teams; Mature teams; Natural work teams; New teams; Permanent work teams; Pilot teams; Redesigned work teams; Self-directed teams; Steering teams; Team implementation; Virtual teams; Work cells

Teamsters, 183-184

Technical Engineering and Electrical Union (TEEU), 151

Telephone support center. *See* Kodak Customer Assistance Center

Temporary cross-functional teams, 10, 200-201, 342-343. *See also* Cross-functional teams; Program teams; Project teams

Tennessee, case-study organizations in. *See* Eastman Chemical Company; Wilson Sporting Goods Company

Tennessee Eastman. *See* Eastman Chemical Company

Termination, 65, 317. *See also* Layoffs

Teverbaugh, L., 281-282, 283, 284, 285, 337

Texas, case-study organizations in. *See* Texas Instruments—Defense System and Electronics Group; Westinghouse

Texas Instruments—Defense System and Electronics Group (DSEG), 248-261; background information on, 251-255, 317; key lessons learned in, 251; results of team implementation in, 1, 250-251, 259-261, 319, 334; summary information on, 5, 248-251; team implementation in, types of, 248; team responsibilities in, 248-249, 309, 312-313, 314, 320; teams in, history of, 252-255; teams in, today, 255-256

Texas Instruments Malaysia (TIM), 264-271; background information on, 265-268, 317; key lessons learned in, 264-265; results of team implementation in, 264, 270-271, 334; summary information on, 5, 262-265; team implementation in, 262, 266-269, 318, 319-320, 321; team responsibilities in, 262-263, 266, 312-313, 318

Tiger teams, 142-143

Titles, 2; as benchmark key point, 13; in traditional vs. team-based organizations, 13

Total Quality Management (TQM): as foundation for teams, 221-233; office, providing managerial support to teams, 194, 195, 202, 204; training in, 292-293. *See also* Quality improvement

Toyota modular production model, 59, 61

Traditional organizations. *See* Functional organization

Training, for team implementation, 324-326; in Ampex Systems, 138-139, 146-147; as benchmark key point, 2, 12-13; in Bord na Mona, 152-153; and in business skills, 159, 160, 256, 271, 282-283, 325, 340-341; in Cape Coral Hospital, 20, 21, 24, 29; in Colgate-Palmolive Company, 165-166, 170, 173-174; in culture change, 21, 33; demands of, on employees, 92; in Development Dimensions International, 36, 42-46; in Eastman Chemical Company, 235-236, 243; expectations about, 108; first-year, 20, 36, 42-43, 54, 55, 67, 68, 80, 91, 92, 102, 107, 122-123, 138, 139, 152, 165, 166, 181, 193, 208-209, 222, 223, 235-236, 249-250, 263, 273, 274, 287; formal programs of, 13; in the future, 340-341; in Hannaford Brothers Company, 181, 189; in Harris Corporation, 193, 202-203,

325-326; vs. implementation of skills, 124, 325; intensive vs. integrated, 131-132, 133; in K Shoes, Ltd., 54-55, 59-60; in Kodak Customer Assistance Center, 208-209, 215-216; and labor cost reduction, 55; management support for, 326; in Miller Brewing Company, 67-68, 77-78; in Milwaukee Mutual Insurance Company, 222-223; in Mine Safety Appliances Company, 80, 85; mission statement regarding, 101; needs for, in heavy work environment, 210, 217, 220; "on-error," 145; and performance management, 332; in Pfizer, Inc., 91-92, 95-99, 101, 102-103; in small business skills, 159, 160; standardization of, 264; of steering team members, 24; in Sterling Winthrop, Ltd., 107, 115, 120; subsequent-year, 21, 36, 43-44, 54, 55, 67, 68, 91-92, 102, 138, 139, 152, 153, 165-166, 181, 193, 194, 209, 222, 223, 236, 250, 263, 264, 273, 274, 287; team involvement in, 313, 326; in Texas Instruments—Defense System and Electronics Group, 249-250, 256, 261; in Texas Instruments Malaysia, 263-265, 267, 270-271; time spent in, 43, 45-46, 104, 115, 189, 214; timing of, 124, 325; types of, 324-325; in UCAR Carbon, 122-123, 131-132, 134; in Westinghouse Electronic Assembly Plant, 273-274, 278, 279; in Wilson Sporting Goods Company, 287, 290, 292-293, 296. *See also* Certification; Cross-training; Training, for team leaders

Training, for team leaders, 325-326; in Ampex Systems, 139; in Bord na Mona, 152-153; in Cape Coral Hospital, 21; in Colgate-Palmolive Company, 166; in Development Dimensions International, 36, 42-46; in Eastman Chemical Company, 236, 246; in Hannaford Brothers Company, 181; Harris Corporation, 193-194, 195, 203, 205; in K Shoes, Ltd., 55, 63-64; in Kodak

Customer Assistance Center, 209, 223; in Miller Brewing Company, 68, 77-78; in Milwaukee Mutual Insurance Company, 222-223; in Mine Safety Appliances Company, 80; pace of, 134; in Pfizer, Inc., 103, 104; in Sterling Winthrop, Ltd., 107; in Texas Instruments—Defense System and Electronics Group, 236; in Texas Instruments Malaysia, 263-264; in UCAR Carbon, 123, 131, 134; in Westinghouse Electronic Assembly Plant, 274; in Wilson Sporting Goods Company, 287, 288, 290, 292
Trust, manager-employee, 255, 344
Turnover, employee, 176, 183, 191, 210, 220, 223, 232, 275, 280, 335-336

U

UCAR Carbon: background information on, 124-126, 317; key lessons learned in, 124; results of team implementation in, 123, 133-134, 334; summary information on, 4, 121-124; team implementation in, 121, 126-131, 305-306, 310, 318, 319, 320, 342; team responsibilities in, 121-122, 312-313; union relationships in, 121, 307
Union Carbide, 124
Union of Oil, Chemical, and Atomic Workers, 121
Union status, of case-study organizations, 4-5; Bord na Mona, 151; Hannaford Brothers Company, 179; K Shoes, Ltd., 53; Miller Brewing Company, 66; Sterling Winthrop, Ltd., 106; UCAR Carbon, 121. See also Unions
Unions: in Australia, 110; and compensation based on performance, 158; and compensation based on team performance, 130; in Hannaford Brothers Company, 183-184, 190; involvement of, in design and planning, 59, 124, 162, 186; involvement of, in review, 163; in Ireland, 156, 158, 159-160, 162, 163; in Miller Brewing Company, 71, 75, 78; and peer review systems, 190; relationships with, 2, 14, 307; and rotating roles/responsibilities, 128, 159-160; team implementation with, 300; training by, 326. See also Union status
United Auto Workers (UAW), 66, 75, 78
United Kingdom, case-study organization in. See K Shoes, Ltd.
United Rubber Workers, 289
US Shoe Corporation, 58-59, 302-303

V

Vacation scheduling: in case-study organizations, listed, 312; team control over, 11, 74, 90, 106, 122, 128, 164, 273
Value-added activities, eliminating non-, 126, 224, 284-285
Vendors. See Suppliers
Videotape equipment, 140-141. See also Ampex Systems
Virtual teams, 342-343, 344
Vision, need for clear, 108

W

Watlow Gordon, 96
Weimels, B., 125-126, 133
Wesray, 289, 295
Westinghouse Electronic Assembly Plant (EAP), 272-285, 301; background information on, 275-277; key lessons learned in, 274-275; results of team implementation in, 1, 274, 283-285, 334; summary information on, 5, 272-275; team implementation in, 272, 277-283, 320-321, 329, 330; team responsibilities in, 272-273, 310-311, 312-313, 315
Westlund, A., 185, 187
Wilson Sporting Goods Company, 286-296; background information on, 288-290; key lessons learned in, 288; results of team implementation in, 288, 295-296, 334; summary information on, 5, 286-288; team implementation in, 286, 290-295, 304, 320; team responsibilities in, 286, 291-292, 312-313

Wisconsin, case-study organization in. *See* Milwaukee Mutual Insurance Company

Work cells, 137, 138, 144, 146, 192

Work environment, employee empowerment over, 11-12

Work teams. *See* Natural work teams; Permanent work teams; Redesigned work teams; Self-directed teams

Workers' compensation costs, reduction in, 181-182, 191, 336

Z

Ziglar, Z., 290